Aspects of
Anglo-Saxon Magic

Bill Griffiths

Anglo-Saxon Books

Published by
Anglo-Saxon Books
Frithgarth
Thetford Forest Park
Hockwold-cum-Wilton
Norfolk, England

First printed 1996
Revised and Reprinted 2003
Reprinted 2006

P.L.

British Library Cataloguing-in-Publication Data. A catalogue record for this book is available from the British Library.

ISBN 1–898281–33-5

And syððan is eac þearf þæt gehwa understande
hwanan he sylf com, 7 hwæt he is, 7 to hwan he
geweorðan sceal

(Wulfstan *Sermo ad Populum*)

And then there is also a need that each should understand
whence he came, and what he is, and what will become of him

CONTENTS

Contents

FOREWORD

A society depends on a concept of a tradition of ideas. Though presented as external and immutable, these ideas will be invented / inherited / borrowed in order to shape society and our interpretation of the world. Within this apparent frame we have a sense of humans as constantly creating and changing things, while themselves remaining catalytically uninvolved and unaltered. But what we cause, and what we only participate in or spectate remains unclear. Conventionally we stress human control over the future by highlighting the achievements of great men though the 'new' may be often a matter of transformation or reaction; novelty and continuity are modes of assessment with little objective distinction. More - that consistent central element in all these calculations – the human itself – may prove to be as mythic and fluid as any of the other factors.

If we work at history in a perceptive maze, the material we take as its basis is hardly any more substantial. Past ideas are fugitive and do not survive in any direct form, only through (records of) the actions and (chance survival of) the artefacts that embody a culture. Contemporary descriptions of beliefs (and even events) may be as partial and party-coloured as our own re-interpretations of them in the present. Our assumptions play with the unities of time and place – yet we should not be happy with concepts of an almost genetic transmission of information that permits all Germanic (perhaps all Indo-European) material to be regarded as a non-developing unity, outside time.

Reducing emphasis on the major gods throws into relief the issues of ancestors, fate and augury as operations of chance, and the importance of animals. Some lesser role would then be indicated for the well-known (to us) pagan deities prior to the Viking Age. The result is something of a challenge to our received perceptions of paganism; it is not an attempt at some new definitive system, but a request for a more flexible and open approach to this fascinating and uncertain area of study, that touches on so many aspects of Anglo-Saxon culture.

Guide to Dates of Principal Texts

Icelandic Texts:

Elder or *Poetic Edda* (alliterating, traditional theme poems): set down in late thirteenth century in Iceland but composed between ninth century and c.1200.

Icelandic family sagas: written down in thirteenth century, telling of tenth–eleventh centuries

Ari Thorgilsson's *Íslendingabók*, a history of Iceland, written in the 1120s, though the surviving text may only be part of a larger work. He may also have had a hand in the *Landnámabók*, an account of the settlement of Iceland, but this only survives in later (thirteenth century) redactions.

Snorri Sturluson c.1179-1241 – wrote *Heimskringla* (1220s? – sagas of Scandinavian kings) and the *Prose Edda*, finished c.1223, which contains the Gylfaginning (the beguiling of Gylfi, a summary of Norse mythology), the Skáldskaparmál (a discussion of skaldic poetic technique), and the Háttatal (examples of the metres put into practice).

Latin texts:

Caesar's *De Bello Gallica* (his own account of his campaigns in the 50s BC)

Tacitus' *Germania* written c.98 AD, probably using earlier first century AD material

Jordanes' *History of the Goths*, written mid sixth century

Penitential of Theodore, apparently seventh century

Bede's *Ecclesiastical History of the English Nation*, completed 731AD

Indiculus Superstitionum, a continental list of prohibited practices, likely eighth century

Confessional of Egbert etc., probably ca.1000 AD

Adam of Bremen's *History of the Church of Hamburg*, written c.1070

Saxo's *History of the Danes* written 1182-c.1210

Aquinas' *Summa Theologica* 1260s, 1270s

Old English Texts:

The Old English version of Bede dates to the second half of the ninth century

Alfred's *Metres of Boethius* are believed to date to the close of the ninth century

The *Leechbook* (BL Cotton MS. 12 D.xvii) was written out in the mid tenth century

The *Lacnunga* (BL MS. Harley 585) was written out c.1000 AD

Ælfric's work dates to the close of the tenth century; the (anonymous) Old English gloss to his Latin *Colloquy* is slightly later.

BL Cotton MS. Vespasian D.xiv is twelfth century, though contents may in some cases be earlier.

Part One

THE UP WORLD

"All clinquant, all in gold, like heathen gods," is an image of (worldly) pomp developed by Shakespeare in the opening scene of *Henry VIII* – perhaps in allusion to the sort of golden idols being recovered from central and south America in the 16th century. Comparably rich images of Germanic gods may once have existed – Saxo for example mentions a golden statue of Odin,[1] but such as survive are predictably modest in scope: in small silver, bronze, wood, bone, textile, etc. More functional everyday images may have been especially perishable – Grimm rather splendidly suggests that bread may once have been designed on religious (god-like?) shapes: "A history of German cakes and bread-rolls might contain some unexpected disclosures."[2] (In support of which we may note the *Indiculus Superstitionum* includes prohibitions against religious images made of moistened flour or of baked dough.[3])

The limited evidence for pagan idols, if not just a trick of artefactual survival, may well reflect a difference between Germanic and Imperial Roman ('Classical') concepts of the roles of the gods. Tacitus is specific in denying the existence of simulacra of the gods or built temples among the Germanic tribes ("...they consider it ill accords with the majesty of heavenly beings to coop them within walls or to depict them in any human shape"[4]) – though he presents the lack as pious rather than primitive. Caesar more radically asserts that the Germans had no anthropomorphic gods at all, only concepts like Sun, Moon and Fire.[5]

Certainly this contrasted forcibly with the practice of the Classical world, where giant images dominated the temples which in turn were the key buildings of major cities. The need for a hierarchical pantheon with one leader god was an essential reflection, surely, of the Greek league of city states, and in turn of a populous, multi-national and diverse society with a centralised administration like that of ancient Rome, where the status of the chief god came to reflect and support the position of the Emperor.[6] Several potential prime deities were tentatively essayed: Jupiter, Dea Roma (favoured by Augustus), the cult of the Emperor as

---

[1] See Grimm, 1900, 1,113.

[2] *ibid.* 1,63.

[3] No.26 "De simulacro de consparsa farina", and no.27 "De simulacris de panis factis"; the MS. derives from the Continent, eighth century, see below, p.96.

[4] *Germania* ch.9 trans. Fyfe

[5] "Solem et Vulcanum et Lunam." *De Bello Gallico* 6,21

[6] Perhaps it was as reassuring to have a human figure at the head of a vast state as it is to have an anthropomorphic god in ultimate control.

god (important from Diocletian's reign i.e. AD 284–305),[1] and then (if not dispensing with at least restructuring the pantheon) the single all-powerful Christian God, with an open number of strictly subsidiary saints. The scale of temples, their enduring creation in stone, the emphasis on large images and use of great riches are all symbols of the power of the god(s) and at the same time of the scope of the state.

This sort of aggrandising motive, or at least the opportunity to express it, was apparently lacking from Germanic society, which we believe to be 'tribal' (i.e. organised in relatively small units[2]) – Bede affirms that "the Old Saxons do not have a king as such but many local leaders put in charge of the people."[3] Moreover from perhaps a century or so before Christ, it would also have been a largely migratory society. In such conditions, permanent or large-scale cult centres would be of little practical value. Such evidence as there is of images at an early period points to processions of idols (or images of some sort) on carts,[4] perhaps appropriate to a culture that laid little emphasis on (or had little use for) Roman stability of concept, building or place, but was preoccupied with agricultural ritual. Here we meet Nerthus, "id est terram matrem" in Tacitus' words[5] – 'Mother Earth' who is noted as having wide respect among the Germans; but a respect, I suggest, founded on common need and agricultural relevance rather than any well-defined concept of universal deism. For the Germanic 'gods' (in this sense 'influences' within rather than above nature) were likely to be relatively local, limited in potential, and connected with a particular need or role, not distinguished by status in some fixed pantheon that assisted and reflected a self-perpetuating and wide-ruling state system.

Even very considerable scholars like Hilda Ellis Davidson, who talk of the worship of "a supreme god of the sky,"[6] consider the role may have been played variously by Tiw, or Odin, or Thor, or Ull (successor to Odin).[7] Tiw is presumably mentioned because his name, in the form *Tiwaz*, seems cognate with Greek

---

[1] See John Wacher *The Roman Empire* (London, 1987) p.178

[2] By 'tribe' (originally a Roman concept) we imply a group small enough to regard itself as a unity (within a larger group?) yet broad enough to provide initial choices of a family partner internally.

[3] "Non enim habent regem idem Antiqui Saxones, sed satrapas plurimos suae genti praepositos." *Ecclesiastical History* Bk.5 ch.10

[4] Via Grimm, 1900, 1, p.107. Tacitus does not however specify an image of Nerthus in the procession in Germania ch. 40; a later Icelandic ritual involved a cart and an image of Frey; and Saxo notes that Frothi's embalmed body was similarly moved around – see Stone, 1996, pp.9–10.

[5] *Germania* ch.40

[6] Ellis Davidson, 1969, p.52

[7] Ellis Davidson, 1969, pp.52,56,57,108; a very few lines of information on Ull (Oller) are given in Saxo Bk.2 ch.4.

Zeus;[1] but if indeed from a very ancient word root, it may only imply some variable concept of 'a god' (Latin, *deus*), not necessarily a paramount or widely honoured divinity with a specific sky-identity. Thus Dickins remarks that "the pl. *Tívar* is used as a generic name for the gods in the Older Edda."[2] Indeed, over the first millennium AD, which is the period for which we have some records of Germanic non-Christian worship, it would be strange if there was not considerable evolution of belief and even of the gods themselves – a variation by place, time and social context. Even Christianity, with the advantage of fixed reference points provided by written records nonetheless shows a measurable development in the role of the Trinity, the Blessed Virgin Mary, or individual saints' popularity.

For if Odin dominates, where do Njord, Rig, Aegir, Ran, and a host of others ("a hundred gods"[3]) fit in? A partial solution could be that there is some redundancy or overlap: thus Grimm equates Phol and Baldur,[4] Ellis Davidson equates Saxnot and Tiw.[5] Turville-Petre[6] discusses as one potential group *dísir, fylgjur,* valkyries, norns, female ancestors and *matrones*. This sort of solutionary linkage is attractive. But what happened to the Alci (compared by Tacitus[7] with Castor & Pollux)? Or to Tuisto and Mannus?[8] Who or what were Nehalennia, Tanfana, Baduhenna?[9] What do we make of the Norwegian temple where Thor was worshipped alongside Thorgerðr and Irpa?[10] Who was Od?[11] Some animals may seem to link to specific gods, but what of trees, springs and rocks also said to be venerated?[12] Is that the same as the "the worship of sticks and stones" attributed to the Anglo-Saxons by Pope Gregory?[13] Where do demons fit in? Or the miniature figures the size of a head of barley or a bee?[14] What is the role of

---

[1] See e.g. Ellis Davidson, 1964, p.57, Branston, 1974, p.74; the continuity of a word is not necessarily a proof of continuity of meaning or of associated beliefs.

[2] Dickins, 1915, p.26, note

[3] Grimm, 1900, 1, 115

[4] *ibid.* p.224

[5] 1964, p.60

[6] 1964, ch.11

[7] *Germania*, ch.43

[8] *ibid.* ch.2

[9] Invoked by Gummere, 1892

[10] *Nialssaga* ch.89 via Grimm, 1900, 1, 113

[11] Derolez, 1962, p.134: "D'Od (vieux-norois Odhr), nous ne savons que le fait suivant; il disparut un jour du monde des dieux..." (Of Od – Old Norse *Odhr* – we know nothing but the following fact: he disappeared one day from the world of the gods...)

[12] Grimm, 1900, 1, pp.110–101

[13] Blair, 1970, p.53

[14] "There is a tiny figure Byggvir, 'barley', who is said to chatter in Frey's ear. His wife, Beyla, may take her name from the bee..." Ellis Davidson, 1969, p.109

possibly phallic columns like the Irminsul?[1] How are we to relate to presumed cults the myriads of small amulets and tokens recovered by modern archaeology for the Anglo-Saxon period?[2] The implication is one of a series of divergent, locally detailed systems rather than one coherent whole: more the sort of complexity and development of unfixed and unrecorded beliefs that might well be expected over hundreds of miles and hundreds of years when no central authority presides.

To reduce this mass of evidence (large in quantity not quality) to some sort of coherent system would be pointless and almost certainly undesirable, if it is simply our own assertion of consistency. The great gods do not, as far as I can tell, offer a useful unifying force to this width of material; ancestors (I will argue) may provide a key to understanding one range of material, but are equally no total unifying theme – perhaps there isn't one. Rather we are left to speculate that as Germanic society expanded its emphasis on agricultural stability to embrace migratory aggression in the early centuries AD, the need for more clearly heroic and personified (male) deities emerged, symbols of war and the justification of war. Nerthus, as Mother Earth, assumes a new or alternative masculine form, Njord,[3] and yields to the new generation Frey (Freyr) and Friga (Freyja), the twin god and goddess of plenty: Freyja is associated also with the war-like boar,[4] yet in turn may yield precedence to major masculine cult-figures like Woden – a transition mythologised in the Vanir family of gods giving way to the newer Æsir.[5]

These quasi-divine figures are nonetheless human in form, and not originally distant (one could almost say alien) or Olympian: Woden is mentioned in quite commonplace situations like the sprained ankle of a horse in the *Merseburg Charm*. They seem to have been instant, familiar (perhaps literally ancestral) resources, through invocation or symbol, of helpful qualities that could be summoned up by the adventurous tribes in their movement into new lands. Woden became associated with wisdom (in the sense of devising workable policies and

---

[1] Grimm, 1900, 1, pp.115–9. I beg to doubt the assertion by Bauschatz (1982, p.5) that "There is little doubt about the central importance of the world tree as a symbol of a large part of the universe as conceived by early Scandinavian people." References to Yggdrasil are part of a later cosmology, and there is little certainty about symbols like Irminsul ('universal column'?) in the Carolingian period that could be early parallels. The concept is discussed further in Stone, 1989, pp.10, 16–8.

[2] Meaney 1981 lists these; in her 1989 article some roles are suggested e.g. as thunder-charms. But apart from obvious links like the hammer to Thor, most amulets and tokens remain unexplained.

[3] See Grimm, 1, 1900, p.256, where conceived of as two different deities; and Ellis Davidson, 1969, p.88.

[4] In Tacitus *Germania* ch.45 the boar is associated, among the Aestii (Estonians?), with the worship of the Mother of the Gods; it is found on later helmets (see Ellis Davidson, 1969, p.92, and illus. Glosecki, 1989, figs 6–8) but continuity of use of the symbol cannot be asserted. Sacrificed horses are attested at pre-migration sites in Denmark (Davis, 1992, p.27), but this need not imply knowledge of Frey or Odin.

[5] See *Ynglinga Saga* ch.4 trans. Morris & Magnússon, 1893

strategies as well as formal knowledge) and with success in battle. Thor, representing thunder, may by origin be a nature god rather than an ancestral figure, and may even be a borrowing from Romano-Celtic religion;[1] he is also called 'the son of Earth';[2] and he was associated with courage and heroic enterprise. The rune 'T', found on some early funerary pots in England may just possibly indicate the god Tiw,[3] but in what role is unknown; unless, as Saxnot, we place him in an ancestral context. These are the sort of figures we assume to be coming to the fore in the period of the Anglo-Saxon settlement, and yet they are clearly distinguished only by the time of the Viking ascendancy; they are apparently new concepts or transformations of old ones beginning to assume a dimension of power not unlike those of Classical deities, and rather than impute some innate Indo-European tendency to create great gods (or possess these *ab initio*), it is worth considering whether this development may not have reflected an increasing influence from (or reaction to) Roman ideology in, say, the second to sixth centuries AD, or even to Christianity in the sixth to tenth centuries. Indeed the role of Latin models as consciously influencing Germanic concepts of divinity was proposed by Saxo in the early thirteenth century, when he made this comment:

> *Sunt qui dicant deos, quos nostri coluere, cum iis, quos Graecia vel Latium celebrabat, solum participasse vocabulum, sed istis tamquam maiestate suppares ab illis cultum cum nomine matuatos fuisse.*

> [Bk.6 ch.5]

> There are some who say that the gods which we worship only shared the title with those whom Greece or Rome honoured, and in effect borrowed from them the rituals and name, as though claiming to be equal in status.

So it struck a later commentator, but the flow of cultural ideas he posits might well have been valid at the earlier date too. As a sixth century commentator noted, "The rich Goth imitates the Roman, the poor Roman imitates the Goth,"[4] suggesting a complex two-way interchange.

I would argue that organised cults and consistency of worship are the concomitant of political stability and centralisation, which only began to emerge in England (at least) as Christianity took over the country and demolished much of

---

[1] Branston, 1974, p.109 considers Thor was adopted in the Lower Rhineland from a Celtic Jupiter Tanarus; cf. the 2nd century AD inscription to Jovi Tanaro at Chester (*ibid.* p.112).

[2] Foote & Wilson, 1970, p.329; on p.389 it is noted he was sacrificed to in cases of dearth and disease.

[3] See Myres, 1977, 1, p.66, who says the name is spelled out in one instance; if this is the Spong Hill pot, see an entirely different interpretation of the runes in Pollington, 1995, ch.4. Tiw is usually equated with Mars, either as god or planet, and may further play a role in legal matters.

[4] In the *Anonymus Velisianus* 12,61, via James, 1980, p.39

the evidence. Such indications as we have of physically larger-scale symbols of worship (implying a higher level of organisation) e.g. the presumed Red Horse of Tysoe,[1] or the temples mentioned in Bede,[2] belong to a period when more settled kingdoms were emerging within Anglo-Saxon England, not impossibly through the example of Christianity on the continent (extant too in Britain?) – suggesting a need for some more organised system of religion among the new settlers. But did this religion centre on gods like Thunor (Thor) or on ancestors or leaders as centres of veneration (consider the remarkable group of royal mounds at Sutton Hoo for example)?

No pagan gods are specifically named in Bede's *Ecclesiastical History*, not even as Latinised equivalents: when Earpwald in Bk 2 ch.15 practices two faiths, he has besides an altar to Christ an "*arulam ad victimas daemoniorum*" (a small altar for sacrifices to demons); when Coifi in Bk 2 ch.13 destroys a shrine, it is a "*locus... idolorum*", a 'place of idols' – and the names we would expect to be associated with such major worship are left unuttered.[3] We cannot be certain what the idols portrayed, if anything more than a conventional word for any pagan maybe abstract symbol. A description of a later pagan temple in Iceland is provided in the *Erbyggja Saga*: at one end is a dais with a gold ring for swearing oaths on and a bowl to collect sacrificial animals' blood; around this are arranged wooden images of the gods, to be sprinkled with the blood.[4] But sites of worship in Anglo-Saxon England are likely to have been typically hilltops, woods, and roadside sites,[5] perhaps with wooden shrines, but lacking elaborate permanent structures.[6] Previously, the role of deities was so ill-defined that Tacitus thinks it worth mentioning that Nerthus was actually believed to intervene in human affairs at all.[7] We need to be aware that we are quite uncertain what is implied by 'god' in

---

[1] Illus. (reconstruction) in Ellis Davidson, 1969, p.72

[2] E.g. *Ecclesiastical History* Bk.2, ch.13 and the 'fanes' assumed by Pope Gregory in his letter, *ibid.* Bk.1 ch.30

[3] Compare Bede's apparent acceptance of Woden as a genealogical figure, Davis, 1992, pp.25-6

[4] This description is given serious consideration by Vigfusson & Powell, 1883, 1, pp.402, 406, as perhaps copied from (lost portions of) the *Islendinga-bok* of Ari. Turner, 1971, p.359, points out there was no suppression of paganism in Iceland with the Conversion in 1000 AD. However one sometimes doubts the serious intent of the *Erbyggja Saga*; consider: "Next morning there was a turf-game going on near the Thorbrandssons' tent. The Thorlakssons happened to be passing by, when a great lump of sandy turf came flying through the air and caught Thord Blig on the neck, hitting him so hard that he went head over heels. When he got back on his feet again, he could see the Thorbrandssons laughing at him." (ch.41, trans. Pálsson & Edwards, 1973, p.133, where also the unbearable footnote: "This game is not mentioned anywhere else; and how it was played is not known.")

[5] Wilson, 1992, pp.7–10

[6] Sites of local assembly (as later at Tingwall) may have had a religious status as well.

[7] *Germania* ch.40

an Anglo-Saxon pagan context; nor can we be sure how far figures like Thor or Woden had become individualised and empowered.

It is only in later centuries, and particularly with the emergence of Viking power,[1] that formal worship and the predominant cult of a single major deity – Odin – takes over. He is plausibly a symbol of the aggressive confidence that inspired these new adventurers, explorers, traders, plunderers and settlers.[2] His power over events like the outcome of battle is transformed into a demonstration of his universal role; warriors turned into 'berserkers' under his patronage; and the heroic dead were received by him in a Germanic 'heaven'. But surely this development shows an awareness of the parallel success of the all-powerful Christian God in the north-west of Europe at much the same time,[3] and may have served to give the Vikings a sense of parity with the Christians and their God.

Such a developmental outline of the possible progression of Germanic worship seems worth giving, and is indeed essential to any investigation of the sort of powers that may lie behind magic ritual; but it must be remembered that no interpretation of the confusing fragmentary evidence will ever be certainly established. Grimm prefers to see the Germanic tribes as worshipping proper 'gods' from the earliest time, with the system "most perfectly preserved" in the far north.[4] His organisation of material into chapters on distinct (and it is implied unchanging) gods is followed by Ellis Davidson 1964 and Turville-Petre 1964; whereas Owen[5] sees the Vikings who settled in England as "exhibiting a polytheism similar to that of their Anglo-Saxon predecessors, although no doubt the myths associated with their gods and heroes were still evolving and continued to develop up to the time when they were written down." The prototype for a rather careful, consistent, and logical mythology of paganism was presented by Snorri Sturluson,[6] and is comparatively speaking, late, i.e. from the 13th century: it may reflect an antiquarian concern, or a move to national identity – in any case a

---

[1] Turville-Petre, 1964, p.69, records that the cult of Odin "spread widely and rapidly in the ninth and tenth centuries."

[2] By this token, a religion is a system that produces optimum commitment – consider the Methodist work ethic.

[3] A sort of pagan trinity, probably in imitation of the Christian concept is noted by Snorri – see Ellis Davidson, 1969, p.97; in Adam of Bremen's view the trinity was Thor, Woden and Fricco (Frey) – see Foote & Wilson, 1970, p.389. In analogy, "Religion among the [American] Indian tribes of the eastern woodlands is reported to include the concept of an All-Father of the type of Odin or Zeus, but it is more probable that this concept had derived from contact with European Christians..." (Burland, 1965, p.73).
Meteorological rather than Christianic seems to be the "concept, found among the Northwest Coast Indians, of a sky house, where an angry old chief lives." (*ibid.*).

[4] Grimm, 1900, 1, p.104

[5] 1981, p.170

[6] Though still involving many inconsistencies and "unsolved problems" – Ellis Davidson 1969, p.17

systematisation that is itself part of the Romano-Christian approach. Even the dramatic concept of the End of the World (related in the Icelandic poem *Völuspá*[1]) need not be some authentic survival of ancient Indo-European mythology: a reasonable line of transmission (or transformation) could be projected from Zoroastrian belief,[2] to Judaeo-Christianity, to later Scandinavian paganism (even if concepts of world-beginning and world-ending are not spontaneous to any human-constructed cosmology).

The problems of interpretation are intensified by the fact that we depend for much of our evidence on written comments by 'outsiders'; such commentators, old or new, inevitably tend to notice and stress those aspects that reflect their own beliefs and preoccupations. Tacitus wanted to use the refreshing piety of the Germans to comment on the debased, superficial and effete, sophisticated attitudes of his Roman contemporaries. At the same time he equated Germanic concepts with Roman 'parallels', in order perhaps to make his evidence seem more comprehensible or reliable. And yet his conventional practice of quoting telling images from previous writers leaves us sometimes doubtful as to the authenticity of his knowledge of the contemporary Germanic world.

Christian commentators variously condemned (in the case of the Vikings e.g. by Wulfstan), ignored (as in Bede's scant material on pagan leaders), or presented as quaint primitives their pagan forebears (e.g. the *Erbyggja Saga*). A more positive technique of 'apology' is represented in the following lines from *Beowulf*:

> *Hwilum hie geheton   æt hærgtrafum*
> *wigweorþunga,   wordum bædon*
> *þæt him gastbona   geoce gefremede*
> *wið þeodþreaum.   Swylc wæs þeaw hyra,*
> *hæþenra hyht;   helle gemundon*
> *in modsefan,   Metod hie ne cuþon,*
> *dæda Demend,   ne wiston hie Drihten God,*
> *ne hie huru heofena Helm   herian ne cuþon,*
> *wuldres Waldend.*

[*Beowulf*, 175–183]

Sometimes they made vows at their idolish temples in worship, asking the Soul-Slayer to lend assistance in some general crisis. For such was their habit, the (feeble) resource of heathens; they envisaged Hell in their hearts and did not know of the (true) Creator, the Judger of Deeds, knew nothing

---

[1] Trans. as 'Song of the Sybil' in Taylor & Auden (1969). The cosmos created from the void (stanzas 7–9) and mankind fashioned from earth (st.14) have parallels in *Genesis*. The world ending through the assault of evil forces (st.41–2), with the Sun and Moon terminated (st.49–50), leading to the re-establishment of a better world (st.51) and the triumph of a resurrected god (?Baldur, st.57) can at least be paralleled in Christian myth.

[2] See Ling, 1968, p.75

of the Lord God, nor even had any idea of how to worship the Protector of the Heavens, the Ruler of Glory.

In general, references in Christian Anglo-Saxon texts to pagan gods are extraordinarily rare and not very informative (an omission or suppression that is not unexpected); those in Old English texts are listed by Stanley.[1]

In the modern period, Jacob Grimm, in his *Teutonic Mythology* (originally published 1835) sought to merge and fix the Germanic pantheon and its attributes into a sort of consistency; in the words of his translator, to present "the prevalence of one system of thought among all the Teutonic nations from Iceland to the Danube."[2] It is no coincidence that this is also the period of emergent modern German democracy and nationalism, in which the Grimm brothers played a prominent intellectual part;[3] a unified system of belief imputed to the Germanic past could become a pattern for a national state in the present. Not just any sort of state, but one with an emphasis on popular consensus and democracy; with paganism evidencing the historicity of this movement as well as supplying a novel lever to use against the entrenched privileges of the contemporary monarchies. Thus Jacob saw his work as one of collecting "what is treasured up in song and story born alive and propagated amongst an entire people,"[4] almost a definition of folk culture, with implications for government as a theory of power arising from the 'folk'. Stallybrass, as translator, tactfully rendered the 'Deutsche' of Grimm's original title as 'Teutonic' rather than 'German',[5] but this in turn may obscure Grimm's tendency to equate the Germanic pantheon with the respected, civilised and ultimately democratic Greek model: "All the divinities, Greek and Norse, have offices and functions assigned them..."[6] – a similarity of role that tends to lend substance and respectability to the sometimes rather "sinister"[7] northern sort of god.

---

[1] E. G. Stanley, 1975, pp.88–9: e.g. Woden mentioned in Exeter Book gnomic verses where "*Woden worhte weos, wuldor alwalda*" ('Woden brought forth idols, the Almighty brought forth glory' – trans. Stanley p.89); Woden also appears in the *Nine Herbs Charm*. Tiw is mentioned in the Old English *Martyrology*, but only as a convenient translation for the Roman Mars.

[2] Stallybrass, Grimm 1, 1900, Pref., p.v

[3] Zipes, 1988, p.63, sees them, slightly differently, as liable (at least in the editing of folk-tales) "to stress fundamental bourgeois values of behaviour and moral principles of Christianity."

[4] 1, 1900, p.99

[5] See his note, 1, 1900, Pref. p.viii

[6] Grimm, 1, 1900, p.335

[7] Adjective from Ellis Davidson, 1969, p.50

Wagner, though we hesitate to ascribe to him the careful scholarship and democratic goals of the Grimms, went a step further. In imitation of the gods of Homer,[1] he portrayed (though possibly with some precedent in the sort of group interaction of gods featured in stories in the *Prose Edda*) the Germanic pantheon as arbitrary heavenly powers with human family attributes and their own domestic hierarchy, who interfere quite unscrupulously in the everyday affairs they look down on, promoting the myth of an Olympian-Germanic fusion that powerfully influences our concept of the pagan past whether we are aware of it doing so or not. His example of pagan as a defining modern 'German' trait was not lost on subsequent German scholars[2] and even politicians, leading to a stern unromantic reaction in the opposing camp of the 1940s. Thus the article by Timmer published during the War in 1940–1, served to challenge the pagan basis for the concept of *wyrd* or (national?) destiny.[3]

The would-be stability of this pagan pantheon (encouraged inevitably by our familiarity with the names of the days of the week[4]) is, I suggest, a modern interpretation of decidedly mythic proportions, and will not help us reconstruct the conditions of a largely unwritten pagan past. It is not just a matter of absence of evidence: but of a different sort of society. Oral records can reflect consensus, but provide a poor basis for hierarchical administration. This may be a clue as to why written Romano-Christian religious and political systems prevailed, for they offered the promise of stability on an alternative basis by establishing systems of reference that can act as 'fact'. And in, I think, every case, the conversion in England was achieved by winning over the king (or king and nobles) of a region, never as a result of popular credence, which was a subsequent detail. For Christianity, however pious and non-worldly its monastic basis may aim to be, is at root a religion of a particular type of state: a system that supplied the educated personnel (the trained thinkers) and the ideology to rule a settled society. Its own rituals and mysteries were at least as impressive as those of any pagan competitors, plus so much more – stone architecture, literacy, art, Latin culture, bureaucracy. It was the missing link in a chain of governmental modernisation. Where organised pagan cults did exist, centring on a particular (tribal) king's 'palace', nothing was simpler than to purge the offending shrine and re-open it as a Christian church to make the change-over complete while encouraging apparent continuity of

---

[1] For a caustic summary of Wagner's amateur enthusiasm for Greek culture, see William Wallace's *Richard Wagner As He Lived* (London, 1925); C. von Westernhagen *Wagner: A biography,* 1978, 2, p.407, neatly encapsulates the duality when he talks of Wagner "Reading Homer and the Edda with Cosima in the evenings..."

[2] As traced by Stanley, 1975. Tolkien, by contrast, uses similar material to evoke a world of settled privilege and land-owning zeal – the apparent portrayal of Gollum in terms of a music-hall Jew, and the 'cleansing of the shires' as a comment on resistance to the reforms of the post-war Labour Government seem often to be overlooked.

[3] The periodical, *Neophilologus*, in which the article appeared, recorded its natural relief at the liberation of Holland in a preface to vol. 30 (1946)

[4] Stressed e.g. even by Ellis Davidson, 1964, p.57, or Stenton, 1947, p.98.

worship[1] and, arguably, an augmentation of authority. Conversely, without the support of a king or tribal leader, no consistent, organised pagan system of belief (if such existed) could arguably survive.[2]

The implication is that any system of powerful, personified individual gods may have been relatively novel to (possibly unformulated among) the Anglo-Saxons who settled in England, and whatever its status easily transformable, when under direct emergent royal control, to a Christian equivalence. Indeed, if religion among the pagan Anglo-Saxons in the early settlement period was in fact some flux between ancestor, hero and emergent central gods, it would scarcely have had the developed consistency to oppose the sophisticated structure of Christianity. In either case, what would be left would be a mass of unorganised popular belief, with only the possibility of oral transmission; and though this can arguably be very persistent, especially when based on ritual, gesture, everyday superstition or valid need, it may not have offered much of a cultural threat to the confident new religion. Pagans, like Coifi in Bede's *Ecclesiastical History* Bk.2 ch.13, gave up in admiration of the new truth, or were content to be passively unhelpful, as the natives who contentedly viewed Christian monks being swept away out to sea –

> *On þe north water banke*
> *Stode many men, were noght to thanke,*
> *For þai had na compassioun*
> *Of þair neghburs confusioun;*
> *Þai scorned þair maner of lovyng,*
> *For it accorded to thairs na thing*
> *And saide þat þai were worthy*
> *To have þat harme and vylany.*

[Late Middle English *Metrical Life of Cuthbert*, Bk.2]

> On the north bank of the estuary stood many people who were not at all sympathetic, for they felt no compassion at their neighbours' danger; they scorned their manner of worship for it was altogether incompatible with theirs, and they said they deserved to suffer injury and disgrace.

The nature of this remnant paganism is indeed 'occult' (hidden), and with minimal political power. But the assumption that some sort of debased tradition of the great gods like Woden and Thor is at the heart of this 'folk' material I beg to doubt; when Ælfric reviews a number of pagan gods in his sermon 'De Falsis Diis', he uses the Viking (Danish) forms of the names – Othon, Fricg – either as more relevant to his

---

[1] As Pope Gregory advised; Bede *Ecclesiastical History* Bk.1 ch.30

[2] Phythian-Adams, 1975, realised the difference in implication between ritual and belief; however to him it was the Reformation that "marked a decisive break with at least a millenium [sic] of evolving and changing ritual activity." (p.10). The enclosure movement of the early nineteenth century with its disruption of population may have put paid to anything that survived the Reformation.

own day, or because there really was little remembrance of such entities among the English. (Literally centuries had passed, after all, though 'Woden' remained in written genealogies and 'Wednesday' and so the authentic forms should have been available to Ælfric.) Perhaps the conversion to Christianity could not alter certain popular beliefs associated with the enduring role of kinship and respect for male descent in society, and certain needs like good harvests and good health; these social 'constants' may earlier have focused on veneration for the (legendary) dead, which would be strictly incompatible with the morality of the new religion, but in other ways tactfully capable of merging with and being accepted into a Christian context – as in the presentation of the story of Weland on the Franks Casket,[1] or in the creation of new saints from members of the ruling dynasty – or in charms for crops and disease.

This 'encouraging' trend is upset in the ninth century when the (pagan) Vikings unsettle and then settle the northern half of the country. Political domination by the dynasty of Wessex was not asserted until the reign of Athelstan in the second quarter of the 10th century, and even then was not uninterrupted. A tighter system of social control (through shire organisation) and religious supervision (through nucleic village as parish) would seem to provide a means of dealing with any new pagan elements; but it may have had the contrary effect, encouraging local contact and fusion.[2] It is to this later period, I suggest, that the concept of pagan god as powerful entity belongs. The Old English charms may represent an earlier stratum of belief ('magic' than organised pagan religion); but whereas the *Nine Herbs Charm* uses the native form 'Woden', and presents him as a benevolent (ancestral?) force, it is equally significant that he appears alone (as appropriate to Viking regard for him), and this later writing down (even fashioning) of charms may owe much to the re-emergence of a pagan influence on culture in England in the ninth to eleventh centuries.

---

[1] For excellent photos of this casket see Branston, 1974, pp.10–13.

[2] As in 'Anglo-Scandinavian' sculpture in the North of England, with pagan images "juxtaposed with Christian iconography." (Lang, 1977)

THE DEAD WORLD

We may reasonably doubt if the pagan Anglo-Saxon concept of 'god' really implied the sort of omnipotence accorded the Christian deity – a creator, external to the world of humans, existing in eternity, with access to all knowledge and all power. This is an unlikely Germanic concept for the period,[1] rather the sort of thing an Augustine of Hippo or a Boethius would be concerned with, in the context of the awesome power of Rome. To the Germanic tribes, a 'god' in the sense of a useful power was surely something more than human, but still had a definite human form, and could pass for human when visiting the world of men. The root of the word 'god' may imply no more than an 'invoked being' from a root IE *ghu- 'to invoke',[2] and provides no guarantee of exact status.

A (selective) Valhalla or heaven above and a (general) Hell below may also be later refinements; for the few references there are suggest a sort of possible after-life, but one in the grave or mound on a quasi-physical plane. As Smithers notes, this Scandinavian belief "is due to a view of the human being as having a single indivisible form and substance, and not a spirit or soul as distinct from, and separable from, a body: at death; he occupies the grave, and there is no question of a life of the spirit (as such) elsewhere."[3] 'Soul' itself is a word common to all Germanic languages, and should plausibly pre-date Christianity; but it has no clear cognates that might explain its original implications;[4] if the analogy with Latin *spiritus*, *anima* is allowed – both words arising from the concept of 'breath' – then *sawol* in Old English might originally imply something like 'life' rather than a separable ghost-like element conjoined with the body.[5] The attributes of an external immortal element might well come to be attached to the word from contact with Christianity – "For most pagan Germans, Christianity meant initially

---

[1] To assume, as Grimm does (1900, 1, 16), that "the Supreme Being is conceived as omnipresent," in the context of the pagan past, from the slim evidence of the form of greetings and valedictions he presents, is unconvincing.

[2] Klein, 1971

[3] G. V. Smithers, 1961, p.8

[4] Klein's etymological dictionary gives a conjectural Old Teutonic source *saiwaló, "that which is related to a lake or sea, from *saiwa-z 'lake, sea'." While there is evidence, especially in Scandinavian, of boat images among rock-carvings, and of pagan boat burials at sea and on land, I can find no justification for Klein's further assertion, "According to ancient Teutonic conceptions lakes used to serve as dwelling places of the soul after death." On the etymology, see also Jente, 1921, p.116.

[5] Jente, 1921, p.67 proposes a meaning of 'breath' (*atmen, blasen*) for the root *ans- of Old English *os*.

a new dimension to their existing beliefs."[1] But if at an earlier stage there was no immortal, immaterial element involved, dependent on some external eternal god for its creation and survival, then life and after-life may have been a more mundane matter. With no eternity, no heaven or hell to supervise, may we not likelier seek the origin for the human-based god, in Germanic terms, in a reliance on ancestors?[2]

Some support of this is recorded as early as Tacitus, whose *Germania* ch.2 mentions Ingaevones, Herminones and Istaevones as examples of 'tribes of divine descent'; and by implication this should mean that ancestors could become heroes/gods in the course of time. The process of transformation may be apparent in the emphasis placed on reputation (*dom*), which we are told is the best sort of legacy a person can leave: 'You have done so well that your reputation (*dom*) will live forever,' Beowulf is told;[3] and in the Exeter Book *Maxims*, after a bleak summary of the fact of death, there is the vivid flash: "Dom biþ selast" (Living on in people's estimation is best). To survive in the memory of the tribe may be both a sort of judgement or valediction, and the first step towards becoming legendary and in the course of time a centre of veneration. Vigfusson & Powell give examples[4] in pagan Iceland where this may have happened within one generation. It took Cuthbert only a decade or so to be revered as a saint; but after probably centuries Weland and Beowulf don't quite make the switch-over to 'divine', though both characters are imbued with powers that seem in effect super-human, and in the latter case are used strictly for the benefit of society, like a good saint. Is it in heroes like this that we have in fact some clue as to how a 'god' was regarded?

Further material on ancestors is provided in Jordanes' *History of the Goths* ch.14:

...proceres suos, quorum quasi fortuna vincebant, non puros homines, sed semi-deos, id est Ansis, vocaverunt. Quorum genealogia ut paucis percurram, vel quis quo parente genitus est, aut unde origo coepta, ubi finem effecit, absque invidia, qui legis, vera dicentem ausculta: Horum ergo heroum, ut ipsi suis in fabulis referunt, primus fuit Gaut....

[Mommsen, 1882, p.76]

---

[1] Van de Noort, 1993, p.70

[2] Such development, as a general trend, or as a method of accounting for the origin of religion, is specifically disallowed by Evans-Pritchard, 1965, as in the theories of Herbert Spencer (pp.23–4) or de Coulange (p.51). I propose no evolutionary determinism, but am unhappy with Evans-Pritchard's critical summariness e.g. judgements like "All this is a little naïve." (p.50)

[3] *Beowulf* 953. However, both Beowulf and the Geats seem in another sense outside the accepted tradition of known heroes and tribes. Was he selected as central figure for the poem exactly because no ancestral cult could be attached to him?

[4] 1883, 1, p.414: the examples are Gudmund in the *Hervar Saga* and Grimm or Camban in the *Landnama-bók*.

For they called their ancestors, to whose good influence they attributed the victory, not entirely mortals, but a sort of semi-god, that is 'Ansis'.[1] And the genealogies of these – as I will briefly relate – and who was born of what parent and where the line began and where finished – to all this, when recited, they give unquerying and credulous audience. Of these heroes, as they tell in their own legends, the first was Gaut [Woden?]...

The key-word here may be *semi-deos*, for in place of the equivalence and status accorded Germanic belief by Tacitus, Jordanes, himself a Goth, seems to be implying the powers of such figures are but half what a Roman would expect of a god.[2]

The transition itself from ancestor to 'god' is attested in the work of King Alfred, who inserts in his translation of Boethius[3] the following material:

> *Wæs se Apollinus   æðeles cynnes,*
> *Iobes eafora,   se wæs gio cyning:*
> *se licette   litlum 7 miclum,*
> *gumena gehwylcum   þæt he god wære*
> *hehst 7 halgost: swa se hlaford þa*
> *þæt dysig folc   on gedwolan lædde*
> *oððæt him gelyfde   leoda unrim*
> *forðæm he wæs mid rihte   rices hirde,*
> *hiora cynecynnes: cuð is wide*
> *þæt on ða tide   þeoda æghwilc*
> *hæfdon heora hlaford   for ðone hehstan god*
> *7 weorðodon   swa swa wuldres cining*
> *gif he to ðæm rice wæs   on rihte boren....*

[*Metre* 26 lines 34–46]

Apollo was of noble kindred, Jove's son, who was formerly the king. He pretended to all, low and mighty, that he was god, highest and holiest. So the master led the foolish subjects into gross error until countless people believed him, for he was after all the rightful guardian of the state, and of their royal kin. It is widely known that in those times every nation considered their lord as the highest god and worshipped him like the King of Glory – if he was legitimately born to the position of power.

---

[1] *Ansis*, incidentally, is the apparent source of Norse *áss*, Old English *os*, 'a god', and so the *Æsir*.

[2] With less emphasis on Woden, Jordanes also says (V, 43): "In earliest times they [the Goths] sang of the deeds of their ancestors in strains of song accompanied by a cithara: chanting of Eterpamara, Hanala, Fritigern, Vidigoia and other whose fame among them is great; such heroes as admiring antiquity scarce proclaims its own to be." (qu. Woolf, 1939, pp.247–8) – the implication being that such ancestors and/or their deeds were invented, a charge oral history can never shake off.

[3] *De Consolatione Philosophiae* Bk.4 Metre 3

Much the same material – suggesting its continued relevance and importance – was presented by Wulfstan and Ælfric in their sermons 'De Falsis Diis'. In Wulfstan's version:

> *Se Iovis wearð swa swyðe gal þæt he on his agenre swyster gewifode, seo wæs genamod Iuno, 7 heo wearð swyðe healic gyden æfter hæðenscype geteald. Heora twa dohtra wæron Minerua 7 Uenus. Þas manfullan men þe we ymbe specað wæron getealde for ða mærostan godas þa on ðam dagum, 7 þa hæðenan wurðodon hy swyðe þurh deofles lare...*

That Jove was so utterly shameless that he married his own sister, who was named Juno, and she was a very exalted goddess in heathen reckoning. Their two daughters were Minerva and Venus. These wicked people that we refer to were accounted as the greatest gods in those days and the heathens worshipped them very much by the Devil's prompting...

A similar line of thought is evident later in Saxo's assessment of the pagan gods:

> *Olim enim quidam magicae artis imbuti, Thor videlicet et Othinus aliique complures miranda praestigiorum machinatione callentes, obtentis simplicium animis, divinitatis sibi fastigium arrogare coeperunt....*

[Bk 6 ch.3]

Once certain men, instructed in the magic art, namely Thor and Odin and many others clever at the marvellous manipulation of illusions, befogged the minds of credulous people and so began to assume for themselves the superlative dignity of divinity.

– to which might be added Saxo's further comment: "..even the intelligent Romans were seduced into worshipping similar mortals with divine honours;"[1] and Saxo's trenchant and satirical account of Odin's career in Bk 1 ch.7. Boniface, in dealing with continental beliefs as a missionary was advised: "Do not waste time wrangling with them about the ancestry of their gods, however false these are... Gods and goddesses born in the manner of men are in fact men."[2]

Of course, all this could be a debasement[3] (or elevation), and a rationalisation, of the concept of a pagan god – an interpretation starting out from the Christian view that such gods both were and were not worth treating as serious; and that any such god would necessarily claim the immense power of the Christian deity, whether this was so or not; yet despite the perceived risks, Woden was not removed from even the pedigree of Christian Anglo-Saxon kings, as though he were someone to be proud of as an ancestor (unthinkable as anything more).

---

[1] Trans. Fisher, Saxo, 1979, 1, p.23
[2] Via Davis, 1992, p.24 note 5
[3] "Heroes, or at least some of them, are fallen gods." Davis, 1992, p.24

For Woden, in particular, was quoted by many royal houses in Anglo-Saxon England as their direct origin, though for decency's sake the pedigree could be continued even further back to one of the sons of Noah, and so to Adam himself. Thus "Later kings of the East Saxons traced their ancestry back to the god, Woden, through the Saxon god, Saxnot."[1] If not a god (and we may be only quibbling over terminology here), a hero at least was required: "later kings of the Mercians included among their reputed ancestors Offa of Angeln, a fifth-century figure of Danish heroic legend."[2] Ing, who appears as a legendary figure in the *Runic Poem*, may be connected with the Bernician royal genealogy, which includes an Ingebrand, and Ing could further be related to the name Yngvi/Ingunar, one of the appellations of Frey;[3] the Geats, central to the Beowulf poem, may be connected with Woden – Gautr being one his cognomens.[4] In a wider framework of ancestral obsession, Saxo named Dan (or Skiold) as the ancestor of the Danes (the Scyldings),[5] and his brother Angul as ancestor of the English; plus, for good measure, Scot or Skott as founder of the Scottish race.[6] These may seem unprofitable notions to us, but a similar preoccupation with memorials and monuments to the great as founders of the present is not unknown in our own day. (The idea is more elegantly put by Vigfusson & Powell[7] in their reference to "the beliefs... which cling so strongly to us still in the honours and reverence which we rightly pay the dead.")

An ancestor would be the natural choice for assistance in supranormal affairs. Who, after all, was in a better position to look after matters of childbirth, health, the welfare of the family, the kin, and the tribe than some personification of ancestral interest? The very title of *cyning*, as leader of the tribe, derives from *cyn*, 'family, kin, species, people', as though political power is regarded as an extension of the standard social bond. Witness also the declarations of personal descent at times of maximum stress in *The Battle of Maldon*.[8] This emphasis may explain in turn why so much surviving Anglo-Saxon legend concerns the continental homeland of the tribes – not as some geographical or historical or personal genealogical concern but from a sense of the past centring on the respect for ancestors.[9] The emphasis in this case is not so much on the descendant as an inheritor of 'genetic' virtue, but on the predecessor as a resource to the living.

---

[1] Kirby, 1991, p.14

[2] *ibid.*

[3] Owen, 1981, p.30; Derolez, 1962, p.118; Jente, 1921, p.93

[4] Owen, 1981, p.37.

[5] Saxo, Bk.1, ch.1; Ellis Davidson, 1964, p.183, notes the further link through Scyld to Woden.

[6] Saxo, Bk.2 ch.2

[7] 1883, 1, 421

[8] Lines 216–223 and 249–253

[9] *Widsiþ* in the Exeter Book is a virtual catalogue of names and tribes e.g. Eormenric, ancestor of kings of Kent – see the genealogy in Kirby, 1991, fig.1. In Fowler's words, "The myth of migration gave the English as a folc a common identity by teaching them

Lesser dynasties were also capable of being formed around a notable (heroic?) ancestor e.g. the Oiscingas in Kent, descended from Oisc,[1] the Wuffingas of East Anglia, from Wuffa; the Icelingas in Mercia, from Icel, and so on. Groups of people[2] could also be formed on this model e.g. the Hrothingas, Stoppingas, and those who gave the present place-names of Reading, Hastings, Sonning , Barking, etc., etc.[3] In the case of Gumeninga Hearh (Harrow-on-the-Hill, Middlesex) such a group is specifically connected with a place of worship, but two other examples[4] show compounds of the element *weoh* (shrine) with the personal names, Pæccel, Cusa – as patrons or as objects of veneration? A further example could be Taplow in Buckinghamshire, where the (treasure-yielding) burial mound of Tæppa may be associated with a putative Anglo-Saxon Christian church[5] suggesting a ritual or religious history to the site. Other examples of churches connected with earlier

---

that they were descended from those who had made the exodus of the mid fifth century." (1989, p.179)

[1] Connected by Kirby, 1991, p.15, to the name Ansehis [Ansis?], "perhaps originally a mythological figure." The role of Oisc is further discussed in Davis, 1992, p.27 and note 23.

[2] May we even take a step into the dangerously mobile world of place-names and query whether those based on the suffix *-ingas* could refer to a group united not only by direct paternity or the leadership of the individual so named, but who also regarded themselves as protected in some way by a single figure's posthumous influence? – for in such a case religion would lend its support to kinship and political organisation, supplying a strong bond that may well have been important in establishing a local loyalty of 'place'. Strictly speaking *-ing* only implies direct descent; thus Ælfric's *Grammar* notes as patronymics forms like *Pending* and *Pendingas* which derive from *Penda* (see Skeat 1884); but it is not impossible that non-related members of a household or community would wish to associate themselves with the principal family, and even a religious group may be implied in the form *Guthlacingas.* Turner notes Old English *sib* as a term suitable for including "a range of persons focused on oneself." (1971, p.364)

On this type of place-name Ekwall, 1962, p.95, notes "What is most striking about the distribution of names in *-ingas* is their frequency in the east, their rarity in the west of England," which could indicate an earliness in keeping with pagan connotations; conversely, place-names with *-ingaham* are concentrated in the Midlands and North, suggesting an Anglian preference in usage. Dodgson (1966) challenged this claim of primacy, in turn to be queried by Copley (1988) who brings forward "the antiquity of this type of name in the Germanic homeland." (p.5) I can assert no correlation, however, between *ing-* place-names and burial mounds.

[3] Bassett, 1989, p.21; Stenton 1947 p.291 adds the Geddingas and Sunningas, though there will be many more. Smaller groups mentioned in the *Tribal Hidage* document, such as the North and South Gyrwe, or the Gifle, though without this sort of name-formation, might also repay study in this light; for discussion of the *Tribal Hidage* see Kirby, 1991, pp.9–12.

[4] Stenton, 1947, pp.101–2

[5] See Fitch, 1996. On the Taplow Mound see Owen, 1981, p.76.

burial mounds (and so perhaps ritual sites) are Maxey in Northants and Berwick in Sussex.[1] Yet if such examples are few (or not easily identified), it is equally hard to trace major cult centres for the great gods, and the connection between Tiw and the Vale of the Red Horse[2] is no less speculatory than my own line of approach.[3] Emphasis has been placed on great gods' names as place-name elements, and the remainder regarded (or disregarded) as name-elements derived from ordinary humans;[4] but might not the Anglo-Saxons have meant something special when they incorporated a personal name in a place feature? For although the 'royal' families provided the most famous ancestor-gods, there is no reason why there should not be local practice of similar rites and beliefs, centring on less august names. Vigfusson & Powell[5] give several specific examples – for Iceland – of an ancestral mound (*heimis-haugr*) located close to a family homestead. This might be special to the dispersed nature of the settlements in Iceland, but similar scattered homesteads might also have been one model of settlement in England.

However, a particular problem is the apparent lack of early mound burials among Anglo-Saxon settlers. Meaney gives the (flat) cemetery as the standard form of early burial (for cremations or inhumations), and dates secondary burials in pre-existing tumuli to perhaps the mid sixth century and rather inland, primary barrow burials as only in the seventh century.[6] Owen[7] similarly comments that "burial mounds were rare before the seventh century." One can insert the caveat that burials of importance are going to be much less frequent than ordinary ones, so that surviving evidence might not give a complete picture, especially as mounds now may only show "between a few inches and two feet high;"[8] and note that barrows and flat cemeteries do occur together,[9] so there is no mutual exclusivity; indeed, at Newport Pagnell the graves in a cemetery have a radial configuration, as though around some central burial of an important person;[10] similarly two nuclei

---

[1] See Aston, 1985, p.50

[2] Stenton 1947 p.99

[3] Concerning place-names it is also interesting to note that there are relatively few place-names evidencing Tiw or Thunor in England (none in Anglian territory), and none at all for Frig (Stenton, 1947, pp.98–99) – a fair number for Woden, but as god or ancestral figure? Tý is found in place-names in Denmark, but place-names with Odin may date to the eighth century; Foote & Wilson, 1970, p.393, 398.

[4] For a barrow perhaps named after a landowner see Speake, 1989.

[5] 1883, 1, 416–7

[6] Meaney 1964, pp.15, 18–9; James, 1980, confirms such row-grave cemeteries as a Germanic marker at this period.

[7] 1981, p.74

[8] Grinsell, 1953, p.27

[9] *ibid.* p.28; so too, Van de Noort, 1993, p.66: "barrows were [often] part of larger cemeteries," both in England and on the continent.

[10] Owen, 1981, p.73. Van de Noort, 1993, p.70, notes that Anglo-Saxon cemeteries could be grouped around prehistoric mounds and Roman tumuli.

are proposed for the large cremation cemetery at Spong Hill, Norfolk;[1] but it is hard to escape the apparent fact that there seems little evidence for the expression of kinship values through notable monuments in the earliest periods of the settlement in England.[2]

The 'well-peopled' cemeteries that are known, with approximate rows of urns or bodies, can be interpreted as either a sign of an egalitarian or hierarchical[3] society, and it must be uncertain how, if at all, they relate to kinship groupings. Hodges recognises such an element when he says "'first-generation' burials appear to be scattered as if in expectation, as heads of families, that others will be joining them."[4] And of burials inland, it is noted, "Seventh-century burials in prehistoric and Roman-period barrows, if the recently excavated Wigber Low (in Derbyshire) is an accurate illustration, comprised family groups, though only for one or two generations."[5] Close groups of barrows as in Kent[6] or Sussex may also have family implications.

Given that kinship is likely to have been an enduring bond in Germanic society,[7] how did this force receive expression, and how could some assumed veneration of ancestors be maintained without clear monumental centres? The society of the settlers would necessarily have been a mobile one, and security of locale (and buried remains) not a practical ambition at first; but an ancestral presence in the home is perfectly viable – connected to the hearth, perhaps,[8] or to transported house-pillars.[9] A small separate wooden shrine (of the kind suspected on top of later burial mounds[10]) may also have served as a focus. In none of these cases are any direct relics necessarily involved, nor do we need to assume that an

---

[1] Hills, 1980, p.206, with pots "buried away from the centre" (p.204). On the possibility of burial mounds as part of the (flat) Spong Hill cemetery, see Hills, 1986, p.167.

[2] Which is odd when you consider that burial in tumuli was being prohibited in Old Saxony in the late eighth century. Van de Noort, 1993, p.67, notes the existence of barrows in the Rhine basin and North Switzerland (i.e. "along the Rhine and the upper Danube") in the period 550–675 AD, and their use in Saxony during the seventh and eighth centuries. Burial mounds were being used in the core area of the Merovingian empire between 550 and 750 AD. Scandinavia had a separate, continuous tradition of mound-building from the later Roman Iron Age. There was also come limited use of burial mounds by Romano-Celts in West Britain and Scotland in the fifth to early sixth centuries (*ibid.* p.69). Nonetheless, the implication in the English context is that the custom was modelled on local prehistoric examples rather than brought over from the continent.

[3] In the sense of imposed equality

[4] Hodges, 1989, p.28 re fifth century

[5] *ibid.* p.64

[6] Grinsell, 1953, p.27

[7] See e.g. Whitelock, 1952, pp.38–42

[8] See prohibitions relating to use of 'oven', below.

[9] See Ellis Davidson 1969, pp.71–2; Foote & Wilson, 1970, p.400.

[10] See Foote & Wilson, 1970, p.413

ancestral 'soul' is inhabiting a piece of wood or whatever; but an article or site could serve as the symbol of ancestral presence.[1] And rather than mounds of eminent individuals, a sense of a group presence could have been important – this could well provide the link between the kin dead and beliefs in elves and *fylgjur*, that is, a general, anonymous grouping of benevolent (ancestral) forces. In this case, the centre of rites could be the home (for a limited kin grouping) or a cemetery (for a more inclusive group), and we can at least assert that some ritual attended even the flatter cemeteries, as the burning of grain there is recorded.[2]

As a greater measure of security developed in England, or new 'dynasties' emerged, and of course as 'immigrant' population grew, incipient respect for the kin could have found expression in more notable burials for particular individuals, either as founders of families or settlements or as political figures, representing the need for a more obvious system of coherence as territory expanded. Later waves of settlers may have brought different customs with them, or Anglo-Saxon practices within the new country may themselves have evolved. The element of reaction and local influence could be strong; so James wonders "are so-called 'typically Anglo-Saxon' burial customs dependent on the circumstances of the area in which the Anglo-Saxons settled rather than being an immutable ethnic attribute?"[3]

No certain consistent picture or interpretation is likely, for any measure of social (even local) uniformity could well take time to build, including the possibility of new consensuses and re-emerging or re-interpreted traditions: not impossibly the need for a more overt ritual could represent a reaction to the remnant Romano-Celtic (Christian) culture and its tenets of immortality in appropriate Germanic terms. Or more elaborate burials may reflect a pagan adaptation of continental Christian grandeur in such matters.[4]

A society organised on kinship is likely to pay greater attention to the burial of a prominent member of the family, and to be capable of venerating ancestors. A society organised on a political basis is more likely to cross kinship lines[5] and stress the glory of its late leaders or an 'impersonal' deity; remembering that that deity may still have an ancestral origin. Neither tendency need be exclusively agricultural or aggressive. Despite all these uncertainties a possible line from general regard for the collective family dead, to specific mounds of local

---

[1] Thus in America, "Instead of sacred places the Indians venerated medicine bundles, which were in effect portable shrines." Burland, 1965, p.87

[2] Meaney 1964, p.18, and see below, p.106.

[3] 1980, p.51

[4] Ellis, 1943, pp.12ff speculates that the elaborate Scandinavian pagan burials of the sixth century and later might owe their inspiration to Merovingian ceremonialism; Van de Noort, 1993, p.66, considers that barrows could be seen as "a monumental answer to the church-graves," and served to express "the opposition of non-Christians to the Christian elite."

[5] Is it coincidental that Odin is associated with warriors, Thor with sailors and thralls?

importance, and on to major mounds of great leaders seems worth proposing. Such a development (especially 550–600 AD) may be implied by Arnold,[1] leading "to the final pattern of... very rich graves removed from the lower groups."

We should at least consider whether the careful burial rituals of the Germanic peoples imply some definite role for the body or (if credited) disembodied 'soul' after death. 'Ghosts' in the Icelandic sagas, be it noted, are seldom see-through spirits with only the power to terrify, they are usually physical forces of some violence and identifiable as the dead themselves reanimated in some way. Indeed the word 'ghost' is supposed to be related to root-words associated with anger, terror, violence,[2] but may only reflect in this emphasis one aspect of the potentiality of the dead or one sense of the word, since 'ghost' can also can be used in a neutral or benevolent sense as of the Holy Ghost. Examples of the dead rising and plaguing the living are particularly common in the *Erbyggya Saga* e.g. ch.34 and 63; *Grettirs Saga* (ch.18) affords an example of a dead body, once disturbed, initiating attacks on the living. But not necessarily always sources of dread: some more personal tragedy seems implied in a translation offered[3] of the right-hand end panel of the Franks Casket: "Here Hos sits on the sorrow-mound; she suffers distress in that Ertae had decreed for her a wretched den of sorrows and torments of mind" – a sentiment not unlike those expressed in the *Wife's Lament*; while in *Njal's Saga*, the sombrely triumphant voice of Gunnar is heard coming from his burial mound singing an encouraging song to his avengers (ch.78). And in the *Eyrbyggja Saga:*

> "Thorolf called that mountain Helga Fell and believed that he and his kinsmen would go into it when they died... One evening in the autumn... Thorstein's shepherd... saw the whole north side of the mountain [Holyfell] opened up, with great fires burning inside it, and the noise of feasting and clamour over the ale-horns... he was able to make out that Thorstein the Cod-Biter and his crew were being welcomed into the mountain, and that Thorstein was being invited to sit in the place of honour opposite his father."[4]

> [trans. Pálsson and Edwards, 1973, pp.41,51]

The afterlife, be it noted, is situated not in some Valhalla (described in the poem *Grimnismál*) or some prison-like Hell but in the ground of the grave; a concept quite unacceptable to Christians as implying doubt about the inferior, physical and corruptible nature of the normal body and the superior, eternal nature of the soul, the separate existence of a soul at all (parting from the body at death) and in some

---

[1] 1980, p.132

[2] See Klein, 1971 s.v. *ghost*

[3] As unattributed text accompanying display of the casket at Laing Art Gallery, Newcastle-upon-Tyne, 1996, based on a transcription in the *Anglo-Saxon Poetic Records* series.

[4] Further details are given in Vigfusson & Powell, 1883, 1, 415

measure querying the reality of Doomsday and resurrection (if the dead just carry on with some sort of uncontrolled existence). Besides the question of imputing saint-like attributes of conscious survival to non-Christians. All this surely lies behind Ælfric's stern comments, on the case of Saul and the witch of Endor:

> *Gyt farað wiccan to wega gelæton*
> *and to hæþenum brygelsum mid heora gedwimore*
> *and clipiað to ðam deofle, and he cymð to*
> *on þæs mannes gelicnysse þe þær lið bebyrged*
> *swylce he of deaðe arise; ac heo ne mæg þæt don,*
> *þæt se deada arise þurh hyre drycræft."*

[*Homilies* ed. Pope EETS 259–60, 1967–8, 2, 796]

Still witches resort to crossroads, and to heathen burial-sites with their evil rites, and call upon the devil, and he arrives in the form of the person who lies buried there as if he had arisen from death; but she can not achieve that, that a dead person arise by her witchcraft.

In other words, even if the image of a dead person were produced (as Saul requested, *1 Samuel* ch.28, seeming convinced that "it was Samuel" in verse 14), it would only be a demon impersonating such a one, for the power of resurrection is strictly the preserve of God alone, not possible by mere magic. Or as Isidore observes: "after certain incantations and the sprinkling of blood, the dead *seem* to come to life, to divine and to answer questions."[1] In much the same way, Saxo[2] lays stress on the "ludificandorum oculorum" – the fooling of the eyes, viewing the pagan gods as conjurers and illusionists almost.

But if the body continued in some sense aware in the grave, or perhaps literally asleep,[3] why did so many early Anglian settlers (e.g. in E. Yorks., E. Anglia, Midlands[4]) practice cremation? This custom was old in Northern Europe, where it was introduced during the Bronze Age (perhaps c.1000 BC).[5] To Derolez[6] it symbolises a belief in a continued existence on a non-material plane, an emphasis on the irreversible nature of the change of death, and perhaps a means of finally releasing some spiritual element from the bonds of the body. Fire can be taken as a symbol of the process of release of the soul, a return to the sky of some element

---

[1] *Etymologia* Bk.viii per Aquinas p.196

[2] Bk.1 ch.5

[3] Relevant here is the bed burial described in Speake, 1989; for Frankish and Alemanic parallels see Vierck, 1980.

[4] Myres, 1969, p.16

[5] Inhumation returns with the Iron Age, c.800 BC and onwards, from which time also boat-motif tombs may date. On the case for continuity of inhumation see Kendall & Wells, 1992, p.xi.

[6] 1962, pp.161–2

that came at birth from above, but there is no external confirmation for such beliefs in the Germanic context. Cremation in Anglo-Saxon England was more a survival of a particular, older custom, perhaps typical of the first Anglian settlers – even a defining tribal feature in common estimate? (And a warning against assuming any great measure of consistency of ritual or religion among the Anglo-Saxon settlers, at least initially.) It is incompatible, clearly, with a concept of the survival of the body in its full form, but where it was practised as a burning off of the flesh and a collecting up of the bones[1] it could be viewed as a sort of preservation of the durable parts of the body, a freeing of the permanent frame from the corruptible element. It is a speeding, as it were, of the natural process of decay. The inclusion of combs, tweezers, little scissors or models of the same[2] with the ashes or bones in a cremation pot seems to attest a continuation of rather than a deletion of a 'physical' afterlife: a possible if bizarre explanation is that as nails and hair of a dead body have been observed to continue a measure of growth after life ceases, it may be that the correct cosmetic tools were provided, even in the context when a body had been reduced to a token form.

To Meaney[3] "the idea behind it [i.e. cremation] seems to be to release the spirit; to dismiss it from the body primarily in order that it shall no longer trouble the living." The dead, in her argument, are a force to be protected against, as in the siting of inhumation cemeteries "well away from the village – the boundary of a territory seems to have been the proper place for them."[4] But a margin could represent a zone of practically unusable as well as indisputably neutral land, suitable for different or special use; if the boundary is earlier, it may have possessed some special reputation; if later, it may have used convenient markers like burial mounds to define its course – indeed there may be a direct link between burials and assertions of land-ownership through family descent.[5] On the whole, I

---

[1] At Spong Hill, Norfolk, a selection of typical bones seems to have sufficed to represent any one body e.g. skull, a few pieces of long bone, pelvis and vertebrae (Putnam, 1980).

[2] E.g. "miniature tweezers, shears and razors… often with a bone comb," at Spong Hill (Hills, 1986, p.166).

[3] 1964, p.16. Against this would seem to be the evidence of Putnam, 1980, who considers examples of multiple burials in one urn as "related to the general pattern of the cemetery which is one of grouping urns together with un-urned bones... strongly suggestive of tribal, kin, or familial groupings." (p.219) i.e. that such a form of burial can indicate a continuing appreciation of social links rather than a severance.

[4] *ibid.* p.20

[5] "Church graves and burial mounds would have created a clear link between the successors of the deceased and their lands, as ties to the ancestors were made visible." Van de Noort, 1993, p.72. The relationship between land and the ancestor is asserted by Pader, 1980, p.162, after Saxe and Goldstein: "Thus the presence of formal, including bounded, cemeteries is consistently associated with corporate groups practising lineal descent. Such a group's communal rights to restricted resources, usually land, are justified by links with the common ancestors who worked the land – that is with the dead."

can find little evidence of abhorrence of the dead (as opposed to the body) in Old English literature, little reference to the malevolent dead before the Icelandic texts noted above, and in general, a regard and respect whether for pagan ancestor or Christian figure of achievement or sanctity from the past. For though Christianity made a show of despising the physical, yet the body was integral to resurrection and the careful burying (and marking?) of the dead was a feature of Christian practice – one that may well have reinforced pagan ancestral beliefs at a stage of initial contact and reaction.

But if we do allow a Germanic belief in some sort of survival after death, attached to physical remains, and beyond this some form of veneration of the ancestor, how, specifically, could the dead be contacted, drawn to involve themselves in the human world again? Firstly, a clear focus is desirable; this could be some relic or symbol; but would be ideally (for Christian or pagan) the bodily remains, and secondarily the site of burial – distinguished not so much as a tribute to the dead as a symbol of location for the reference of the living. "The dead man continues to exist in his grave-mound as in a house, and there sacrifices may be made to him, and possessions laid in the howe beside him, so that he may have the use of them as he dwells there."[1] Thus the *Indiculus Superstitionum* starts with warnings about misuse of burial sites: no.1 "De sacrilegio ad sepulchra mortuorum" (About sacrilege (committed) at the tombs of the dead); no.2 "De sacrilegio super defunctos i.e. dadsisas" (On sacrilege practised upon the dead i.e. dirges); while no.3 "De spurcalibus in Februario" (On defilements (practised) in February) is connected by Saupe[2] with a similar provision about "epulas ad parentum suorum tumulos apponerent, quas nocte daemones consumebant," (feasts placed on the burial mounds of their parents, which are in fact eaten by demons during the night). It may be because of pagan beliefs associated with such mounds that Charlemagne, for Saxony, ordained that Christians (*alias* the whole Saxon population, under duress) be henceforth buried in church cemeteries, "et non ad tumulus paganorum"[3] (and not in the tumuli of the pagans.) Laws surviving from Norway in the twelfth century prohibit veneration of a mound or a cult-structure.[4] In *Beowulf* also we have the curious feature of the hero being buried not where he fell (though a ready-made mound was on site) but being carried elsewhere for the funerary rites – to a location of more traditional relevance to his tribe?

Though mounds, perhaps even re-used pre-existent mounds, are a clear signal of a burial, it seems a standing stone or cairn could also play a similar marker role. Thus the Icelandic *Hausbok* (early fourteenth century) criticises "women... so stupid as to take their food to stonepiles and into caves. They consecrate it to the *landvættir* and then eat it, believing that the *landvættir* would be friendly to them,

[1] Ellis, 1943, p.61; Meaney notes items of food sometimes deposited with inhumation, 1964 p.18.
[2] 1891, p.9
[3] Pertz, 1835, p.49
[4] Foote & Wilson, 1970, p.396

and they will be more prosperous."[1] Vigfusson & Powell[2] cite the *Kristni Saga* as containing an example of a 'family spirit' which dwelt in a monolith. Here the monumental marker may parallel the Christian grave-marker, a focus, as it were, not incompatible with the requirement in *Exodus* 20:25 to use unhewn rock for an altar; and not impossibly there may be a clue here to alleged early worship of trees and stones – if these were considered capable of providing a focus (a symbol of contact) for an ancestral or sacred presence because of their uncorrupted form. In the *Ynglinga Saga* (ch.8) Odin is portrayed as encouraging not only cremation, but burial in mounds or a place marked with a standing stone.

The ritual of burial itself may play an important part in establishing the way to continued future mutual contact. An account of a tenth century Viking burial on the Volga, preserved by an Arab writer, Ibn Fadlan,[3] portrays the cremation of a chief, accompanied by sexual rituals and human sacrifice – in this case involving a young slave-woman. The victim has visions, just before her death, of firstly her own parents, then "all my dead relations sitting together,"[4] and lastly the recently deceased master in some green paradise – though whether she is a messenger, an 'object' to be transferred or part of a ritual to benefit her dead lord is not clear. Nor is this so alien an example: some pagan graves in England have been interpreted as suggesting burial of wife with husband at time of his death.[5] At Sutton Hoo, one major modern excavation (completed 1992) of a grave perhaps attributable to Wuffa, was reported to be accompanied by numbers of human sacrifices.[6] In other cases, the position of limbs may indicate burial alive.[7]

Sacrifice from among the losers in battle seems well attested,[8] in the Germanic context: in Saxo (Bk 9), Sivard, the son of Ragnar Lothbrok, when so badly wounded that ordinary doctors gave up on him, was miraculously healed by "an amazingly tall person," an "old man, ...providing he would consecrate to him the souls of those men he was to strike down in war;"[9] in another, Hading, having unwittingly killed a superhuman being who had taken on the shape of a sea-

---

[1] Trans. Turville-Petre, 1964, p.233

[2] 1883, 1, 416

[3] See Ellis Davidson, 1964 p.52; in Ellis, 1943, p.42 she singles out the account of Baldur's cremation in Snorri's *Prose Edda*, less alarming, but thoroughly vivid. The Ibn Fadlan account is translated in Foote & Wilson, 1970, pp.408–10.

[4] Foote & Wilson, 1970, p.410

[5] Wilson, 1992, pp.71–3; for continental examples see Foote & Wilson, 1970, pp.411–2

[6] Stone, 1994a, discusses the suggestion that this is untypical, perhaps a reaction to encroaching Christianity.

[7] Wilson,1992, p.77

[8] Ellis Davidson, 1969, pp.36–9; 1964 (Sidonius' evidence of sacrifice by drowning of captured slaves to note a successful voyage)

[9] Trans. Fisher, Saxo, 1979, 1, p.283

monster, is obliged to make annual human sacrifice to Frey;[1] such sacrifice is always purposeful, in its own terms, an offering of some kind to secure the good will of a supernatural force or power, not just a marker of the violence of battle or some symbol of destruction[2] (though please remember there is a circuit of self-deception by which we manage to rationalise any act). Indeed, in *Beowulf* (lines 2940–1) we have a possibly related account of how the Swedish king, Ongentheow, threatened to hang his captives when trapped and surrounded. Nor solely by hanging: Adam of Bremen heard accounts (eleventh century) of animals and humans sacrificed by hanging in a sacred grove at Uppsala;[3] and at the same site, "There is also a spring at which the pagans are accustomed to make their sacrifices, and into it they plunge a live man."[4]

Even the rather 'wholesome' (to modern eyes) links with nature, implied by respect for trees, wells, etc., may include a sacrificial element. Among Picts, for example, drowning was the standard method of execution: the elaborate Burghead Well may be such a site, and the cross-slab at Glamis Manse in Angus, with human being thrust head-first into a cauldron, may illustrate the very act of sacrifice.[5]

In Germanic context, there is the regrettable example of Fiolnir, a son of Frey, who was drowned, accidentally as it seems, in a vat of mead.[6]

There is considerable evidence for sacrificial rituals among Germanic peoples from all periods and areas, indicating a significant tradition of enaction.[7] Tacitus noted the use of human sacrifice amongst the Semnones, who would have an intertribal meeting and mark this with "savage worship by a public human sacrifice";[8] in ch.9 he mentions the propitiation of Mercury (Woden? as emblem of ancestry or – like the Roman god – of commerce?) on certain days with human victims. It may indeed have not stopped there. Saupe assumed a reference to cannibalism in the *Indiculus Superstitionum* item 30, "De eo quod credunt quia femine lunam comede[n]t, quod possint corda hominum tollere iuxta paganos"

---

[1] Saxo, 1979, 1, pp.29–30, indeed Frey is attributed with initiating "a morbid and unspeakable form of expiation... the slaughter of human victims."
   trans. Fisher, *ibid.* p.73
[2] In the *Erbyggja Saga*, ch.10, there is the perhaps fanciful figure of victims having their backs broken upon a sacrificial stone, called Thor's stone, during the course of an Assembly.
[3] Foote & Wilson, 1970, p.400
[4] Quoted by Bauschatz, 1982, p.60; cf. *Indiculus Superstitionum* no.11 "De Fontibus Sacrificiorum" (On springs used for sacrifices).
[5] Ritchie, 1989, p.15
[6] *Ynglinga Saga* ch.14
[7] For Celtic parallels e.g. Vortigern advised to sacrifice a child to secure the building of a safe fortress, and a monk interred alive in the foundations of the monastery at Iona, see de Jubainville 1905.
[8] *Germania* ch.39, trans. Fyfe

(Concerning the belief among the pagans that because women might eat the moon, they might also be able to remove the hearts from human bodies) and there is a curious similar reference in Charlemagne's Capitulary of 797 AD (for Saxony):

> *Si quis a diabulo deceptus crediderit, secundum morem paganorum, virum aliquem aut feminam strigam esse et homines commedere, et propter hoc ipsam incenderit, vel carnem eius ad commendum dederit, vel ipsam commederit, capitis sententiae punietur.*

[Pertz, 1835, pp.48–9]

> If anyone, deceived by the devil, believes, after the fashion of the pagans, that a certain man or woman is a witch and eats people, and because of this burns the woman or gives her flesh over to be eaten, or themselves eat the flesh, let them suffer capital punishment.

The implication of such sacrifice in the case of an ancestor could be that the offering of a human life was a method of conveying a quantum of life-force to the dead; either at the time of burial (as in Ibn Fadlan's account, though this was presumably a make-shift on-journey affair), or at stated periods thereafter,[1] or (perhaps) on special occasions of need. This implies in turn that blood was regarded as a life-force, a universal elixir that could impart or sustain life; and I think some support for that view can be gleaned from Saxo, where Bjarki, having killed a great bear, "told Hialti, his comrade, to apply his mouth and suck out the beast's blood so that he might achieve greater strength; for it was believed that this type of drink afforded an increased bodily vigour."[2] In the context of the dead, a libation or pouring on the ground, of liquor or blood might have the same intention.[3] Animal sacrifices would of course be much commoner than human ones, and we may note here the death of Thorstan Rednebb in the *Landnámabók*, which was accompanied by all his sheep leaping of their own accord into a waterfall and ending up drowned.[4]

The sort of help received in return might be in the form of intervention in that other world, for healing, perhaps; or – if the action were the responsibility of people in this world – a message i.e. directions of what to do or how to cope with a pressing problem – either as voice message from beyond, or dream or vision. (Paralleling in the political world, the emphasis on councils, discussion and *ræd* –

---

[1] "In Germany and Scandinavia it was said that they [the dead] came back either at Halloween or at Christmas." Ellis Davidson,1988, p.114

[2] Bk.2 ch.6, trans. Fisher, Saxo, 1979, 1, p.55; the *Confessional of Ecgbert* ch.31 provides against the use by a wife of any of her husband's blood "pro aliquo remedio" (as any sort of remedy.) cf. P106 below on the tasting of blood. Ælfric (quoted below p147) also equates (animal) life with blood – in contemptuous reference to some pagan belief?

[3] On libations, see Derolez, 1962, pp. 189–90

[4] Vigfusson & Powell, 1883, 1, p.421; see further de Jubainville, 1905.

i.e. the duty of advice,[1] and the importance of omens and auguries in affirming or negating decisions; thus at Uppsala in Sweden and Tingwall on the Isle of Man, important burial mounds mark the site of the local assembly.) "There are indeed many scattered references in the literature to kings and seers sitting on burial mounds, not only in order to make a claim to the title of a former king after his death, but also when they desired to seek inspiration."[2] One King, Hrollaugr, rolled down a royal mound to signify his subjection to a higher political power.[3]

From the *Flateyjarbók* comes the story of the shepherd Hallbjörn, who sought poetic inspiration by sitting and even sleeping on the mound where the poet Thorleif was buried. Appropriately, the shepherd thought he would start with composing a poem in Thorlief's honour, but found the technical aspects daunting. One night as he slept, he dreamed that a figure came out of the mound and showed him how to compose such a poem properly. And as he woke afterwards, he thought he saw his instructor returning truly into the interior of the mound. Hallbjörn's dream poem was a success, and his subsequent poetry as well.

Mound-sitting need not be a matter of special ritual or special need, however. In *Hallfred's Saga*, the yeoman Thorlaf "was wont, as was much the habit of the men of old, to sit for hours together out on the howe not far from the homestead."[4] An impressive example of coercive communication is recorded by Saxo: Hading and his female companion Harthgrepa seek shelter for the night at a house –

> "where they were celebrating in melancholy manner the funeral of the master, who had just died. Desiring to probe the will of the gods by magic, she inscribed most gruesome spells on wood and made Hading insert them under the corpse's tongue, which then, in a voice terrible to the ear, uttered these lines..."
>
> [Saxo, Bk.1 ch.6, trans. Fisher, Saxo, 1979, 1, p.24]

But there are other examples: of Odin, in the *Ynglinga Saga* ch.7 it is said, "whiles would he wake up dead men from the earth, or sit down under men hanged;"[5] seemingly as one of his many methods of gathering information.

---

[1] *Regin-* in compounds may convey a similar sense of advice, decision (Jente, 1921, equates Gothic *ragin* with 'Rat, Beschluss').

[2] Ellis Davidson, 1969, pp.86–7

[3] Ellis, 1943, p.106

[4] Vigfusson & Powell, 1883, 1, 416; see further Ellis Davidson, 1988, p.130.

[5] trans. Morris & Magnússon, 1893, p.18

In the *Elder* or *Poetic Edda*: *Hávamál* (The Words of the High One) stanza157:

> *Þat kannk et tolfta   ef sék á tré uppi*
> *váfa virgilná:*
> *svá ek ríst   ok í rúnum fák,*
> *at sá gengr gumi*
> *ok m⇒lir viþ mik.*

I know a twelfth (spell): If I see on a tree a corpse swinging, then I cut and colour runes so that the man walks again and talks to me.

The word for spells in this poem is *ljóþ* cf. Old English *leoð* 'song, lay, poem'. – cf. "diris admodum *carminibus* ligno insculptis" in Saxo.[1]

On another occasion, Odin, needing advice on ill-omened dreams affecting Baldur, raises a seeress from the dead for questioning:

> "On Woden rode... till he came to the lofty hall of Hell. Then Woden rode to its eastern gate, where he knew the Sibyl's [*vælo*] barrow stood. He feel to chanting the mighty spells that move the dead [*val-galdr*], till she rose all unwilling, and her corpse spake..."

> [*Baldur's Dreams* trans. Vigfusson & Powell, 1883, 1, 182]

Whether by ritual of blood or command, some control over the dead as ancestral force is implied. The obligation of the dead to the living is not always recognised: in *The Waking of Angantyr* in the *Elder Edda*, Hervor summons her father Angantyr from his grave with this invocation:

> 'Angantyr, wake! Hervor calls you,
> Your only daughter whom you had by Tofa....
> Hervard, Hjorward, Hrani, awake!
> Hear me, all of you, under the tree-roots...'

When this does not seem to be having effect, she curses them if they do not respond:

> 'May ants shred you all to pieces,
> Dogs rend you; may you rot away.'

This brings Angantyr before her, apparently of his own free will, for he claims:

> 'Your words are mad, without meaning to them.'

> [trans. Taylor & Auden 1973]

---

[1] Bk.1, ch.6.

The return of the dead in this case is accompanied by searing flames, appropriate to volcanic Iceland or some image of Hell. Yet in a curious possible parallel, the Old English translation of *Deuteronomy* 18:10 seems to substitute for 'pass through the fire', the element, 'do not seek for solutions from the dead' – and this in turn serves as part of a proverb in the *Distiches of Cato*: 'Ne acse þu nanre wicce rædes, ne sech þu riht æt deaden; soðlice God ascuneð swylce þing.' (Do not ask any witch for advice, nor seek solutions (or justice?) from the dead; truly God despises all that kind of thing.) The link is perhaps slight, but did fire in the Biblical text evoke some association with attempts to contact the dead in the Anglo-Saxon translator?

The importance of the voice, as messenger between different levels of existence, in combination with a practical recognition of the head as the source of hearing, speech and sight (and perhaps intelligence) may lie behind the well-attested cult of the head. This is apparent in Celtic tradition e.g. the cult centre at Roquepertuse (Bouches-des-Rhône), with its many skulls inlaid in sockets in stone.[1] And is indeed universal, as with the even more bizarre ritual consumption of ancestors' brains in, for example, New Guinea.[2] In Anglo-Saxon tradition, we have the Christian cult of the head of St Oswald, the chief part of his body recovered; the apparent concern of the Vikings to dispose of the head of Byrhtnoð at Maldon;[3] heads were also severed from statues and thrown into rivers.[4] The importance of the head as containing the organ of speech is attested in the case of Mimir, whose head was returned to Odin during a primeval hostage crisis:

> "Then Odin took the head, and smeared it with such worts that it might not rot, and sang words of wizardry thereover, and gave it such might that it spake to him and told him many hidden matters."
>
> [*Ynglinga Saga* trans. Morris & Magnússon, 1893, ch.4 (p.14)]

Not dissimilarly, in the *Erbyggja Saga*, a severed head chants a warning verse (ch.43).

To a Christian the head in isolation could be a focus of veneration; to the pagan its removal seems to have been a gesture of control or a precaution to stop the later reanimation or magical use of the body.[5] In Ellis Davidson's assessment: "The

---

[1] cf. the small "stone 'severed' head" found in Romano-Celtic context at Corbridge, possibly third century AD, with a hollow on top for "ritual purposes" (Laing Art Gallery exhibition, Newcastle-upon-Tyne, 1996). For unusual treatment of skulls in late Roman levels at Wroxeter, see Hills, 1986, p.136.

[2] Of particular note, since it causes the disease *kuru*, which has factors in common with scrapies in sheep and B.S.E. in cattle – see Wilkins, 1995, pp.170–172.

[3] See Griffiths, 1991, intro.

[4] Merrifield, 1987, p.101

[5] Thus *Grettir's Saga* ch.18, *Svarfdaela Saga* ch.18, and Saxo Bk.1.ch.7; compare the preservation of the skull of the Mahdi as a drinking-vessel by the victors after the Battle

custom of preserving and honouring the heads of kings and respected enemies must surely have been based on the belief they could bring luck and power to the living, who might inherit their heroic qualities."[1]

This quasi-cannibalistic transfer is not expected in Christian contexts. Yet the story of the head of St Edmund is a graphic example of the importance that continued to be attached to what is literally head-hunting :

> Well then the pirate fleet-force   fared back to ship
> and hid the head   of the holy Edmund
> in the thick brambles   to prevent its burial.
> After a period   when they had departed,
> then the folk of the region   – such remnant as was left there –
> came to where their lord's body   lay without its head;
> and they were very distressed   in their hearts for his death
> and the more so that they had not   the head to the body.
> Then said some witness   (who watched it all earlier)
> that the Vikings had   the head with them
> and it seemed to him   as was certainly the case
> that they had hidden the head   somewhere in the holt.
> Then all went   in unison to the woods,
> seeking everywhere   among the scrub and brambles
> in the hope they could   discover the head.
> Now as a great wonder   a wolf had been sent
> by God's guidance   to guard the head
> against the other dangerous animals   by day and night.
> They went on casting about   and always calling out
> as is usual   with those who often go to the forest
> 'Where are you now, friend?'   And them the head answered:
> 'Here! Here! Here!'   and so it continually called
> until they all were collected   together by the calling.
> There lay the grey wolf   that guarded the head
> and with his two paws he had   clasped the head,
> being greedy and hungry   and yet for God not daring
> to nibble at the head   but held it safe from all animals.
> Then they all marvelled   at this wolf's vigilance
> and carried the holy head   home with them
> thanking the Almighty   for all his miracles.
> But the wolf pattered after them,   kept pace with the head
> until they came to town,   rather as though he were tame,
> then at last went back   to the woods once more.

---

of Omdurman in 1898, and see E. V. Gordon *An Introduction to Old Norse*, 1957, pp.lxix–lxx, on this supposed tradition.

[1] 1988, p.129

Then the local people   laid the head
to the holy body   and buried Edmund
as best they could   considering the need for hurry,
and raised a church   upon the site, in time.

[trans. from Ælfric's Lives of Saints]

In one bizarre case, an Anglo-Saxon cemetery at Mitcham in Surrey, of the mid fifth to late sixth century yielded "a number of what might be called cranial anomalies: inhumations with an extra head; skeletons with no head; the head at the feet; and skulls buried alone."[1] So extraordinary are the implications, that meddling by Victorian archaeologists has been posited to explain the situation. But a similar example, with the skull laid by the ankles, in the case of two female bodies, is reported at the Romano-British cemetery at Guilden Morden.[2] A female skull buried ritually on its own was found at Bidford Wa.[3]

Here, too, we might consider whether the lugs or crude pulled 'handles' on funerary urns indicate a sort of symbolism of pot as head, an indication that communication is still possible; but in general, representative ornament on such pots is rare.[4] As Derolez points out,[5] the urns used for funerary purposes do not seem to differ from everyday ware, except in the case of a few special designs of pot – as a house, or as a face. And there is "the deliberate holing of certain Anglo-Frisian urns, or the provision of windows of glass in some of the early urns of Kent, Lincolnshire and Cambridgeshire."[6] Not as gestures of escape or dismissal, but as symbols of communication?

Such ancestral beliefs, if admissible as likely, and if persisting into the Christian period, would be a special target of attack by the authorities as almost a parody of the cult of saints. Hence *Indiculus Superstitionum* no.25 "De eo, quod sibi sanctos fingunt quoslibet mortuos." (of the practice in which people fashion for themselves saint-like images of any dead person.) To the Church, the average dead were at best neutral, discounted until the Last Judgement; and perhaps a sort of morbid fear of the dead body was encouraged to sever any surviving regard, as in the Exeter Book and later Middle English *Soul & Body* poems. The exceptional dead, the saints, whose souls were conveyed to heaven straight at death, were a different matter: and the veneration of their relics may seem to possess (and may have been feared or even encouraged to possess at the time) something of the sort of superstitious regard for ancestral remains I assume for the pagan Anglo-Saxon

---

[1] Wilson, 1992, p.93

[2] South-west of Cambridge; see Saxo, 1980, 2, note, p.33.

[3] Meaney, 1964, p.17

[4] See Myres, 1977, vol.1, 67

[5] Derolez, 1962, p.162

[6] Meaney, 1964, p.16; in the *Ynglinga Saga* ch.12, Frey is buried in a great mound with a door and three windows, but only to persuade the Swedes he was still alive and receiving taxes.

period. The parallel is the more striking if we assume for ancestors not the role of 'god' but of a more limited but benevolent, assisting power. If so, the irregular, local or family-level competition was to be discouraged or re-channelled, and a potential link between family ancestors and elves may well have led to the bad reputation accorded elves in Christian medical texts.

For the dead were to be consigned in many cases to Hell as evil, and without this clear sign of punishment hereafter it might have been difficult to enforce the Christian message clearly and effectively: that is, draw people to a particular morality through establishing the principle of an ultimate (and sometimes immediate) settling-up.[1] Though it adopts a Germanic name, and in the following description has a distinctly chilly northern atmosphere, the collective punishment in Hell is a Christian concept unlike the neutral survival in the grave likelier in pagan tradition.

> ...*him helle gescop,*
> *wælcealde wic   wintre beðeahte;*
> *wæter in sende   and wyrmgeardas,*
> *atol deor monig   irenum hornum,*
> *blodige earnas   and blace nædran,*
> *ðurst and hungor   and ðearle gewin,*
> *egna egesan,   unrotnesse;*
> *and æghwilc him ðissa earfeða   ece stondað*
> *butan edwende   a ðenden hie lifigað.*

[Solomon & Saturn 2, 289–296]

for them (i.e. the sinners) He (i.e. God) created Hell, a death-cold dwelling obscured with wintry (mists); water He sent in, and snake-pits, many a poisonous beast with iron horns, bloodied eagles and black adders, thirst and hunger and fierce conflict, apprehensions of all terrors, and great sadness; and each of them must forever endure these hardships without relief for as long they live.

Reinforced with such imagery, the Anglo-Saxon priest could present the uncertainty of life and death in an effective way, with hope of some response:

> *Uton nu geþencan þis sceorte lif and georne clypian to þam ælmihtigan*
> *Gode þæt he us geunne þæs ecan lifes þe nænne ende næfð, forðæm þe nan*
> *mann nat þyssere worulde geendunge ne furðon his agene geendunge.*

[Rogation Homily 7, Bazire & Cross, 1989, p.99]

Let us now think upon this short life and call keenly upon the almighty God to grant us the eternal life that has no end, because no man knows (when) this world will end nor indeed (when) his own life will end.

---

[1] For the origins of eschatological belief in the Zoroastrian dualism of good and evil see Ling, 1968, p.82.

THE AROUND WORLD

Elves, etc.

The gods of the Anglo-Saxons, whatever their exact form, had to share the Middle Earth not only with men, but with a number of (apparently) unseen beings, which could be called demons, fairies, elves, and the like. They are seemingly unconnected: gods are human-like in many ways, the others only semi-human in form; but by origin, there could well be some parallels. Gods like Thor and Frey may be connected with agricultural success,[1] and elves, too, could be viewed as nature spirits or elementals; from another view, Woden seems an ancestor god, and elves may have a connection with the home and family too, and an even greater involvement in everyday affairs. But nature spirits are not considered ancestral by origin: they concern a sort of animistic belief by which various features of the natural world become viewed as forces imbued with consciousness, and even personified as actual beings.[2] Vigfusson & Powell[3] claim this sort of role for spirits known as *vættr* in Iceland – the word corresponds with Old English *wiht*, which can equal 'demon' or more usually any entity with movement.[4] Of the strictly inanimate, swords are often accorded names as though they have some inner power of their own; while the *Riddles* in the Exeter Book open with a dramatic vision of a storm as a human-thinking phenomenon. But the humanisation of objects and processes may be a universal (as well as a literary) tendency, as is a trust in local approachable super-human arbiters[5] (even in the saints of Christianity or the modern trend for Ombudsmen), and it is probably a coincidence that the evidence for fairy beings in Britain survives best at the Celtic edges; there is no reason to suppose that Germanic beliefs in this field were derivative,[6] though we have to be aware that elements can be

---

[1] Foote & Wilson, 1970, p.389

[2] Curiously, the sense of presence need not be individualised: thus "The [American] Indians of the great forests had a wider concept of nature, and their thinkers postulated a supreme spirit, all-embracing, but without form and having little contact with men. The concept was more like an abstract notion such as Time…" (Burland, 1965, p.73).

[3] 1883, 1, 419

[4] See Jente, 1921, pp.153–4

[5] We should however take warning that it may be too easy to imply the presence of a spirit from archaeological or folk record: "In the ancient custom… of wassailing fruit trees, the farmer and his labourers not only drank a health to the orchard trees, but also urged them to be fruitful." (Phythian-Adams, 1975, p.15) A clear case for a breathalyser?

[6] Derolez suggests a Celtic source for elves, 1962, p.226, but without presenting any clear evidence.

adapted and endowed with entirely new roles and properties that can make them hard (perhaps pointless) to trace.

To the Romano-Celts, we are told, "...any form of water, either a spring, a pond, a lake, a river or even a bog, seems to have provided a focus for some sort of spirit which represented the power and movement of the water, and which was often endowed with healing properties."[1] In such cases we might assume a non-ancestral spirit, but one whose help would still need to be 'paid for', and this is a possible reason for later apparent offerings of Anglo-Saxon objects by discarding them in rivers, a practice of some popularity throughout Europe during the Viking era – an offering? – or a tributary/disposive gesture with a dead man's weapon? – at least some "unrecorded sacrificial custom."[2] However, in Anglo-Saxon charms, dangerous items are sometimes disposed of by placing them in running water, or handing them over to an itinerant vendor, simply as a means of losing them, so it may be that it is not some spirit that is being invoked, as the erosive and disposive virtue of water in this case.

Such 'misunderstandings' of natural processes were ridiculed by the Christians:

Sume men synd swa ablende þæt hi bringað heora lac
to eorðfæstum stane and eac to treowum
and to wylspringum swa swa wiccan tæcað
and nellað understandan hu stuntlice hi doð
oððe hu se deada stan oððe þæt dumbe treow
him mæge gehelpan oððe hæle forgifan
þone hi sylfe ne astyriað of ðære stowe næfre.

[Ælfric *Lives of the Saints* Bk 1 no.17 *De Auguriis*]

'Some men are so blinded that they bring their offerings to an earth-fast stone, and eke to trees, and to well-springs, even as witches teach, and will not understand how foolishly they act, or how the dead stone or the dumb tree can help them, or give them health, when they themselves never stir from the place.'

[trans. W. Skeat]

The same criterion was not applied, understandably, to Christian images, endowed with symbolic dignity by the operation of art, or to holy relics, that represented contact with the favourites of an active as opposed to a false god – for it is not miraculous action that is criticised but perception of the source of power. And whatever the concept of God, for early Christians (as for modern scientists) the world was pregnant with uncertainties, and all manner of unseen influences. As demons (the preferred Christian evaluation), these might be classed as beings of the air, incorporeal, and therefore invisible. A Scottish Highland explanation is

---

[1] Wacher, 1987, p.186; Hatt, 1970, pp.133–4 discusses the possibility that the cult of springs was ultimately Mediterranean in origin.

[2] Merrifield, 1987, p.108

that they are 'the hidden children of Eve'. In this legend, Eve had so many children she was ashamed to admit to them all before God; He in response declared, 'Let those who were hidden from me be hidden from all Mankind.'[1] Their invisibility could be as plausibly attributed to nocturnal habits, remote haunts, or shyness.

The initiated or gifted could see them, as a matter of course, though some special act of viewing could be necessary: "Bring your gaze nearer and look through my arm akimbo. You must first hallow your eyes with the sign of victory to recognise the war-god safely face-to-face," is the advice someone receives in Saxo;[2] if sight were granted, such beings could be distinguished by virtue of their stature or some other clear visual attribute. For example, they could be as small as half an inch high,[3] or medium small – in keeping with the "prehistoric earth dwellings which were popularly supposed to be the home of the fairies."[4] (Arthur Machen supported a historical interpretation, that legends of fairies were actually memories of smaller stature inhabitants of this Island driven into hiding by larger succeeding races. His source seems to have been David MacRitchie's *Testimony of Tradition* (1890).)

But they could be equally unduly large, like the Irish 'sidh': "The opalescent beings seem to be about fourteen feet in stature... an old schoolmaster in the West of Ireland described them to me from his own visions as tall, beautiful people, and he used some Gaelic words, which I took as meaning that they were shining with every colour."[5]

An attempt to explain such forms is made by Saxo (early thirteenth century), who calls supernatural beings in general "apparitions marked by a false pallor whose momentary corporeal substance was borrowed from insubstantial air,"[6] foreshadowing Prospero's "baseless fabric." Gervase of Tilbury's *Book of Marvels* (c.1200) similarly mentions *fadae* or a sort of fairy, who form an aerial body to become visible to men [ch.86]. A much later, but thoroughly intriguing account, is that in *The Secret Common-Wealth*, by Robert Kirk, completed in 1691, drawing on folk beliefs among the Lowland and the Gaelic Scots. Kirk saw these subterranean and (usually) invisible spirits as conforming to the Christian scheme, for (according to his recent editor) "it accorded with belief in the orders of the spiritual world of Christianity as they are described in medieval theological commentaries and their descendants."[7] – i.e. not so gross as man but not so ethereal as angels, though the more standard view would place them intermediate between man and Satan i.e. as lower demons. In Kirk's words: "Their

---

[1] Briggs, 1978, p.31
[2] Trans. Fisher, Saxo, 1979, 1, p.63
[3] Briggs,1967, p.3, quoting Gervase of Tilbury
[4] Briggs 1978, p.28
[5] quoted by K. M. Briggs, 1978, p.28
[6] trans. Fisher, Saxo, 1979, 1, p.44
[7] Stewart Sanderson's introduction, Kirk, 1976, p.39

Chamaeleon-like bodies swim in the air, neer the Earth with bagg and bagadge,"[1] perhaps as "spirits which assume light aery bodies,"[2] or again, "light changable bodies (lik those called Astrall) somewhat of the nature of a condens'd cloud,"[3] or "congealed air."[4] Fortunately, "They do not all the harm which appearingly they have power to do: nor are they perceived to be in great pain, save that they are usually silent and sullen. They are said to have many pleasant Toyish Books... They have nothing of the Bible, save collected parcels for Charms, [i.e. bits of holy scripture as amulets] and counter-Charms; not to defend themselves withall, but to operate on other Animals: for they are a people invulnerabl by our weapons."[5] Primitive arrow-heads are seen as their work: "So I have had Barbed arrow-heads of yellow flint, that could not be cut so smal, and neat, of so britle a substance by all the art of man."[6] Mostly they engage themselves in work: "Wherefore in this sam age they are somtimes heard to bake bread, strike hammers, and to do such like services within the little hillocks where they most haunt."[7] Also there are well-disposed types, such as "The Brownies who in som Families as Drudges clean the houses and dishes after all goe to bed, taking with him his portion of food, and removing befor day break."[8] Perhaps in the relatively safe, busy, and increasingly controllable world of the seventeenth century, the idea of malignant opposition to human progress was bound to yield to a quainter view of a neutral and industrious fairy folk, for who could seriously oppose the will or pattern of man?

The Anglo-Saxon world was a good deal less predictable and dependable, and we should expect a more pronounced, efficacious role for these invasive beings. But in surviving records of Old English, the references are few and not always informative...

ælf. 'elf' is recognised in many varieties: *dun-elfen, feld-elfen, wudu-elfen, wylde-elfen, sae-elfen, land-ælf* – but mostly these occur as interpretations of Latin peculiarities in *Ælfric's Glossary*, and may indeed correspond with the categories for 'demons' established by Proclus in the fifth century AD.[9] It is not safe to assume that Anglo-Saxon elves themselves came in such neat categories – this is likelier a function of the need to find an equivalent for a Latin term. Yet it may be significant that *ælf* is the standard cover-all term resorted to in such cases. In

[1] Kirk, 1976, p.51
[2] *ibid.* p.53
[3] *ibid.* pp.49–50
[4] *ibid.* p.50
[5] *ibid.* p.57
[6] *ibid.* p.88
[7] *ibid.* p.50
[8] *ibid.* p.88
[9] Cavendish, 1975, p.244

Storms' opinion[1] "*Elves* was the general name for spirits among the Germanic peoples. They are neither good or bad spirits, they help or hurt." In medical recipes,[2] their role is less balanced and the elf is clearly cited as a cause of illness: in the view of Bosworth & Toller, as a source of nightmare (as *ælfsiden*, 'the influence of elves or evil spirits, the nightmare'[3]); but in one case[4] the elf is cited as associated with, perhaps equivalent to, "*yfel costung... oþþe nihtgengan*," which has a more sinister ring, and may recall the occasional use of elf to gloss *incubus*[5] (a type of demon). The occurrence of the term 'elf-shot' (in the charm, *Wið Færstice,* below, Pt 2, no.10) is indicative too; it would not be so called if it were a normal wound caused by a mortal weapon. The implication is that this is a 'magical' wound, an infection caused by an invisible arrow or dart, and by consequence, that the Anglo-Saxon elf is an invisible being also. In more than one Old English text such magic weapons are elaborated as demoniac:

> *Þa deofle fihtende scuten heora fyrene flan ongean þa sawle, ac þa deoflice flan wurden þærrihte ealle adwæscte þurh þæs gewæpnodon ængles gescyldnysse.*   [Vision of Furseus, Warner 1917 p.110]

The demons attacking shot their fiery arrows against the soul, but the devilish arrows were instantly totally quenched by the armed angel's defence.

And:

> *Ða he þa se eadiga wer mid þære gesettredan streale gewundod wæs þæs awerigedan gastes....*   [Prose Life of St Guthlac, ed. Gonzer, 1909, p.120]

Then was the holy man (Guthlac) wounded by the carefully prepared arrow of the accursed demon...

Thus illness becomes associated with temptation and moral health:

> *Se ungeseowenlice feond... ongann þa sænden his ættrige wæpnen, þæt synd costnungen, togeanes þan halgen were.*   [St Neot, Warner 1917, p.130]

The invisible fiend.. began then to launch his poisonous weapons, which are temptations, against the holy man.

And the invisibility of such attackers is again a factor in the phrase "ðone ungesewenlican mancynnes feond"[6] (the invisible enemy of mankind) for the Devil.

---

[1] 1948, p.229

[2] See survey of such references in Thun, 1969, pp.387–390

[3] cf. German *alp* 'nightmare'; the second element may be related to Icelandic *seiðr*, see Thun, 1969, p.388

[4] *Leechbook*, pt.3 item 61

[5] See Bosworth & Toller s.v. *ælf*; for comment, Thun, 1969, p.389

[6] Rogation Homily 7, Bazire & Cross, 1989, p.97

Is it possible that the aggressive, human-harming aspect of elves, as disease-causers or (to give them their formal title) "projectile-discharging supernatural beings,"[1] comes from fusion of elf and demon, in a Christian context, and relates to a strict dichotomy of good and evil typical of Christianity?[2] If so, Thun's reasonable assertion,[3] "An important aspect of the Anglo-Saxon conception of elves is that they were thought of as bringing disease," would both be confirmed and need qualifying to refer only to 'the Christian Anglo-Saxon conception of elves'.

For considered as an element in human names,[4] *ælf* takes on a more attractive aspect: *Ælf-red* means wise as an elf (or possessing the wisdom of an elf), *Ælf-ric* equals rich or powerful as an elf, and the adjective *ælf-scinu* (as brightly beautiful as an elf), applied to the biblical heroine Judith, also conveys a favourable impression.[5] Does such popularity imply the antiquity of the concept of 'elf' or simply attest to their good reputation, in one manifestation? It may be, indeed, that names convey the older more traditional concept of elf as neutral or even benevolent; and that they are cast in the role of bringers-of-illness specifically to fit them into the Christian model of the world, and this accounts for their malevolent causative role in the ecclesiastical charm.

A later division into good and bad, as in the *Prose Edda*, is considered by Cavendish to exemplify a basic contrast between the 'light elves', living in *Alfheim*, and the 'dark elves' who live underground, and are "black and sinister because there were the dead."[6] Similarly, Grimm notes of the far north, "When the elf is red he brings people gold; when blue, corn or ill-luck."[7]

Elves in some aspects have a family or household role and may have had a connection at some stage with the familiar or communal dead (as greater figures may relate to royal ancestors). In this case they would not be nature spirits at all, and we run into contradictory evidences on such points. Elves are associated with

---

[1] Thun, 1969, p.386. We would assume that the projectiles were hurled by hand or shot from a bow, but Ælfric in his Homily for the 4th Sunday after Easter has a ?biblical-based reference to children "þe sceotiað mid reodum on heora geonglicum plegan on heora plegstowe" (who shoot with reed-pipes in their childish play in their playground).

[2] Originally Zoroastrian; see Ling, 1968, 78–80

[3] 1969, pp.380–1

[4] *ælf-* is an element in some 35 personal names; see Jente 1921 pp.170-1 viz. *Ælf, Ælfa, Ælf-beorht, ~cytel, ~flæd, ~frið, ~gar, ~geard, ~geat, ~gifu, ~god, ~gyð, ~heah, ~helm, ~here, ~hild, ~hun, ~mær, ~noð, ~red, ~ric, ~run, ~ryd, ~sig, ~stan, ~swið, ~þryð, ~waru, ~weald, ~weard, ~wen, ~wig, ~wine, ~wulf, ~wynn;* Thun, 1969, p.379, considers the form *ælf* as probably West Mercian, *ielf* or *ylf* that appropriate to West Saxon.

[5] There is also one plant-name, *ælf-þone* 'elf-vine' or Woody Nightshade, see Thun, 1969, pp.390–392.

[6] Cavendish, 1975, p.239

[7] A Lithuanian superstition recorded in Grimm, 1888, 4, p.1847. On black elves and white elves see Grimm, 1883, 2, 444–6; dark elves, he thinks, might be the souls of dead men. They are all inclined to be thievish, it seems.

hills and mounds; and could need simple offerings of milk and meat[1] – factors suggesting a parallel with the dead,[2] but no ancestral context is mentioned in Old English texts, unless this is a case of deliberate reticence or loss of an already remote tradition. There is one possibly significant later example:

> 'She [Thordis] said, There is a knoll a little way from here where the Elves dwell; thou shalt take thither the ox that Cormac slew, and sprinkle the blood of the ox on the outside of the knoll, and give the Elves a banquet of the meat; and thou shalt be healed.'
>
> [*Cormac's Saga* via Vigfusson & Powell, 1883, 1, 414]

This links elves with both (burial) mounds and the process of healing – in contrast to Christian Anglo-Saxon texts that suggest elves as a problem to health.

In Sweden an *álfablot* or offering to elves, in the interest of future harvests, is known,[3] which could support an elemental or an ancestral interpretation – Vigfusson & Powell[4] suggest such rituals were "collective sacrifices to what we take to be spirits of the dead, male and female, 'Alfa-blót' or 'Dísa-blót', held every year to gain good seasons." The *dísir* are female entities of uncertain role; they may play some part in deciding events (like valkyries or norns[5]), but later become associated with family spirits, *fylgjur*, suggesting a considerable measure of flexibility in the attributes and functions of such beings.

(Two enigmatic beings in this class of supernatural entities, that should perhaps be considered parallel to elf, are represented only in personal names: **os** and **ceol**. *Os* is usually interpreted as 'divine-' in name compounds, but if we recall Jordanes' assertion of *ansis* as ancestor or demi-god, might be better rendered 'ancestral-'. It is found in combination with an impressive range of secondary elements[6] that attest to its popularity. *Ceol* is found in combination with a similar range of qualities,[7] and it hard to agree that it means simply 'boat' on the assumption that Anglo-Saxons joined name elements irrespective of sense. But Merovingian *childe-* (cf. Old English *hilde-* 'battle-'), *chilpe-* (cf. Old English *helpe-* 'help') do

---

[1] Ellis Davidson, 1964, p.156

[2] As affirmed in Ellis, 1943, p.115–6, Ellis Davidson, 1969, p.117

[3] Derolez, 1962, p.226

[4] 1883, pp.413–4

[5] See Turville-Petre, 1964, pp.221–2

[6] E.g. from Searle, 1897: *Os-beald, ~bearn, ~beorht, ~beorn, ~burh, ~cytel, ~dæg, ~fereth, ~fram, ~frida, ~frith, ~gar, ~geard, ~gearn, ~geat, ~gifu, ~god, ~grim, ~(g)yth, ~helm, ~here, ~lac, ~laf, ~mær, ~mod, ~mun,d, ~red, ~ric, ~thryth, ~weald, ~weard, ~wio, ~wig, ~wine, ~with, ~wulf, ~wynn*. Jente, 1921, para.54, adds *~ecg, ~waru* and *~weda (wido, widu)*.

[7] Again, from Searle, 1897: *Ceol-beald, ~beorht, ~burh, ~flæd, ~frith, ~gar, ~hæth, ~heah, ~heard, ~helm, ~here, ~lah, ~mær, ~mod, ~mund, ~noth, ~red, ~ric, ~sige, ~stan, ~swith, ~thryth, ~uht* (i.e. -wiht?), *~weald, ~weard, ~weorth, ~wig, ~wine, ~wio, ~wulf, ~wynn*.

not seem relevant; and Irish *col-* forms too alien. There remain other possibilities in Old English,[1] and a posited root meaning of 'something vaulted or rounded' (cf. Dutch *koll* 'head', Middle High German *kule* 'ball') permits Tengvik to envisage an Old English *coll* = 'hill'[2]. Might Latin *coelum* 'heaven' be relevant?)

The **dweorg** or dwarf implies small size, and in Old English it glosses Latin words like *nanus, pygmaeus, pumilio*. In recipes, it may be mentioned not so much as an agent of disease, as an equivalent for disease, *dweorg* being used in the sense of a convulsive fit or fever, but without the role of dwarf as such in causing the attack being clearly explained. Cameron[3] favours a shift in meaning from 'dwarf' to 'fever', and de Vriend[4] notes the quote: "hwile he riþaþ swylce he on dueorge sy," (and for a while he trembled as though he were in a fever) – which lends some support to this. The Old English Charm '*Wið Dweorh*' ('Against a Dwarf'; see page 190 no.9) may also be connected with fever. Another occurrence in the Old English *Herbal* ("Dweorg onweg to donne..."[5] (To get rid of a 'dwarf'...) is not any more revealing, for here *dweorg* represents the Latin *verrucas* (warts).

The element 'dwarf' is used in the case of one plant: *dweorge-dwostle* (pennyroyal or flea-bane, properly *Mentha pulegium* L.), described in the Old English *Herbal*[6] as having two types, "*wer 7 wif*" (male and female) with different colours of flowers, and having the strange attribute that 'they bloom with the greatest colour when other neighbouring plants wither and fade.' The second element in this plant-name is obscure;[7] nor do we do know if the Old English name was formed after some attribute in the Latin or independently awarded.

Dweorg is not an element in Anglo-Saxon personal names, whether from unfamiliarity or dislike. Such few mentions as we have of dwarvish characteristics come from Scandinavian legend, including their reputation as metal-workers; in Derolez' summary "Ils habitaient les montagnes et les rochers, et craignaient la lumière du soleil...,"[8] which Grimm[9] saw as mountains and caves, recording the evocative Norse kenning *Dvergmál* 'dwarf-talk' for an echo. One plausible

---

[1] Including the enigmatic "þec, Crist cyning, ceolas weorðian" (you, Christ, King, *ceols* venerate) in *Azarias* line 103, where *ceolas* is conventionally translated 'cold winds' by collation with the following "forst ond snaw." There is also Old English *ceole*, 'throat' or 'beak of a ship'.
[2] Tengvik, 1938, pp.142, 299.
[3] 1993, p.152
[4] 1984, p.310
[5] *The OE Herbarium*, ed. de Vriend, 1984, p.266
[6] *ibid.* no.XCIV, p.136
[7] There is the possibility it is a corruption of *ðistel* (thistle) in mimicry of the *dweorg* element.
[8] Derolez, 1962, p.224
[9] 1883, 2, 452–5

illustration of dwarves, on a hog-back stone coffin is also Scandinavian in inspiration.[1] The dwarves there look rather like featureless ginger-bread men.

Some other terms are also recorded from the Anglo-Saxon period:

puca or *pucel*, the later Puck of 'A Midsummer Night's Dream'; the word has cognates in Irish (*puca*), Welsh (*pwci*), Icelandic and Danish.[2] A *boggart* or *bogle* seems related to the Welsh word *bwg*, and modern 'bogie-man'. Both *fairy* and *goblin* are French (ultimately Latin) in origin. Fairies seem to take on many of the attributes of elves: "Indeed, half of our ideas about fairies are derived from the heathen beliefs as to the spirits of the dead, their purity, kindliness, homes in hillocks..."[3]

An *orc* is a sort of demon, glossing Latin *orcus*, a name of Pluto, and hence used with the sense of 'death' in Classical Latin verse. There is mention of the worship of Orcus in seventh century Gaul,[4] but this could be a Latinisation of some other god. In one Old English gloss for Latin *orcus*, it is rendered "*orc, þyrs vel hel-deofol*." (Orc, giant or demon of hell.) *Orcneas* in *Beowulf* is seemingly a variant of this, perhaps via the Latin adjective *orcinus*.

Scucca (pronounced with initial 'sh-') is a word for demon, favoured by Ælfric, where the demon has the expected Classical role of communciator.[5] It glosses both *daemon* and *zabulum* (the Greek form of *diabolum*). As a survival in later folklore, it is Shuck, the demon in form of a dog – the 'Shock' of Suffolk;[6] indeed Briggs' *Dictionary of British Folk-Tales* opens its section of folk legends with 19 pages of 'black dog' stories, including the powerful black dog of Bungay who terrified church-goers during a storm in 1577.

His origin is uncertain, and there is little obvious link between dogs and pagan Germanic lore. Turville-Petre[7] associates the dog with wolf and so with Odin; Ellis Davidson[8] sees him as a Cerberus-like "guardian of the underworld, and one reason for putting a dog into a grave might be to provide a guide for the dead."[9]

A similar manifestation is found in Yorkshire, called Pad-Foot: "about the size of a small donkey, black, with shaggy hair and large eyes like saucers; and he

---

[1] An example, from Lancashire, is illustrated in Ellis Davidson, 1969, p.122–3.

[2] Per Bosworth & Toller; see further Jente, 1921, pp.177–8.

[3] Vigfusson & Powell, 1883, 1, 418

[4] Dalton, 1927, p.248 – perhaps from a sermon of St Eligius, see Grimm, 4, 1888, pp.1737-9

[5] At *Beowulf* 939, "scuccan 7 scinnan" it is paired with *scinna*, a word for an apparition or evil spirit perhaps deriving from *scinan* 'to shine, show'.

[6] Briggs, 1971, p.17

[7] 1964, p.60

[8] 1988, p.57

[9] Examples of Anglo-Saxon burials with horse or dog are noted by Meaney, 1964, p.18, with dog by Green, 1992, p.84.

follows people by night, or waylays them in the road which they have to pass."[1] – which may go back to an apparition recorded in Reginald of Durham's Book on the Miracles of St Cuthbert, ch.17:

Subitoque, et improvide, canis nigerrimus permaximae magnitudinis pedibus anterioribus superius per parietem irrepsit.

Suddenly and unexpectedly a black dog of huge size sneaked into view, placing its front paws on the wall.

Typically the Northern *padfoot* is "a huge black mastiff-type dog with eyes shining red or green."[2] He is a solitary night-time visitant, bringing help or bad luck, in different circumstances; but whether as some animal manifestation of the Devil, or an older pre-Christian (even pre-Germanic) element, it is hard to determine. There are otherworld dogs in Welsh mythology, but white, with red ears; such are also reported from the Hebrides.[3] Celtic deities often did have a dog as companion,[4] but perhaps no specific source for man-and-dog coupling is necessary.

Dogs in a hunting pack might seem a similar line of tradition, but here too there is some confusion. Apart from the uncommon god Ull[5] who is sportsman and hunter *par excellence*, it is hard to identify hunting with dogs with any particular deity. The *Peterborough Chronicle* for 1125 AD has a famous account of 'the wild hunt' where "The huntsmen were black, huge, and hideous, and rode on black horses and black he-goats, and their hounds were jet black, with eyes like saucers, and horrible."[6] The goat, identified with Thor, or through Pan with the Christian concept of the Devil, is not a clear clue; and the image of a hunt may be no more, in this context, than a blatant satire on the Normans and their habits.[7] Hunting through the sky was attributed to Diana,[8] and even to the angel Gabriel;[9] but it is commonly associated with Odin (e.g. in Danish legend, see Fitch, 1994, p.77), or the mysterious figure of

---

[1] Henderson, 1925, p.273
[2] Linahan, 1994, p.33
[3] Per Linahan, *ibid.*
[4] Green, 1992 pp.82–3; remember also the delightful 'Pais Dinogad' stanza from the *Gododdin*, where the father is pictured setting off hunting, with perhaps just two dogs.
[5] Whose worship is recorded in Norway and Sweden – see Turville-Petre, 1964, p.183, and Foote & Wilson, 1970, p.394
[6] Trans. Garmonsway, 1953, p.258; dwarves riding on goats are noted by Grimm, 2, 1883, p.465.
[7] Going about with "an heep of houndes at his ers as he a lord were," in Langland's *Visio* passus X (B-text).
[8] The General Council of Ancyra issued a decree against women riding through the night sky on animals in honour of Diana. Crawford, 1963, p.110, dated this tentatively to the ninth century, but the Councils at Ancyra were held in the fourth century.
[9] Linahan, 1994, p.34

Herne.[1] Similar legends turn up in Holland, Switzerland,[2] and were carried to the New World to inspire the cautionary song, 'Ghost Riders in the Sky'.

To return to our catalogue: as well as the 'little folk', Old English attests various larger-than-life beings, the **ent**, **fifel** and **þyrs**, attributed, among other things, with the origin of great Roman ruins – as though only superhuman beings could need or construct homes of such strength and impressive proportions.

> Well-wrought is this wall of stone, now broken down by time;
> the structures of the city have fallen apart, the handiwork of giants decays.
> Roofs are collapsed, towers ruined,
> and the barred gate wrecked...   [opening of *The Ruin*]

Giants were perhaps associated with the Vanir group of gods[3] and occur in myths of creation and origin, as if underlining their ancient role. *Thurs*, in both the Icelandic and Norwegian *Rune Poems* is associated with "women's anguish" and "women's illness" – as some sort of incubus? In the apocryphal Biblical book *1 Enoch* giants breed with women but produce monsters – and so might be viewed (in Christian context) as a cause of misbirths.

A quasi-historical account of giants supplanted by the more acceptable (if pagan) gods is given by Saxo in Bk 1 ch.5. The giants are remarkable only for their size, the gods for their skill in divination and their general sharpness of mind. The contest between these two lasted a great time, but the gods eventually won supremacy and came to rule the world.

The giants accordingly retracted their sphere; thus in Derolez:[4] "Dans le Nord, ils habitaient Jötunheim, le monde des géants, qui se situait quelque part au nord-est, probablement dans les montagnes sauvages de la péninsule scandinave." They seem to play no part in Anglo-Saxon medicine or charms.

As to a theory of such beings, the *Beowulf* poem, examining the ancestry of the monster Grendel, notes that from Cain "were born all evil broods: ogres (*eotenas*) and elves (*ylfe*) and goblins (*orcneas*) – likewise the giants (*gigantes*) who for a long time strove against God;[5] he paid them their reward for that."[6] This neatly suggests both a corporeal origin for such monstrosities, while at the same time emphasising their separateness from humanity and accounting (via the feud of Cain and Abel) for their malevolence towards mankind.[7]

---

[1] It may even contribute to Alfred's image of death as a hunter that I cite below p.68.

[2] Fitch, 1994, pp.77, 21

[3] Ellis Davidson, 1969, p.93, re creation role see p.114

[4] 1962, p.229

[5] i.e. by building the Tower of Babel.

[6] Lines 111–4, trans. Swanton, 1978 (my annotations in brackets)

[7] Saxo also seems to affirm their physical basis when he refers to 'monstruosi generis viri quos gigantes antiquitas nominavit' (men of monstrous type whom Antiquity called giants). 1979, 1, Bk1 ch.6

Medicine

Whether motivatedly and maliciously interfering with human activities, or simply colliding, as it were, with the human world from time to time, elves and the like are assumed to provide an acceptable interpretation of many processes. Christian (and perhaps pagan[1]) detected in such forces a lacking causative element that "answered the questions of the untimely death of young people, of mysterious epidemics among cattle, of climatic disasters, of both wasting diseases and strokes, of infantile paralysis and of the birth of mongol and otherwise deficient children."[2] After all, we cannot see germs, but we are very clearly aware of their effects and so take their existence on trust; and we make catalogues of and hand out doses of dangerous substances much as Anglo-Saxons did their herbs, oblivious alike of side-effects.

The analogy is only partially true, of course, since our success rate in dealing with germs, based on a model that corresponds workably with external reality, must be assumed to be more effective than arbitrary rituals of magic, if still, to some critics, rather an adversarial approach to health.[3] Yet, to the patient, the processes are not so easily distinguished. As Mauss[4] notes: "...a doctor's drugs and potions and a surgeon's incisions are a real tissue of symbolic, sympathetic, homeopathic and antipathetic actions which are really thought of as magical." The groundwork is 'scientific', but in many cases modern science provides the same sort of perception of an arcane solution that we trust implicitly (and perhaps have to) for it to work. "When human beings are ill they require magic *and* medicine: both are essential components of almost every healer-patient contact."[5]

This trust is particularly disturbing in early notions of 'hygiene':

> *Ðonne snottrum men snæd oððglideð,*
> *ða he be leohte gesihð, luteð æfter,*
> *gesegnað and gesyfleð and him self friteð.*

> [Solomon & Saturn 2, 224–6]

---

[1] I hesitate to be definite about the cause of disease in the Anglo-Saxon pagan context: a dwarf? an intrusive element like a poison or arrow? the malicious dead (perhaps as 'worm')? an enemy spell? ill-luck alone? While I have proposed ancestral aid as a remedy, the action expected is unclear, though they would most easily a combat a personified force, and an animal form is suggested in the '*Wið Dweorh*' charm.

[2] Briggs, 1978, p.28 after Prof. Chistiansen

[3] The fear is that an escalating contest between germ and remedy results: "Antibiotics have not seen off the micro-organisms: indeed, the proliferation of drug-resistant strains of microbes has ensured that many diseases, widely regarded as long since conquered, are busily staging a deadly renaissance." Wilkins, 1994, p.xv

[4] 1972, pp.20

[5] Buckman, 1993, p.235

When a morsel of food slips from [the plate of] some wise man, and he locates it [on the floor] in the light, he bends down after it, signs it [with a cross] and seasons it and eats it himself.

Similarly,

Gif on mycelne wætan hwelc mus oððe wesle afealle, and ðær dead sy, sprencge man mid hæligwætere 7 ðicge.

[Confessional of pseudo-Egbert]

If some mouse or a weasel fall into a large [vessel of] liquid, and is [discovered] there dead, sprinkle on some holy water and consume it [as normal].

It is notable here that the sign of the cross, or holy water, is being used much as we believe disinfectants and antibiotics to have effect in our own world.

Illnesses without an obvious external causative factor might be attributed, as we have seen, to hostile elements shooting small (invisible) spears or darts at someone.[1] This in turn may give us some clue as to how the Anglo-Saxons regarded the body and the question of invasive disease. The frequent images using the word *hama* for the outer shell or coat of the body[2] suggests a concept of an exterior continuous whole 'skin', a sort of physical boundary, which is somehow penetrated by an undetected 'wound', as it were, paralleling actual wounds. A disease could be seen as a breach of the integrity of this defence, which had to be located and neutralised. This is not so strange and primitive as it may seem:

'As part of its defence against these forces [i.e. disease], the organism walls itself off from alien elements in the world. The skin of the body is such a wall, forming a natural border between the individual and the environment. No barrier, however, can be completely effective. Large communities are always vulnerable to sneak attacks and the human body, a vast community of cells, is no exception.'

[Pfeiffer, 1969, pp.163–4]

The protection might be achieved by magic formulae, by 'prayer' or offering, by some correct series of actions (a ritual), or by applying herbal drugs or remedies – or any combination of these; in short by a net of special knowledge and action that might be appreciated equally by both pagan and Christian. The Christian practice in relation to the integrity of the body is well illustrated in a special prayer called a

---

[1] The image is an enduring one and not always hostile: "The Lord was wonderfully present," he [Wesley] writes in his diary, "more than twenty persons feeling the arrows of conviction." Timothy Eden *Durham*, 1952, p.391.

[2] e.g. *flæsc-hama, heort-hama, lic-hama; græg-hama;* 'grey-coat' is presumably a wolf, as *feðer-hama* represents the plumage of a bird, and the unity of phrase may carry implications for shape-changing, as though outward appearance is the true identity.

lorica or 'breast-plate' – a sort of spiritual armour against the attack of disease, or other temptation, as applicable. The concept is probably derived from *Ephesians* 6.13–17 ("Wherefore take unto you the whole armour of God..."). As an example here is part of an Old English Lorica attributed (in its Latin form) to Gildas:

> *Crist mid me were fæste trume gefæstnige, ege [7] fyrhto ða sweartan weorud abrege. God unþurhsceotendlicre gescyldnesse æghwonan mec gescild ðinre mæhte mines lichoman lewera alle, alæs gesundum plegscylde gescyldendum anra gehwylc þætte nalæs ða sweartan deoblu in min sidan leligen swa swa gewuniað scytas [7] flanas: þone hnoll, ða heafodpannan mid þæm loccum ond eagan, ondwleotan, tungan, teð, ða næsþyrlu, swiran, hryncg, sidan, lendenu, ðyoh, micgern ond ða twa hond...*

> [*Lacnunga* cf. Grattan & Singer, 1952, pp.135–7]

May Christ confirm a fast covenant with me, that terror and fright disturb the dark troop (of demons). O God may you with your impenetrable defence and power shield me on all sides; free my body's parts all, protecting each of them with your safe defensive shield so that the dark demons may not launch, as is their custom, their darts and arrows at my sides. (Protect) my top, my skull with the hair and eyes, my face, tongue, teeth, the nostrils, neck, back, sides, loins, thighs, fatty parts, and both hands...

There then follows a detailed list of body parts, from head to toe; the same order adopted in the *Leechbook* parts 1 and 3 for listing ailments of the body and their herbal remedies, in the realm of 'serious' medicine.

Christian medicine had access, through the Graeco-Roman tradition, to some interesting observations on the biology of the body and possibly effective traditions of herbal drugs,[1] in addition to native knowledge of herbs. But the operation of the chemical constituents of these organic elements was not fully appreciated, as witness the curiously complex vocabulary for infection and counter-action in the *Nine Herbs Charm*. Old English *lybcræft* can mean alike the skill in applying drugs or the employment of magic or surgery. The processes of practical and mystical aid, in short, were one and the same, and the charm/prayer still played a large part in Christian healing: "Ne wyrta gaderunge mid nanum galdre, butan mid paternoster and mid credan, oððe mid sumum gebede þe to Gode belimpe."[2] (Nor any gathering of herbs with any charm, but with the Paternoster (Lord's Prayer) and the Creed, or with some prayer that belongs to God.) It is unlikely that many people could afford the attentions of a physician, if such a specialisation existed outside the richest of households, but some might spare a little gift to a local priest for whom compilations of charms may well have

---

[1] But difficult to obtain in England sometimes, see Cameron, 1993, p.29.
[2] *Penitential of pseudo-Egbert*

been made. This healing role for the clergy is spelt out in one Old English recipe[1] – 'and a mass priest shall perform the leechdom if a man hath means to get one.' Which suggests that even the parish priest might come expensive. For example, the price for tending to a troubled cow, including herbs and recital of the Paternoster was a tenth of the value of the beast.[2] Whether profit or orthodoxy were the motive, the Church aimed to keep a close eye on medicine: Ælfric's homily *De Auguriis* notes "Læcedom is alyfed fram lichamena tyddernysse and halige gebedu mid Godes bletsunge, and ealla oðre tilunga syndon andsæte Gode."[3] ('Medicine is granted for bodily infirmity, as are holy prayers, with God's blessing, but all other aids are hateful to God.' – trans. Skeat). The Church was, of course, the compiler of herbals and medical texts, and the preserver of a number of charms, some overtly Christian, some with a traditional element. If there was some flexibility here, it may well have been intended to encourage a switch from 'self-help' or confidence in a charmer to use of Church resources, but this only stresses the underlying problem that health was a major area of concern for everyone – with no obvious dependable solutions.

The charm cannot be claimed, therefore, as an exclusively pagan resource, and because of this it is hard to deduce a definite pre-Christian theory of medicine from such texts. In the probably pagan context, we have Woden as a healing force in the *Second Merseburg Charm*, and as a powerful champion in *The Nine Herbs Charm*; grouped but unspecified 'women' are called upon in the '*Wið Færstice*' charm (associated with a burial mound, be it noted) and the *First Merseburg Charm*; the plants of *The Nine Herbs Charm* seem imbued with power according to their own history or experience; the power (of the charmer?) to transform seems emphasised in '*Against a Wen*'; and several charms depend on or aim at power over animals. In general, good knowledge or good forces are invoked to expel or neutralise some adverse factor, seldom specified.

To the radical Christian, neither a physical nor an elf-based explanation nor a charm-dependent solution was necessary: disease could be viewed as the punishment for sin,[4] and such punishment could be visited on subsequent generations.[5] In treating of Christ healing the blind man,[6] an Old English homilist feels it necessary

---

[1] Quoted by Bonser 1963, p.227
[2] See Bonser, 1963, p.424
[3] *Lives of Saints* Bk.1 no.17
[4] *Deuteronomy* 28:58–61
[5] *Deuteronomy* 5:9 "…for I, the Lord thy God, am a jealous God, visiting the iniquity of the fathers upon the children even unto the third and fourth generation of them that hate me." And contrariwise, *Ezekiel* 18:20. Ling, 1968, p.124, feels that the emerging personification of evil in the Devil externalises this guilt, but the responsibility in that case remains with the individual not to submit to devilish temptation.
[6] The story opens ch.9 of St John's gospel: "And as Jesus passed by, he saw a man which was blind from his birth. And his disciples asked him, saying, Master, who did sin, this

to defend what might seem an unjustified remittance of punishment: "Nes ðe blindæ man swa þeah buton synnum on life – forþan ðe monig blind mon bið swiðe manful – ac he nes for his synne oððe for his magæ blind acenned."[1] (However the blind man was not without sins in his life – because many a blind man is very evil – but he was not born blind because of his sins or his parentage.) In the Old English *Phoenix* (lines 447–50) disease (*atre* – 'poison') is the surviving proof of the enmity of the 'ancient foes' (*ealdfeonda*), suggesting again an equation between infection and temptation, and illness and guilt. There are many cases of illness miraculously healed in the New Testament; particularly revealing is the man with palsy in *Luke* ch.5, for he is cured when Jesus says to him, "Man, thy sins are forgiven thee."[2] – a clear case where illness and sin are equated, opening the way to healing through confession and atonement.[3]

What of the case when a virtuous person falls ill? This exact scenario occurs in an episode in the *Life of Cuthbert*, when a husband of good status is so ashamed of his wife's illness that he hardly dares mention it to the saint, as retold in Ælfric's *Catholic Homilies*: "A certain pious man also had close acquaintance with the holy Cuthbert, and often attended his preaching. Then something worse happened to his wife than he ever expected, in that she became much troubled with madness. When the pious man approached the blessed Cuthbert... he could not for shame openly tell him that his pious wife lay in the grip of madness..." Nor is it any easier to accept, when Cuthbert guesses what the matter is, for "Then the man began to weep bitterly, deploring the misfortune."

Some explanation of the suffering of the good was clearly needed, and supplied in passages like the following:

> *Ac wite ge to wissan þæt se wælhreowa deofol*
> *ne mæg mannum derian mid nanre untrumnysse*
> *ne heora orf adydan butan drihtnes geþafunge.*
> *God is eall godnyss and he æfre wel wile*
> *ac manna yfelnysse mot beon gestyrod*
> *þonne geðafað God þam seoccan for oft*
> *þæt he men geswence for heora misdædum...*

> [Ælfric *Lives of Saints* Bk 1 no.17 De Auguriis]

But know ye for certain that the cruel devil cannot hurt men by any sickness, neither destroy their cattle, without the Lord's permission. God is all goodness, and He ever willeth well, but the minds of men may be excited

---

man, or his parents, that he was born blind? Jesus answered, Neither hath this man sinned, nor his parents: but that the works of God should be made manifest in him." etc.

[1] Warner, 1917, p.66

[2] *Luke* 5:20

[3] The Latin *Anonymous Life of Cuthbert* has that saint healing by forgiving sins (Colgrave, 1940, pp.117–9, discussed by Bonser, 1953, p.154)

to evil; then God permitteth the devil very often to afflict men for their misdeeds. [trans. Skeat]

Later in the text, this is ameliorated into a general statement of two main reasons for suffering: "Either God so punisheth our perverse deeds, or He proveth us through the peril..."[1] Note there is no consideration in the Christian view of disease being 'accidental' or the blameless consequence of human physical frailty, it is explained in well-defined terms of personal targeting by external agencies, motivated to attack mankind.

Incomprehensible cases of madness could be attributed to possession by a demon. This concept is met with in the New Testament and accepted as part of Church tradition by Anglo-Saxon Christianity. In the familiar story from the end of *Matthew* ch.8 ("...there met him two possessed with devils, coming out of the tombs, exceeding fierce"):

> *Ure Drihten adræfde deoflu mid his hæse of anum wodum menn;*
> *Þa wæs ðær gehende an heord swina*
> *and hi sona bædon þæt hi moston faran into ðam swynum*
> *and Drihten geðafode þa ðam deoflum þæt.*
> *Hi ða into þam swynum and hi ealle aweddan*
> *and urnon to ðære sæ and sona adruncon."*
>
> [Ælfric *Lives of Saints* 1, 17 De Auguriis]

'Our Saviour drave devils by His hest out of a possessed man. There was then nigh at hand an herd of swine, and they straightway prayed that they might go into the swine, and thereupon the Lord granted it to the devils. They then (entered) into the swine, and they all became mad, and ran to the sea, and forthwith were drowned.' [trans. Skeat]

The case Cuthbert was involved in – mentioned above – turned out to be possession by a demon, though here he was able to effect a cure at a distance:

Cuthbert then comforted him in words, said that the demon who wished to hurt her would give up on his approach and flee away with much fear, and the wife, full-witted and speaking normally, would come up to him and take his bridle. Then it turned out according to the teacher's words...

[Ælfric's *Catholic Homilies* 2nd series, no.10]

Such views must be relevant to any consideration of trepanning. Parker (1989) surveys 13 known examples (all adult) from the Anglo-Saxon period, from pagan and post-conversion cemeteries. As some 9 showed signs of subsequent healing, it is to be assumed the intention was not murderous or cannibalistic;[2] but whether it can be called religious/magical or medical in inspiration remains unclear. On the

---

[1] Trans. Skeat

[2] Though this motive is considered, Parker, 1989, p.79

medical side: "This man may have suffered from some mental abnormality in life, occasioning the trepanning of his skull, pehaps to release what was thought to be an evil spirit."[1] And: "Trepanation was probably carried out for two major reasons: as a surgical treatment after head injuries... or for the alleviation of headache, epilepsy, mental disease and coma, disease attributed to evil spirits, which escaped through the hole ground in the skull by a stone or flint."[2]

Yet the irrational is not always viewed as a disease; it can seemingly play a constructive role in society.[3] This is less likely with ailments with no positive aspect (headaches, coma, adult blindness, paralysis, stroke, etc.) and such might have seemed to justify drastic remedies.[4] In those cases, might we view trepanning as parallel to the holing of cremation urns – as a means of restoring communication? It would be hard, whatever the exact circumstances, to separate medical action from sacrificial or punitive motives – a point not without its relevance to the more drastic psychiatric remedies of the present day.

'Devil' and 'demon' are loan-words (and loan-concepts) from Latin Christianity, and appropriately liable to trouble the pious. Cuthbert had to confront demons when seeking to live as a hermit on Inner Farne; and similar opposition was met by Guthlac, the East Anglian saint and hermit, though in this case an added sinister element is noted – the demons talk in British (Welsh)!

> Þa onbræd he Guðlac of þam slæpe, and eode þa sona ut, and hawode and hercnode; þa gehyrde he mycel werod þara awyrgedra gasta on bryttisc sprecende...
>
> [Prose Life of Guthlac ch.6]

> Then Guthlac started from his sleep, and went straight out and looked about and listened; then he heard a great troop of cursed spirits speaking in British...

Those who overcame such assaults by demons (a sort of shamanistic initiation trial?[5]) attained both a reputation and a value to the Church. If illness were associated with sin, then healing could be a matter of forgiveness and sudden transformation to good health by, literally, a miracle – part of the lottery of God's grace. This sign of favour could not be controlled by man but might be channelled

---

[1] Wilson, 1992, p.82

[2] Wilkins, 1994, p.3

[3] E.g. shamanism as a form of 'arctic hysteria', see Eliade, 1989, pp.24–5; for shaman as 'epileptic or liminal psychotic', see Glosecki, 1989, p.3. Relevant too is Adam of Bremen's assertion, 'Wodan, id est furor' (Woden, meaning frenzy). *Wod* is the standard word in Old English for 'mad, furious', and one compound, *woden-dream* (madness) may extend this sense specifically to the god.

[4] A coma, I am told, if caused by intercranial pressure e.g. a tumour or internal bleeding, *might, just possibly,* be relieved by trepanning, which would not be the case with epilepsy or many psychiatric disorders.

[5] Interestingly, this seems to be Glosecki's view (1989) of Beowulf's earlier adventures.

through a living saint and encouraged through his or her relics thereafter. The Council of Nicaea, 787 AD, recommended the presence of relics in a church; this may have been one factor in encouraging the promotion of local English saints for whom a supply of relics could be provided at little cost and effort. Saints from whom such benefits were to be expected could command great popularity, and might incidentally become centres of pilgrimage and a source of income for churches that contained their relics.

> *Binnon tyn dagum þær wurdon twa hund manna gehælede*
> *and swa fela binnan twelf monðum þæt man hi getellan ne mihte:*
> *se lictun læg afylled mid alefedum mannum*
> *swa þæt man eaðe ne mihte þæt mynster gesecan*
> *and þa ealle wurdon swa wundorlice gehælede*
> *binnan feawa dagum þæt man þær findan ne mihte*
> *fif unhale menn of þam micclan heape.*
>
> > [Ælfric *Lives of Saints* Bk.1 no.21, Swithhun]

'Within ten days two hundred men were healed, and so many within twelve months that no man could count them. The burial-ground lay filled with crippled folk so that people could hardly get into the minster; and they were all so miraculously healed within a few days, that one could not find there five unsound men out of that great crowd.'

Later, in the same text:

> *Seo ealde cyrce wæs eall behungen mid criccum*
> *and mid creopera sceamelum fram ende oð oþerne*
> *on ægðrum wage þe ðær wurdon gehælede*
> *and man ne mihte swa ðeah macian hi healfe up.*

'The old church was hung all round with crutches, and with the stools of cripples, (from one end to the other, on either wall), who had been healed there, and not even so could they put half of them up.'

> [trans. Skeat]

This recalls the *Indiculus Superstitionum* item no.29 on the subject of cures: "De ligneis pedibus vel manibus pagano ritu" (Concerning wooden feet or hands in pagan ritual) – possibly personal images hung up in trees in encouragement or in acknowledgement of healing? Similarly, offerings of votive wax limbs in churches to attract cure were also common.[1]

Riches accrued to monasteries: from cures, from donations of lands by patrons, from pilgrims and the expenses extractable from any such tourist, and even mutually beneficial donations of individual coins: "To the accompaniment of a prayer calling on the saint for help, a coin would be bent above a sick person or

---

[1] Merrifield, 1987, pp.88–90

animal, or one might be bent at a time of danger to avert some catastrophe."[1] On the passing of the risk, the coin would later be presented to the invoked saint's shrine. Hence we may note the interdict against "vota reddentes nisi ad æcclesiam Dei"[2] (fulfilling vows except in the case of the Church of God) which left the procedure available in proper context.

In some sense, the Church might be seen as in competition with physical medicine and folk charms alike, for dependence on forgiveness for healing became a matter of ecclesiastical income. May such a motive lie behind the advice, "Se ðe geuntrumod beo, bidde his hæle æt his Drihtne, and geðyldelice þa swingla forbere..."[3] (He that is sick, let him pray for his health to the Lord God, and endure the pain patiently...)? Such advice might be appropriate to discouraging 'self-treatment' with un-Christian remedies for those unlikely to have access to a 'proper' doctor. Not that they were missing much.

The more Classical tradition was based on Empedocles' (fifth century BC) theory of the four elements, extended by the fourth century BC to the (Hippocratic) four humours of the body. King Alfred, regarding the four elements, makes special note of their combinatory ability and balance:

> Each element that we are talking about has its own proper place, apart, yet it is with the others also commingled, and none of them could exist without the others, though they only combine unobviously: so now earth and water, though it is difficult to demonstrate to anyone ignorant, is present in fire,[4] as is evident to the wise; similarly fire is present in water[5] and also quietly hidden in stones,[6] invisibly – but it is still there. The Father of Angels has bound in fire so securely that it cannot escape back to its home station where that other fire dwells[7] naturally high above all this world: very quickly this transitory world would be overcome with cold if it were ever to abandon us and return to its home!
>
> [*Metre* 20, 142–158]

---

[1] *ibid.* p.91
[2] *Penitential of Theodore*, heading to ch.27
[3] Ælfric *Catholic Homilies* ed. Thorpe, 1844, i, 474–6
[4] Since earthy materials, like wood, burn and give off smoke; and water turns to steam
[5] Or there would be no hot water (only ice?).
[6] Flint, perhaps, or coal.
[7] The Sun

This was also the basis of the science of the body, through the medical theories of Hippocrates and Polybus (fifth–fourth centuries BC), and Democritus' theory, of the same period, that the body represented the universal situation in miniature. Bede's *De Temporum Ratione* ch.35 summarises the concept:[1]

> Man himself, who is called by the wise a microcosmos, that is a miniature world, has a body mixed throughout with these same humours... Blood, which increases in the Spring, is wet and warm; red cholic, which favours summer, is warm and dry; black cholic, which favours autumn, is dry and cold; phlegm, which favours winter, is cold and wet... When blood predominates it makes people joyful and glad, sociable, laughing and talking a great deal; red cholic makes them thin, though eating much, swift, bold, wrathful, agile; black cholic makes them serious, of settled disposition, even sad; phlegm renders them slow, sleepy, forgetful.

Disease was viewed as an imbalance of the humours, and introducing some item of diet or removing blood from the system could help restore a healthy balance. Inasmuch as blood-letting is likely to reduce (temporarily at least) the symptoms of fever, the treatment had a certain demonstrable validity; but one would have to be very strong of constitution, it seems, to survive the regime of purges, leeches, venesection, etc., that predominated from Graeco-Roman times into the nineteenth century.[2]

A parallel tradition[3] attributed parts of bodies to the government of individual planets or zodiacal signs; this would effect timing – when herbs were to be gathered, when applied; how different ailments affecting different parts of the body could be distinguished in cause and treatment. The Stoics' belief in a united universe, with 'sympathy' linking its details, permitted plants to be associated with planets,[4] while from Pliny came "the doctrine of signatures according to which each animal, plant or mineral had some mark indicating its hidden virtues or uses."[5] The shape of a flower might resemble some part of the human body and so indicate its application – '*similia similibus curantur*' (like is cured by like). This was exploited by Paracelsus in the sixteenth century, at which time a walnut because of its resembleance was good treatment for the brain (for example[6]). Similarly the Anglo-Saxon poking an 'ear' of barley into a patient's earhole.[7] Or,

---

[1] There is a later exposition of the same theory in *Byrhtferth's Manual*, Crawford, 1929, p.10

[2] See, for example, the casual references to leeches in Jane Austen's *Sanditon* chapters 5, 12; according to Wilkins, 1994, p.136, some 5 million leeches were imported to England from France in 1824, as a sample year.

[3] Evidenced in the pseudo-Hippocrates *Libellus de Medicorum Astrologia* – see Means p.72

[4] Second century BC to first century AD – Tester p.24

[5] Crombie, 1961, p.17

[6] For others, see Robbins, 1993, p.12

[7] Cameron, 1993, p.137

the claim that plantain (*wegbrade*) will resist illness as it resists physical pressure as a plant (in the *Nine Herbs Charm*). Or again: the use of mulberry was considered appropriate to treat a discharge of blood, with a play on the colours of white skin and red blood:

> *Wið blodes flewsan: þonne eallum mannum sy seofontyne nihta eald mona, æfter sunnan setlgange ær monan upryne cyme to þam treowe þe man hateþ morbeam, 7 of ðam nim æppel mid þinre wynstran hande, mid twam fingrum, þæt is mid þuman 7 mid hringfingre, hwitne æppel þe þonne gyt ne readige; ahefe hyne þonne upp, 7 upp aris: he bið brice to þam uferan dæle þæs lichaman...*

[Medicina de Quadrupedis de Vriend, 1984, p.238]

> For a discharge of blood: when the moon is seventeen nights old – this applies to everyone – then after the sun has set but before the moon rises, get to the tree called mulberry and from it take a fruit with your left hand, with two fingers only – that is the thumb and ring-finger – chose a white fruit that has not yet reddened, lift it up, and yourself arise: it will be effective for the under part of the body...[1]

"Many treatments must have given some comfort to patients, and a few were positively useful," Cameron hopefully concludes.[2] In some cases of tested and tried remedies, this could be so. It is even possible that helpful treatments were arrived at by accident, using false premises and theories. But on the whole Anglo-Saxon medicine (like that of many other periods) was a chancy business; and even the defensive Cameron, considering one especially brutal form of treatment, has the grace to ask, "Did the man with the 'folded' skull ever recover, especially after being pounded with a sledgehammer?"[3]

---

[1] For comment see Meaney, 1989, p.25; she considers the text applies to menstrual blood, which seems likely, though *eallum mannum* (if not just a conventional phrase) also implies a wider relevance.

[2] Cameron, 1993, p.186

[3] *ibid.* p.40

Agriculture

Though still uncertain of date, it was probably during the Anglo-Saxon period that the heavy plough was introduced,[1] with clear advantages in coping with a range of soils, and with an investment in machinery and oxen that could well favour larger estates or co-operative farming, and large open-field systems. Well-timed action (implying practical knowledge) was essential to agricultural success and it is not surprising to find close connections between Church calendar and agricultural seasons.[2] As Ælfric's glossator states in the *Colloquy*, in answer to the question, which is the most important secular art: "Eorðtilþ, forþam se yrþling us ealle fett." (Agriculture, because the ploughman feeds us all.) Yet nothing was known about the patterns of climate or disease that might crucially affect a crop.

When Cuthbert set up as hermit on Inner Farne, his first crop failed, and his second was raided by ravens. If even a saint had problems, it is no wonder the average estate needed an elaborate[3] charm like the Land Ceremonies one [see page 175] to safeguard the proper germinating of the seed. Such agricultural ceremonies are typical of many civilisations, and recall especially the Roman *Ambervalia*. "There are certain religious or ridiculous superstitions of some who we see ceremoniously bless their Garden to preserve them against the witchcraft and sorcery of spiteful and envious persons," noted Pliny.[4] And it was perhaps a procession descended from the like that St Martin came upon in fourth century Gaul,[5] when could be seen rustics "dragging pagan images through their fields and vineyards in order to protect them from injury and loss."[6]

The Germanic peoples had agricultural rites and processions too, and some sort of processional shrine on a cart is recorded as late as the Icelandic settlement;[7] three headings in the *Indiculus Supersitionum* refer to related practices: no.23 "De sulcis circa villas" (Of furrows cut round villages – as a supernatural or protective barrier?); no.24 "De pagano cursu, quem yrias nominant, scisis pannis vel calciamentis" (Of the pagan procession which they call '*Yriae*', with rent clothes or shoes); and no.28 "De simulacro quod per campos portant" (Of the simulacrum they carry through the fields).

---

[1] I hesitate to accept Lynn White's opinion (1962, p.53) that this plough was a Viking contribution on the evidence of word-derivation alone; Norse *lagu* 'law', replacing Old English *æw* as a word, does not mean the absence of law in pre-Viking England.

[2] See Phythian-Adams, 1975, pp.21–2

[3] One might feel over-elaborate; this adds to the challenge of performance. In pagan Rome "we hear of an occasion when a sacrifice had to be repeated thirty times until the liturgy was perfect." Wilkinson, 1975, p.30

[4] Philemon Holland's translation of Pliny's *Natural History* (2 vols., London 1601) 2,10

[5] Sulpicius Severus' *Vita Martini* ch.6

[6] Dalton, 1927, vol.1 p.247

[7] In the *Flateyjarbók*, see Vigfusson & Powell, 1883, 1, 407, Stone, 1996, p.9.

Crop disease or drought could be attributed to malicious influences, and the power of God invoked to neutralise any such effect. So we have in effect pre-modern explanations of the causes of disease in crops, and appropriately pre-technological means of averting them. If the ritual didn't work, it in some measure proved the theory that malign influences existed. But the approach to such problems need not be adversarial. On a positive level, the ideal cycle of crop-life is to be hoped for, and initiated through some approach to benevolent supervisory powers, to guard against poor results. Most of the *Land Ceremonies Charm* is indeed of this positive nature, asking for encouragement of growth rather than protection from harm.

How much understanding there was of growth as a natural process is not clear. The *Old English Herbarium* notes that different plants are likely to be found in different sorts of ground, implying some awareness of habitat. The relationship of growth and season must have been clear, yet the *Land Ceremonies Charm* makes no appeal for special weather; rather it seems pre-occupied with the quality and 'luck' of the seed itself. Only very briefly is the theory of it all tackled, in Alfred's version of Boethius:

> Hæfð se ælmihtiga   eallum gesceaftum
> ðæt gewrixle geset   þe nu wunian sceal,
> wyrta growan,   leaf grenian
> þæt on hærfest eft   hrest 7 wealuwað...

[*Metre* 11, 55–58]

Has the Almighty for all creation established that state of (cyclical) change, so that plants grow (and) leaves become green which in turn in the autumn will die down and wither away...

Growth was one part of a cycle that included decline and death. Applied to the human lot, this produced one of Alfred's most memorable Boethian images (present but not developed to any extent in the Latin source), portraying human vulnerability as a cogent argument for social collaboration:

> Hwy ge þæs deaðes,   þe eow Drihten gesceop,
> gebidan ne magon   bitres gecyndes,
> nu he eow ælce dæg   onet toweard?
> Ne magon ge gesion   þæt he symle spyrað
> æfter æghwelcum   eorðan tudre,
> diorum 7 fuglum?   Dead eac swa same
> æfter moncynne   geond ðisne middangeard,
> egeslic hunta,   a bið on waðe,
> nyle he ænig swæð   æfre forlætan
> ær he gehe[n]de   þæt he hwile ær
> æfter spyrede.   Is þæt earmlic þing
> þæt his gebidan ne magon   burgsittende,

ungesælige men!   Hine ær willað
foran to sciotan.   Swa swa fulga cyn
oðð e wildu dior,   þa winnað betwuh,
æghwylc wolde   oðer acwellan –
ac þæt is unriht   æghwelcum men
þæt he oðerne   inwitþoncum
fioge on færðe,   swa swa fugla oðð e dior,
ac þæt wære rihtost   þætte rinca gehwylc
oðrum gulde   edlean on riht...

[*Metre* 27, 6–24]

Why can you not await that death that the Lord has destined for you, bitter enough in its own way, since now with each day it speeds towards you? Can you not see how he is always pursuing all of earth's species – beasts and birds alike? In just the same way, Death, the dreadful hunter, is on the track of mankind throughout the world and he will not give up on any spoor until he has laid hands on that he has been chasing so long. It is a wretched situation that the inhabitants can never bear to wait for him, luckless beings! But they must always try to get in first. Just like birds or wild beasts, that fight among themselves, each would kill the other – but it is not proper for any of us to hate another with malicious thoughts in his mind, like birds and animals do, but it were more proper for each person to respectfully yield the other his due in justice...

THE EMPTY WORLD

In almost shock contrast to the world around being thronged with invisible supernatural beings, and every facet of life accountable in terms of divine intervention, a number of Old English texts seem to place emphasis on an almost vacant supernatural world, a bleak reality, where events hardly have meaningful shape at all, so that all share in a world where happy endings cannot be counted on, where neither gods assist nor demons deter.

This is indeed a trenchant sort of 'realism', a disillusioned or liberated view of the human condition, without the intervention at the last minute of some god who will favour the virtuous or brave. Instead the human is left to his or her own resources, which may well be inadequate; and one's own conviction of what is proper behaviour has to serve in place of access to communal approval (*dom*) or official morality (*æw*). In *Njal's Saga* this very problem becomes a religious lesson: that the uncaring divisive outlook of paganism cannot solve inevitable social disputes in the way Christian forgiveness and co-operation can.[1] Yet the same sort of bleakness can be a theme in itself in the Judaeo-Christian tradition, notably in the cynical and unconsoling thoughts of the book of *Ecclesiasticus* ('The Wisdom of Jesus the Son of Sirach') in the Apochrypha, whose comment is close to nihilistic at times.[2] (But that is not a popular Christian view and unlikely to be an influence here.)

In Old English texts, the condition of social doubt (the 'dilemma' – of which Hengest's case, *Beowulf* 1063–1158, is a classic statement) is clear within the few examples of heroic poetry, and is not related to any positive Christian message or philosophical standpoint, though arguably it could represent an indirect consequence in the sense that Christianity subverted the pagan reliance on the personal link to kin-leader or ancestor as spiritual authority,[3] and replaced it with an impersonal concept of quasi-national authority dependent ultimately on a remote super-deity.[4] (Despite the attempts to present martyrs, saints and even Jesus

---

[1] Turner, 1971, p.370, sees the Saga in a later interpretative context: as contrasting the 'anarchy' of the thirteenth century with the order possible through Norwegian overlordship of Iceland.

[2] And thoroughly disturbing: e.g. 'Keep words to yourself and be very watchful: for you are walking about with your own downfall' (13:13); or 'When one builds and another tears down: what do they do but toil?' (34:23)

[3] A local headman or *goði* had spiritual as well as secular status in Iceland, 'chieftain-priests' in Turner, 1971, p.359

[4] The Augustinian God, in particular, existed prior to and outside the known cosmos, as the ultimately alien being.

in a respect-winning heroic mode.) This severance is paralleled by the reliance placed in law not on kinship but on loyalty to a lord as land-owner or royal official.[1] Previously, some coincidence of interest might be expected (e.g. with *cyning* as leader of the *cynn* or kin at local level), and the first clue to a dilemma of this sort[2] is notably precipitated by conflicting loyalties to lord and kin.

But the classic statement of this sense of abandonment comes from Bede's image of the flying sparrow, and its context is exactly that of Christian truth exposing pagan inadequacy.

> 'Thus,' he said, 'to me seems, O King, the life-span of humans at present on earth, in comparison to time as a whole, of which we know so little: it is like when you are in your hall feasting with the war-leaders and councillors in the cold season, and a fire has been kindled in the centre of the hall, warming the chamber, while outside the whirlwinds of winter rain and snow rage over everything – then at great speed a sparrow flies through the chamber, coming in one door and exiting soon after by the other. During the time it is inside the building it is unaffected by the wintry weather – but only a fraction of time is passed in comfort before it must leave, and repassing speedily from winter into winter, it is hidden from your eyes. Such the life of man on earth seems to me. What follows it or what comes before, we have no way of knowing....'

> [Bede *Ecclesiastical History* Bk.2 ch.13]

No wonder so magnificent a paragraph (sentence?) is employed on such a significant image, for its implications go far beyond the context of Northumbria, and may represent a transition of view that is apparent in heroic literature thereafter as the certainties of pagan existence are increasingly challenged. The grim need for self-reassurance among the warriors in *The Battle of Maldon* after Byrhtnoth's death is an example – whether their motivation is that of positive loyalty or negative grief. The heroic despair and resolution, couched in sardonic, darkly humorous terms, in the *Finnsburg* fragment is another example. Beowulf's fatal perseverance against the dragon might also be cited. Common to all of these is the determination to be seen to behave well as an individual in overwhelmingly adverse circumstances, even when no witness of behaviour is ever likely to appreciate act or motive.[3] The stern Anglo-Saxon continued to trust in his own power, and when this was obviously not enough, still kept on trying. It is a theme familiar from endless cowboy movies, and curiously, involves much of same sort

---

[1] E.g. loyalty to secular lord in Alfred's *Laws* ch.1, use of group oaths in *5 Athelstan*, and general oath of allegiance in *3 Edmund*

[2] *Anglo-Saxon Chronicle* A, 755; the opening item in Sweet's *Reader*

[3] This is a bit of a paradox, for of course it is precisely *why* the poet has chosen to record this selfless heroism.

of ironically pungent dialogue.[1] Not impossibly the negative of lack of help can convert into a positive stoical self-dependence: 'they realise that fortune is fickle, while bravery can be depended on,' Tacitus declared.[2] That is, cut off from the social reinforcement of consensus, the individual has to make his or her own decision in circumstances that are necessarily unforeseen and confusing. It is as though the responsibility has shifted from external dictation (by a god or a society) to an isolated personal level where each has to determine what are the core values of the human; and a sense of betrayal by the standard gods is sometimes credited as the source of such disillusion and consequent self-reliance.[3] (Might we suspect Christianity, as throwing more responsibility on the individual conscience, as playing a role here? But it would be a dangerous double-edged weapon to bring into play.)

Less clear is whether the 'victim' is determined despite his own abandonment and isolation, or whether he is submitting actively to destiny, a force of fate that gives some a good, some an awful future. Christian tradition was aware of this potential stability of personal destiny, as in the Exeter Book poem we call *Fortunes of Men*:

> One shall hunger get at; tempest will remove another; one shall the spear finish; another, war shall destroy...

> One in the woods shall fall, wingless, from a high tree; yet he is flying, spinning through the air, till he is no longer part of the tree like a fruit; then he lands among the roots, with mind blacked out, bereft of life he falls to the ground; his soul is away...

> One, in his youth, shall work through all his hardship, through God's powers, and in full age become fortunate again, enjoy times of pleasure and obtain wealth, riches and the mead-cup in his familiar home...

The implication in such a Christian text is that the human fortune is directly controlled by God and each individual has to submit to His will. Indeed, predestination in any formal sense depends on a Boethian deity, an inhabitant of eternity, all-knowing, in whose consciousness events are already mapped out. Some have interpreted *wyrd* as having just such a Christian implication. Thus Stanley notes the link with Christian providence,[4] and warns against turning an abstraction into a (pagan) divinity;[5] rather, like Timmer (1940–41), he stresses the neutrality of any

---

[1] Skarp-Hedin in *Njal's Saga* is the great exponent, e.g. his ominous "Are you thinking of doing some cooking?" in ch.129, but the ironic questions that open the *Finnsburg* fragment come a close second.

[2] *Germania* ch.30 trans. Fyfe, re the Chatti

[3] Ellis Davidson, 1964, p.50, specifically, of *Hrólfs Saga*, where Odin is belittled for deserting his heroes. Egil takes it upon himself to reproach Odin in the *Sonatorrek*, see Foote & Wilson, 1970, p.403. For fuller references see Saxo, 1980, 2, p.84, note 102.

[4] Stanley, 1975, p.119

[5] *ibid.* pp.95–6

Old English concept of *wyrd*: it derives, after all, from the verb *weorðan* (to become) and so should mean 'that which happens or has happened, an event, occurrence, incident fact';[1] in verse, it can mean 'final fate, doom, death'.[2]

Isidore of Seville presents us with a Classical picture of three ladies spinning the fates of men in thread.[3] Snorri in the Prose Edda has a similar image:

> 'A hall stands there, fair, under the ash by the well, and out of that hall come three maids, who are called thus: Urdr, Verdandi, Skuld [past, present, future]; these three maids determine the period of men's lives: we call them Norns; but there are many norns: those who come to each child that is born, to appoint his life; these are of the race of the gods, but the second are of the Elf-people, and the third are of the kindred of dwarves.'

> [trans. Brodeur 1929, pp.28–9]

An example of birth-norns is given by Saxo:[4] a king consults an oracle about the fate of his new-born son: there he finds three maidens, but they do not so much foretell as bestow gifts, good and bad, like the fairies in Sleeping Beauty, and may be closer to the family *fylgjur*[5] or house-elves than shapers of destiny. They seem to be 'awarding' character rather than disclosing future events. Indeed, the concept of external forces with the ability or power to predict or shape seems to me appropriate to a later stage than the Migration or Settlement; that is, to the developed paganism of Scandinavia in which Christian influence, directly or indirectly, encouraged a sense of fixed condition and determined future as a feature of the ideal of social control. Apart from occasional use of *wyrd* in Old English as equivalent to Latin *parcae*,[6] explicit references to any active non-Christian agency of destiny are lacking from the texts, and in the heroic poetry there is often a sense of a dilemma, a choice or option, which of course would not exist if destiny were already decided.[7]

I suggest that we are dealing with a concept of the accidental here, an acquiescence in the sense of a positive response to a set of inescapable conditions, but not necessarily something pre-planned, not some agreement in the working of

---

[1] *ibid.* pp.93–4

[2] *ibid.* p.93

[3] Bauschatz, 1982, p.8; Latin text in Grimm, 1883, I, p.405 note; while stressing the antiquity of the Norns in Teutonic lore, he admits the limited scope of the attribute of spinning, *ibid.* p.413

[4] 1979, Bk.6, p.169

[5] "The family wraiths (*ættarfylgjur*) were protective spirits who were often seen in female form." – *The Saga of Gunnlaug*, ed./trans. Foote & R. Quirk, 1957, note, p.42; see also Turville-Petre, 1964, ch.11.

[6] Stanley, 1975, p.92

[7] For an interesting discussion of the problem, see Stone, 1989; he concludes, "there is very little to suggest that the northern Europeans had much of a belief in an exorable and predetermined Fate." (p.39)

fate as a dictat of the gods. Perhaps it indicates a society (like that after the Conversion in England) whose standards had been subtly but decisively altered or undermined (but whose undoubted subsequent success only served to bring upon themselves the curse of the Vikings). Even Wulfstan in his famous *Sermo Lupi* comes close to the language of despair, though far from atheism, for Wulfstan of course can explain misfortune in terms of God's retribution for ill-doing[1] and use even adversity to good purpose in an almost Churchillian manner.[2] A simpler reaction might be, there is no god, no power for good, just endless accidental happenings, through which the individual applies his own resources as best he can. Faith becomes a matter of trusting in one's own self and religion reduced to the most basic definition of a 'proper' human and 'proper' human values. This is far from the ideological, aggressive[3] certainty with which the Christian martyr faces death, convinced that his or her deed is justified in terms of the eternal validity of God and paradise on hand as a reward.

Looking back in time, we may risk connecting this sense of an open future with Tacitus' remarks on the Germanic obsession with chance: 'Gambling, with dice, it is strange to find, they reckon as a serious occupation. They play while sober, and show such recklessness in winning and losing, that, when all else fails, on the last throw of all they stake their liberty and person.'[4] A similar 'trust' in chance may underlie the use of runes (or other symbols) for divination: for here again serendipity seems the important element.

Does such belief in augury and fortune-telling imply that there is a fixed course of events which we can cheat by peeping at in advance? In short, a sort of predestination? In the Germanic context,[5] we may be dealing not so much with a glimpse of destiny as with a sense of parallel accidents: chance operating one way in observed bird or beast 'sign' may indicate a parallel in the case of something happening or about to happen in another sphere: a matter of good or bad luck applying to a series of events, circumstances or times, rather than a firmly directed course of future history.[6] In this, I realise I am close to Brian Bates' assessment of *wyrd* in his book, *The Way of Wyrd* (1983). His compendium of Einsteinian, Chinese and shamanistic material can seem too eclectic, but his analysis of *wyrd* as an interconnective, non-causative pattern is intriguing: "A sorcerer can read omens as

---

[1] A line of interpretation pioneered by Alcuin, see Howe, 1989, pp.25–6.

[2] Is the revival of interest in Wulfstan in the 1940s a coincidence?

[3] For a notable example of a martyr irritating his persecutors see the story of Saba the Goth, retold in Stone, 1996, pp.11–12.

[4] *Germania* ch.24 trans. Fyfe

[5] This is also proposed for the Latin culture; thus Stevens (1985, p.31) explaining Bede, says, "*Sors, sortis and accedens*... may be understood as referring to events occurring to some extent due to indeterminate contingencies rather than due to a friendly or malevolent Fortuna."

[6] It may be relevant to point out here, with Bauschatz, 1982, p.157, that Germanic languages have no ready-made future tense, only past and present.

pattern-pointers… from which connections between different parts of patterns can be assumed."[1] This sympathetic sense of immediate unity leaves a more open set of possibilities than a predetermined fate: "The pattern of life is not woven ahead of time, like cloth to be worn later as a tunic. Rather, life is woven at the very instant you live it."[2] Equally, it is strictly not necessary to propose some (constructed?) web of events to permit incidents to link together: an omen might be an indication of personal luck status, somehow conveyed to external phenomena:

> "In the Viking world, this quality was called 'hamingja': an abstract conception, that of something belonging to an outstanding person which is partly a matter of character and partly of personality, and partly something more than either – that strange quality of 'luck' or 'lucklessness' which attaches itself to certain individuals more than others."
>
> [Ellis, 1943, p.134]

Turville-Petre[3] associates this quality of personal luck (Icelandic *gipta, gæfa*) with the *fylgja*, not in this context as some sort of attendant spirit (literally 'an accompanier'), but as "a kind of inherent, inborn force." Such a concept, according to Jente[4] could indeed lie behind the positive force accorded the Old English word *hælig*, later 'holy'. They would link aptly, I feel, with a world in which ancestors or deities exist not to combat some conspiracy of evil, but to help[5] towards the correct solution (health, good harvest, victory) in a context where nothing is certain, but nothing either has to be feared. In general, such concepts of luck (however vague) seem in stark contrast to the Romano-Christian trust in rational processes and planning ahead (evident still today in the doubts expressed by Churchmen on the morality of the new British lottery,1995+). To both cultures, arrogant action could invite disaster: Hrothgar's 'sermon' to Beowulf may indicate the risks of depending too much on one's own sense of success, a lesson well learned in Heorot, where happiness had provoked Grendel's attention.

---

[1] Bates, 1983, p.74

[2] *ibid.* p.113. I am less happy to extend trust to the point of leaping off a cliff (p.187) or extending one's throat to the knife (p.195); these are symbols of cultic submission that will only appeal to the severely historically committed.

[3] 1964, p.230

[4] 1921, pp.252–3

[5] Effort is assisted by benevolent forces, and what is *bad* is something good not happening. It follows that there is no need for a (personified) force of evil, in the way the Zoroastrian-late Hebrew-Christian tradition assumed; the assaults of elves, demons and the like could easily be a post-pagan phenomenon (an adversarial view of the world that still motivates the rational West?). The nearest to a Germanic 'devil' is Loki, but he is a trickster at base, or a cause of the unexpected, rather like a joker in a pack of cards. That a culture need not posit a force of evil seems attested in West Africa, where Anansi, the spider, plays a Loki-esque provocative role; and cf. Coyote ('the trickster-creator') in Navajo myth (Burland, 1965, p.103).

THE RATIONAL WORLD

To the modern critical mind it is not only most convenient to study Anglo-Saxon England positively in the light of a Christian state, it becomes almost possible, for the period, to dispense with paganism altogether.[1] For if there is no self-documentation from the pre-Christian ambit, how can its identity or influence be seriously asserted? What is pagan almost becomes what we are reluctant to let Christianity take the credit for.[2] Conversely, it is reassuring to find that that what was once deemed pagan can often be better explained through Christian analogy: most of Beowulf, for example.[3] There, the non-standard element has become viewed as folkic or secular, without any non-Christian import, though this may be largely a debate on categories. What we can label 'pagan' has dwindled in what may be a major interpretative shift; and yet we cannot be certain this sort of label-and-dismiss strategy is not some rather ancient device laid by those who well knew the value of seeming progressive *and* humane. The lavish Benedictine culture of the late tenth-eleventh centuries may appeal to modern sensibilities and adequately proclaim its own glories, but what if it achieved this status by replacing and rewriting the information we would have had on the earlier pagan period?

For the priorities of the early Church[4] seem seldom to have coincided with our modern (overtly) humane aspirations: then it was more the discipline of religion and the anxiety of survival that informed ecclesiastical policy; if Church authority were not extended in the West in the seventh century and thereafter, then the advance of Saracens in the south and Hungarians and others in the east would leave little scope for the exercise of the finer virtues. Security, it seemed, came first, and the assertiveness of an Augustine or Wilfrid did little to harm the cause.

The Conversion undoubtedly implied a switch to a form of government depending on written records, and access for a selected class to the collected knowledge of the Graeco-Roman tradition. It is likely that in the Christian ambit, writing became a much more powerful tool than 'magical' runes ever seem to have been: in standardising correct belief, formalising laws, recording grants, payments, dues and land-holding rights, issuing orders (by writ) and disseminating and/or

---

[1] The cautious Crawford, 1963, p.99 will only go so far as to concede that "Some form of Germanic heathenism was most probably well established in England when the first Christian missionaries arrived…"

[2] Consider Stanley's (1955–6 p.450) "*The Seafarer* is a Christian poem: *The Wife's Lament* is not."

[3] See Stanley 1975 and 1994, especially 1994, p.218: "'Pagan or Christian?': that old contrariety has long been laid to rest, one had hoped given decent burial…"

[4] Constantine did not abolish gladiatorial games but only execution by crucifixion.

controlling/synchronising all manner of information (which ultimately defines the legitimacy of power and proper rule). It can be no coincidence that the first English law-code was promulgated under the influence of the Gregorian mission c. AD 602–3, for writing brought government within the reinforcing context of Roman continuity in Europe, and offered a path to local stability, increasingly effective kingship, and supernational co-operation (in theory, at least).

The importance of this system of ideas and wider context was grasped by key figures like Alfred, but it is to be feared that many texts promulgated were credulous copies of late Antique belief, and not always accurate copies, so that it is hard to be certain how much use this access to theoretical material was. Intellectually, it is said, if the 'medieval spirit' introduced a new element, it was that knowledge must have a moral dimension: "The primary interest in natural facts was to find illustrations for the truths of morality and religion... The moon was the image of the church reflecting divine light, the wind an image of the spirit..."[1] Everything must have a purpose in a world created in one definitive set of acts by God, presumably a purpose that assisted or at least affected man, and science consisted in discovering the key to every particular inbuilt function. "This preoccupation with the magical and astrological properties of natural objects was, with the search for moral symbols, the chief characteristic of the scientific outlook of Western Christendom before the thirteenth century."[2] For example, it provides a key to Alfred's respect for Boethius, who is already presenting Classical science as a unity in which the natural world acts as it does because of God's moral intentions.[3]

Any information, whether observed, empirical (practical), traditional or theoretical could be given the status of fact by this added religious dimension. The line between science and magic may not be an objective one, and 'science' in the Medieval context may mean little more than approved information. Thus in surveying Middle English texts about predictions from the phase of the moon, Means[4] notes: "One must assume from the evidence that, for most of its users, the lunar-prognostic text was a scientific document." Manuscripts of such works are known to have belonged to monks and priests in the fourteenth century and to doctors (for apparently quite 'practical' purposes) in the fifteenth to seventeenth centuries.[5] Does the modern sensitivity over what is put forward by the media and keenness to find out how language influences people reflect a similar notion that information is only too readily transmuted into fact or truth?

---

[1] Crombie, 1961, p.15. It can be argued that information always has a moral dimension - as our present concern with 'political correctness'.

[2] *ibid.* p.17

[3] A process perhaps started by Boethius himself, who is re-presenting Classical science in a framework that we recognise as Christian.

[4] 1993, p.69

[5] *ibid.* pp.72–3

Technology is not easily assessed from literary or linguistic evidence, but has some artefactual base. Building in stone (and re-used brick) and a high quality of wood building work are apparent; earth-shifting for burial mounds, boundaries and defence-work was possible; and metalwork for jewellery, tools and weapons was of a good standard; simple pottery and glassware was available; there was the (innovative) use of waterwheels for power; carts and boats were available for bulk transport, horses for human vection; oxen were used for traction, especially to power the new heavy plough, capable of turning efficient furrows; yeast was applied to the grain product for bread and beer, meats smoked or pickled to preserve them; herbs were used for their preserving or medicinal powers; weaving and leather-work would be employed for clothing, and the art of curing skins was relevant to the production of manuscripts. How much of this was owed to the Church as communicator or entrepreneur is hard to assess; but if trade and contact were advantages claimed for Christianity, they were also a feature of the rival Viking – was the clash commercial as much as religious?

Economic development there was, but its benefits are not easily assessed. Whether from new forms of agriculture, or organisation, or simply a propitious climate, large estates seem the key to later Anglo-Saxon England, with law codes by the tenth century a medium of subordination with collective oaths of loyalty; while the subjection of freemen to the ordeal as a method determining guilt[1] must have blurred the line between slave and free. And if you were not free, the laws recommended stoning to death for a male slave offender, with burning to death for a female, as in the law-code *4 Athelstan*. Christianity outlawed human sacrifice as a deliberate act of religious ritual,[2] and in so doing severed a rival pagan tradition that may have contributed to maintaining the link to ancestors or proto-gods; yet hanging[3] as a penal measure survived without Christian objection.

The justification of torture in the Old English poem *Elene* is far from reassuring, nor is the suffering of martyrs in poems like *Andreas* and *Juliana* much different. Bede quite calmly accepts, even seems to justify the slaughter of some 1,200 (British) monks at the Battle of Chester;[4] and in the following excerpt from the Old English poem *Solomon & Saturn 1*, when the letters of the Pater Noster attack a demon, we wonder if the new dispensation has done anything more than lend violence a new direction:

---

[1] E.g. 4 Athelstan, 1 Ethelred

[2] The rejection of human sacrifice seems to have been an issue in the prime period of Athenian culture e.g. concern expressed in Euripides' plays such as *Iphigenia in Aulis*, or *The Women of Troy*; but not necessarily shared in Hebrew tradition, see Tierney, 1989, ch.19. Perhaps the revulsion centred on the greater respect for the potential of the individual in an urban milieu? Ling, 1968, p.80 posits an origin in the Zoroastrian opposition to wilder nomad practices.

[3] Probably associated with Odin, see Ellis Davidson 1969, pp.33–36 and illustrated p.29

[4] *Ecclesiastical History* Bk 2 ch.2

So too ᛃ.Q. and ᚾ.U. bring him low with pain, bold leaders, advance upon him; they have bright spears, long poles, to drive him relentlessly; they do not restrain their strokes, severe blows; to the devil is hateful... then ᚠ.F. and ᛗ.M. press round the guilty trouble-maker; they have sharp spears, vicious discharge of arrows; they send fire into the fiend's hair, darts scattering over the comfortless phantom.

[trans. Griffiths in Kemble, 1991, p.70]

According to your viewpoint, the Christian world may have been just as brutish as the pagan, or the pagan as the Christian. The Anglo-Saxon world, we may say, was (necessarily) a more painful place than the modern one; yet then as now a surprising amount of suffering involved conscious and self-justified action by human against human.

The new religion also had strong views that must have served to influence human sexual perspectives, asserting the ideal of virginity and re-evaluating the reproductive act. Marriage was a civil contract or family arrangement, a *weddung*, that is a pledge or personal agreement; it was not a formal sacrament of the Church until Lutheran times, though Charlemagne seemed in favour of a benediction from a priest to make the act more solemn and official. Divorce (confirmed in the Eastern Empire in the sixth century by Justinian) was also a simple matter in Anglo-Saxon England, with the wife retaining her share of the property if a couple split up. In such conditions, there was little for the Church to do but stress the importance of sexual fidelity, limit the degree of consanguinity proper in marriage (incidentally undermining the kin-bonds of the extended family unit), and query the right to remarry.

Within the monastic rule, sexuality was not a recognised or tolerated factor, and exemplary saints presented to the laity a humourless picture of sexual continence, as when the heroine Juliana faced martyrdom rather than take a husband (alright, a pagan one). Or Aldhelm's idealistic compendium of female virgin martyrs. Beyond this, the Penitentials claimed to exercise control over the sexual practices of lay folk as well as clerics e.g. *The Penitential of Theodore*, ch.28, lays down heavy penalties for incest and homosexuality for all classes, from archbishop (13 years' penance) to lay person (5 years' penance), "and [they] shall never sleep with anyone else ever again" – a markedly different tradition from that of the general ritual of sex recorded at the Viking funeral by Ibn Fadlan; or the collective nature of even later (not necessarily Anglo-Saxon-derived) mating customs on May Day as recorded, with delicate concern, by Philip Stubbs in his *Anatomie of Abuses* published in 1585 in London.[1].

---

[1] "...every parishe, towne, and village, assemble themselves together, bothe men, women, and children, olde and yong, even all indifferently: and either goyng all together, or deuidyng themselves into companies, they goe some to the woodes and groves, some to one place, some to another, where they spende all the night in pastymes, and in the mornyng they returne, bringing with them birche bowes, and braunches of trees to deck their assemblies withall. I

Taboos on sexual delinquency may well have existed previously: Tacitus talks of Germanic intolerance of 'evil-living' in *Germania* ch.12, and in ch.2 of *Gisli's Saga* two recognisable wooden figures are set up, one standing "close behind the other,"[1] as a slanderous accusation against those so portrayed. But only Christianity conceived the paradox of setting up exclusive one-sex communities[2] and then punishing homosexuality and onanism. Pope Gregory's answers to Augustine of Canterbury's queries (Bede *Ecclesiastical History* Bk.1 ch.27) included detailed material on clerical personal purity, and *Theodore's Penitential* ch.28 established what might seem an impossible ideal of non-sexual neutrality in every aspect of monastic life, including accidental night-time promptings, with what would now seem a remarkable concern for the trivial private experiences of young monks.

In practice, through membership of the priesthood – a privilege of the utmost importance – there would be an implicit assertion of the superiority of the male over the female,[3] though this is more pronounced in the post-Conquest period.[4] It is an inequality that becomes institutionalised with marriage and property regulations in the period of Protestant ascendancy in the sixteenth to nineteenth centuries.

The advantages or disadvantages of the Conversion will depend necessarily on how you assess (if at all) matters of social or intellectual 'progress'. To the Anglo-Saxon, the world was part of a moral progress towards Doomsday, a transformation operating in the world of ideas and judgements, and it is rather likely that they were encouraged to this end to feel ashamed of their pagan past. But should we be accepting such self-judgements on 'improvement', and be content with the picture of Christianity leading feckless Germanicules towards the goal of modernity? Does this do anything more than celebrate our own cultural climax? – a determinism we would reject angrily if applied against us by some other culture.[5] Perhaps such biases are inescapable and the most objective scholar can hardly resist the urge to interpret historical figures as embodiments of modern

---

have heard it credibly reported (and that viva voce) by men of great gravitie, credite, and reputation, that of fourtie, three score, or a hundred maides goyng to the woode ouer night, there have scarcely the thirde parte of them returned home againe undefiled." (p.94)

[1] Trans. Johnston, 1963, pp.3-4; see further material in Stone 1994 on *seiðr*.

[2] Though the Jomsburg Viking pact also provided that no man should keep women in the stronghold – see Ellis Davidson 1964, p.69 – to avoid rivalries or in imitation of monastic lifestyle? A translation of this text is included in Auden, 1937.

[3] Stressed by Meaney 1989 p.30. This does not preclude a similar dominance in the pagan ambit, however.

[4] For example the legends of Cuthbert's hatred of women, as forbidding them to enter his monastery or church, in the *Metrical Life of Cuthbert* – an attitude not borne out and indeed contradicted by the earlier accounts of his life.

[5] For example, Gandhi's "medical science is the concentrated essence of black magic," per Rosita Forbes, *India of the Princes*, 1939, pp.44–5 – though we might enjoy the paradox.

ideals: Bede as the prototype of the painstaking, humble scholar[1], Alfred as the successful, far-planning leader,[2] and Ælfric as some symbol of social conscience.[3] *En suite* with this, the move from paganism to Christianity in Anglo-Saxon England can be too easily assessed as a switch from the superstitious to the rational – a triumph, as it were, of emergent logic and science, a sort of recognisable 'progress', and a conscious rejection of the crude and cruel customs of the past in favour of unison with the enlightened Roman tradition.

This creating of historical perspective is apparent as early as, and particularly in, Bede. Nick Higham's recent study (1995) emphasises the political content of his historical writing, as implementing a sense of a super-tribal power-base in England, with Anglo-Saxons (and especially Northumbrians) playing the role of heirs to the Roman *imperium*, at the expense of the native British. "[Bede's] work is both less even-handed, and more politically charged, than has often been imagined."[4] The events Bede thought to preserve are functional to his picture of a nation moving towards an admirable Christian goal, as though information has to demonstrate divine purpose to make sense at all. Events to be included are selected therefore on a particular criterion.[5] The growth of Roman Christianity and the nobility of Northumbria's record is paralleled by the diminution of the Welsh British (emphasised in the closing chapter of the *Ecclesiastical History*) in both religious and political terms, which may warn us against taking Bede's own 'modest style'[6] at face value.

Now Bede often does distinguish the sources of his information, giving the impression he is keen to assert, or as appropriate, leave open, the authenticity of the material according to the reliability of the source,[7] but this could be seen as the

---

[1] Largely through the work of Plummer, 1896, in a late nineteenth century context of Conservative caution versus Liberal action. Higham, 1995, has at last managed some challenge to this myth.

[2] We have little certain knowledge on Alfred's decision-making process, however, or even his aims, though he may have realised (in the Preface to the *Pastoral Care*) that the success against the Vikings had paradoxically all but led to the extinction of Christianity in Wessex.

[3] His inclusion of the predicament of the slave plowman and hoarse, chilled plowboy in the *Colloquy* is curiously ambiguous: the monastery might be the one profiting from such labour, after all; and what better warning could there be to keep novices at their calling?

[4] Higham, 1995, p.9

[5] Thus the pagan Penda was excluded from Bede's list of *bretwaldas* who are exclusively Christian overkings – see David Nicholas, 1992, p.66; Higham analyses Bede's bias against Constantine, 1995, p.30.

[6] *sermo humilis* – see Higham, 1993, p.9

[7] The use at all of 'primary' sources is something Bede had little choice about, for there were few written records about the past of England available. In the matter of Bede's sending to Rome for a copy of Pope Gregory the Great's original instructions to Augustine of Canterbury and Mellitus, we may be seeing less a concern with the scrupulous accuracy of historical sources, and more a care to establish the constitutional

attribution of responsibility as much as a check of validity. In the Preface to Bede's prose life of Cuthbert it is notable that his *finished* text is read out to assembled clergy as if to involve them in the process of critical approval (a 'public consultation'?); but it is then found that their comments cannot be incorporated, as it would be a pity to change the text at this late stage. No better scheme for spreading responsibility while retaining control of content could be devised. It exhibits a sensitivity that could well have arisen from a need to defend himself from charges of invention or inaccuracy or heresy as much as any instinct to assess the objective integrity of information.

Such a charge of heresy was indeed brought by a fellow monk[1] over Bede's assessment of the number of years remaining before Doomsday in his *De Temporibus*, and lodged with the influential Bishop Wilfrid; Bede's reply or defence of 708 AD survives, and uses strong terms to discredit his accusers.[2] This incident may have left an enduring effect on Bede's writing – and his career. Northumbria had been the scene (AD 664) of a dramatic reversal of belief over the way of celebrating Easter only decades before Bede's time. That would serve as a warning to Bede's generation to be very cautious about what could be affirmed as doctrinally correct, and time and again, Bede is seen to exhibit exactly such caution e.g. he will not say what sort of voice Cædmon, the pioneer poet, heard in a dream inspiring him to compose verse – for is secular poetry the realm of God or of demons? Similarly, he will not ascribe the source of miracles to physical components of relics, e.g. a possible chemical or medicinal element, laying emphasis instead on the role of divine grace, for to imbue an object with 'magical power' might perhaps seem idolatrous.[3]

The acceptance of miracles alone provides a major stumbling-block to the 'modernisation' of Bede. The problem is aptly if ingenuously summarised as follows by David Nicholas:[4] "Although Bede believed firmly in miracles and used them to illustrate the lessons of history, he was a critical historian who examined his sources carefully." To a more sceptical eye, this would seem a contradiction in terms. Again, does it help to assume, as Colgrave & Mynors do,[5] that "theologians, such as Bede, knew well the difference between true faith and mere faith in the marvellous" – and so included miracle stories to tempt the credulous?

Such defensive strategies may be significantly reducing Bede's claim as a creative writer and political stylist; and even in his scientific writings, there is no

---

basis of the English Church, a rather important legal and doctrinal subject, and imbue his history with the reflected status of Rome itself.

[1] Named David, in Jones' view, but this is queried in Stevens, 1985, p.36.

[2] See Plummer, pp.xli, cxlvi, Jones 1943, pp.132-5; we are talking here of un-Bede-like words that translate as 'greatly annoyed', 'up-starts', 'drunken rustics', etc.

[3] Even more curiously, he will not ascribe any miracles to Wilfrid, thereby obstructing *his* path to sainthood, while promoting the more favoured Cuthbert.

[4] 1992, p.79

[5] 1969, p.xxxv

clear pursuit of new knowledge in the modern sense,[1] but a persistent concern with using safe authorised material to clarify the process of calculating Easter. Thus the early work, *De Temporibus*, was commissioned in 703 apparently because a challenge on the dating of Easter in 704 was expected from Adamnan.[2] The later (725 AD) *De Temporum Ratione* is an expansion of the earlier work,[3] with much fuller detail on all manner of meteorological points. But there is also by Bede a *De Natura Rerum*,[4] unhappily omitted by Jones from his 1943 edition of Bede's *Opera de Temporibus*, which is again information taken on trust from the authority of previous writers (especially Isidore of Seville and Pliny the Elder), but exhibiting less sign of discrimination and an admixture of material we would consider today rather arbitrary e.g. stars and moon alike borrow their light from the sun (ch.5); Saturn is cold by nature (ch.13); plagues arise from foul air (ch.37).[5] Nor is a sense of astrological influence absent:

> *Cometae sunt stellae flammis crinitae, repente nascentes, regni mutationem, aut pestilentiam, aut bella, vel ventos, aestusve portendentes.*
>
> [*De Natura Rerum* ch.24]

Comets are stars with fiery hair, swiftly appearing, portending a change of ruler, or plague, or war, or storms, or drought.

– which is exactly the sort of material that Jones will not allow as Bede's in a text on prognostication by thunder.[6] *De Natura Rerum* chapter 36, on weather predictions, seems more conventional, but is just as difficult to defend on grounds of observation or logic, and is indeed cautiously handled by Ælfric in his redaction.[7] Granted, Bede avoids the more calamitous pitfalls of astrological credulity and exaggeration, but he may be shunning not so much the irrational as trying to steer clear of the heretical and controversial.

If not by Bede, the reservations expressed in the Preface to *De Tonitruis Libellus*[8] aptly seem to summarise that sort of viewpoint. Stress is placed on being commissioned to undertake the work by others (a shift of responsibility?); and aims to disarm criticism by expressing ahead the fear that he may perhaps be

---

[1] Stevens' assertion (1985, p.19) that "Beda... explained natura phenomena on the basis of observation and reason" can only refer to the timing of tides, and here "Beda's contribution was to clarify" as Stevens himself notes, p.18.

[2] Jones 1943, p.130

[3] New sources seem to have included Irish seventh century scientific writing, see Stevens, 1985, p.12

[4] Text *Patrologia Latina* vol.90 cols.187-278; Stevens, 1985, dates the work to about 701 AD.

[5] "Pestilentia nascitur ex aere" - cf. examples from Aldhelm in Griffiths 1995, 1996

[6] Jones, 1939, p.45; and see below, pt.2 no.30, p.230.

[7] See pt.2 no.29, p.229, no.33, p.236.

[8] Text in *Patrologia Latina* vol.90 cols.609-614

considered to be inspired "diabolico (quod absit) spiritu, aut iniqua magicae excogitatione artis... non sancti Spiritus gratia" (by a demoniac spirit – which is absent – or by some evil invention of the magic art... not by the grace of the Holy Spirit). This work is removed from the Bede canon by Plummer[1] and Jones,[2] as 'a most contemptible work and clearly spurious' or because Herefrid should have the title of *frater* not *pater,* as well as for its suspicious manuscript descent. While the Latin of the text is grossly over-flowery for Bede, and the content unacceptably dire, the matter at least of the Preface is relevant, and Jones is realistic, I think, in seeking an alternative early context for the work (perhaps Herefrid, Bishop of Auxerre, d.909 – thus his 1939, p.47).

I have spent some time on Bede (too much, some may think, if all I can do is to threap), because it may be that Plummer's assessment of him has formed the keystone of a particular version of Anglo-Saxon culture that we have come to accept as absolute and real. The myth of the passage from pagan to rational continues to dominate even now, and seems to haunt even the most recent works on Anglo-Saxon medicine. Thus Cameron,[3] having appealed against a view of all Anglo-Saxon medicine as anti-rational, raises a new division into "its magical component" and "its rational component," which is hardly more helpful. It implies the Anglo-Saxons saw these criteria in the same way we do e.g. "When all else failed,[4] the Anglo-Saxon physician could resort to charms..."[5] But surely the charm was essential to the administration of medicine in many cases, as practical and as Christian (or pagan) as any of the rituals that are prescribed in endless recipes, and as rational, in its own terms, as any other remedial action – given that the first hint that germs might exist does not occur until 1722,[6] and anti-biotics were not available until the 1930s. Indeed, we may well agree with Buckman[7] that "Magic *or* medicine is a false dilemma." Trust and optimism are essential to ritual, and are implicit in cures of all ages, not opposing strands to 'true' medicine.

I necessarily query the assertion that the Anglo-Saxon physician's "approach to medicine was predominantly rational *in spite of* his use of charms and magic for

---

[1] 1896, pp.l, clviii

[2] 1939, p.45

[3] 1993, pp.2–4

[4] A simple practical remedy e.g. a dock-leaf for a sting, was likely to be common knowledge, and not the subject of writing down or referral to a 'specialist' then or now. However oral information does not bother to distinguish between the effective and the fanciful e.g. a child is just as happy to believe that the reflected shine of a buttercup means it likes butter. (At least I was.)

[5] *ibid.* p.24

[6] In the work of Benjamin Marten on tuberculosis; see Wilkins, 1994, p.78. There is earlier a connection supposed between foul air and contagious disease, but leading only to a dependence on herbal nosegays or incense and use of perfume.

[7] 1993, p.235

conditions intractable to rational treatments."[1] The manuscripts, to my understanding, make no distinction between cases suitable or unsuitable for treatment including spoken words (whether Christian prayers, Latin or 'gibberish' formulae, nominally pagan references, or alliterative verse charm – all of which form arguably one genre): the opposition of practical and rational to magical (and verbal?) cannot easily be projected on the past in this way. It implies that 'serious' minds in the Anglo-Saxon world very well knew the real or scientific truth (just as we do), and that the less appealing texts (to us) were the province of a less enlightened class and so may be safely relegated or disregarded. Thus Cockayne (perhaps defensively) in the Preface to vol.3 of his *Leechdoms*[2] asserted that "The unfounded hopes, scruples, and alarms of the ignorant, ignorant by comparison, are justly regarded by the wise with a copious contempt..." The very texts he so usefully edits afford "an insight into the notions and prepossessions upon scientific subjects of the less instructed portion of Saxon society."[3] This is indeed 'the modest style'.

Beliefs in astrology were prevalent at the highest level, and were part of the very Graeco-Roman system that also advocated what we accept as theoretical and rational science; there is no indication that Anglo-Saxon manuscripts containing such material were in any way inferior – on the contrary charms and prognostics are found in very respectable company. Cotton MS Titus D.xvi/xvii[4] which contains a text of the Old English *De Temporibus* (Ælfric's summary of Bede), recipes, computistic texts, prognostications and devotional material was the personal property of Ælfwine, Abbot of New Minster, Winchester in 1035. Christ Church College Cambridge MS.391,[5] once considered to be a handbook belonging to St Oswald, but likelier to be associated with Bishop Wulfstan II of Worcester (1062–95), includes prayers, hymns, and ecclesiastical material in Latin as well as prognostications. Cotton MS. Caligula A.vii,[6] an early eleventh century MS. which contains the text of the German poem 'Heliand' and the *Land Ceremonies Charm*, was believed by Sir Robert Cotton to belong to King Canute.

To dismiss material that does not appeal to us, as magical or anti-rational, must be resisted. A pagan Anglo-Saxon surely believed he/she was as sensible, and holding beliefs as normal as any Christian to come. That we have lost the substructure that justified their practices can leave them seeming odd, but the same could well be said of Christian ritual to outsiders. Worse, locked in its own book-dependency, the only guarantee to the Christian of value of information became the status (preferably antique) of the author.[7] So that

---

[1] Cameron, 1993, p.24, my italics

[2] 1866, pp.vii-viii

[3] *ibid.*

[4] Ker, 1959, no.202

[5] *ibid.* no.67

[6] *ibid.* no.137

[7] Hence frequent misattributions, and even 'forgeries'! This two-way relationship between status and credibility is explored by Elizabeth Tonkin, pp.25–35 in *The Myths We Live*

restoration and multiplication became the touchstones of Anglo-Saxon taste, looking ever backward to the standards of Classical Rome; also, it may be, in new creative ventures. Rational has ceased to imply curious or inventive in such a context; it is an era of recovery rather than adventure, forever piling up renewed evidence of the past.

Sometimes this trust in accumulated knowledge was well placed. For example, we have in *Bald's Leechbook*[1] a text that is an impressive work of anatomical analysis. This is its apt description of the liver:

> *Sio biþ on þa swiþran sidan aþened oþ þone neweseoþan; sio hæfð fif*
> *læppan, helt þa lendenbrædan; sio is blodes timber 7 blodes hus 7 foster:*
> *þonne þara metta meltung biþ 7 þynnes þa becumaþ on þa lifer þonne*
> *wendaþ hie hiora hiw 7 cerrað on blod; 7 þa unsefernessa þe þær beoþ hio*
> *awyrpþ ut 7 þæt clæne blod gesomnaþ 7 þurh feower ædra swiþost onsent*
> *to þære heortan 7 eac geond ealne þone lichoman oþ þa ytmestan limo.*
>
> [*Bald's Leechbook* ch.17]

> The *liver* is extended on the right side as far as the pit of the belly, it hath five *lobes or* lappets, it has a hold on the false ribs, it is the material of the blood, and the house and the nourishment of the blood; when there is digestion and attenutation of the meats, they arrive at the liver, and then they change their hue, and turn into blood; and it casteth out the uncleanness which be there, and collects the clean blood, and through four veins principally sendeth it to the heart, and also throughout all the body as far as the extremities of the limbs.
>
> [trans. Cockayne, 1864–6, 2, p.199]

The importance of the heart, here, is not as a pump, but, in Aristotle's terms, as the centre of intelligence, with presumably a prior claim on the fresh blood. Nonetheless, we have here the voice of authentic Classical observation[2] – but was it perceived at the time as more reliable than the *Medicina ex Quadrupedis* or any of the other dubious efforts of late Empire medicine? Or more real than witchcraft? For if key intellectual Latin texts were selected for translation into Old English by thoughtful patrons like King Alfred, so also others clearly considered that texts on dreams, astrologically favourable times, and auguries were just as important and just as needful to be accessed in the vernacular.

By ed. R. Samuel & P. Thompson (1990) e.g. "very often, we accept that an account must be true because its author is authoritative." (p.29)

[1] With an internal reference to King Alfred. "Almost certainly, too, the original fair copy, presumably written for Bald by Cild, would have been produced in a Winchester scriptorium, during Alfred's reign." Meaney, 1984, p.236

[2] Or experiment? The allegation of human vivisection was made against Herophilus and Erasistratus in Greek Alexandria.

In the medicine, in the very heart, as it were, of Anglo-Saxon applied science, just as in the mix of history and miracle, it seems as though rationality and credulity were not incompatible. We would like to have it so, but a wider appreciation of Old English texts leads us to a more complex world, where there may be very little to chose between the ethics of pagan and Christian, or science and prejudice, and relatively little left if we discard that which does not seem to us rational and proper.

It is as if we had set up a fantasy of the Christianity of the age, and a fantasy of its paganism, diminishing our perception of either in the delight of attributing the past our own ways of thinking. But the Anglo-Saxon period had a very different set of 'facts' from our own, a quite alien set of evidence about reality – one whose effectiveness was limited by resources and knowledge; magic was not an alternative to knowledge but in its broadest sense part of a way of understanding and coping with the external world; faith too (Christian or pagan) was part of the rational (that is intellectual) process, for 'fact' could ultimately only be useful as it coincided with the truth of a religious perspective which made sense of the world. As to where they were headed, the apparent endorsement of state aggression at the opening of *Beowulf* is counterbalanced surely by the note of uncertainty over Scyld's funeral and afterlife – growth and increase were not sustainable ambitions.

There is the consideration also that while logic is potentially available to all humans, the strict system of deduction we depend on is a specialised art implying a degree of training; so much so that we hardly regard it as a tool[1] to an end, but have come to see it as the prerogative of the educated soul, associated with a thought-action causal relationship special to the Christian West.[2] This Logic is solutional and predictive, but can also be aggressive and destructive; while the language in which it is expressed has a built-in set of cultural values that makes objectivity additionally difficult. These are limitations best appreciated before placing overmuch trust in any interpretative conclusion; is it perhaps better to open up options than use logic to narrow them down?[3]

Pardon this semantic (quasi-homiletic) detour; but how else could we clear the ground for any consideration of so vexed a subject as magic...

---

[1] It cannot, for example, validate the material you select or accept as your starting point, or where you are headed.

[2] See for example John Garrett Jones *Tales and Teachings of the Buddha*, (London 1979) where (p.56) he proposes that "the deed is father to the thought." The emergent western grammatical system of 'sense order' of words i.e. subject-verb-object acts to reinforce the view of causative action and human as prime causative agent.

[3] Our own certainties have proved, at best, relative. "In 1800 the world was deemed to be governed by stern necessity and universal laws. Shortly after 1930 it became virtually certain that at bottom our world is run at best by laws of chance." (Ian Hacking, p.34 in *The Probabilistic Revolution* ed. L. Krueger et al., Cambridge, Mass., 1987.) A point, I have suggested, the Anglo-Saxons had worked out for themselves.

THE WORLD OF MAGIC

'Magic' as a word is allied to *magus* 'wise man', originally an Old Persian word denoting a member of a priestly caste; from there it spread to Greek, Latin and French, and even appears in the Bible as the *magi* who visited the infant Christ.[1] In modern parlance, the adjective *magic* can imply something sham or inexplicable, but most often something splendid or amazing. As a word it is absent from Old English, where a range of terms apply to supernatural transactions, but the Latin form would be familiar through the encyclopaedia of Bishop Isidore where "Magicians (*Magi*) are those that are commonly called evil-doers (*malefici*) on account of the magnitude of their crimes: they stir up the elements, confuse the minds of men, and can kill without any administration of poison by the violence of their chanting."[2]

In Old English the terms were *scinn-lac* (magical action), and *scinn-cræft* (magic skill) from *scinn(a)* (phantom, illusion, demon?); *galdor-cræft* (skill at enchanting); *wiccecræft* and *wiccedom* (witchery); *lyb-lac* and *lyb-cræft* (drug-based magic); *wigle* and *wiglung* (divination); *bealocræft* (sorcery or evil art); and *tungolcræft* (star-skill) which glosses both *astrologia* and *astronomia* (and need not imply ill-doing, though most of the above are terms of condemnation).

The darker side of magic is partly defined by evil intention[3] or the more political fact that it is something forbidden. "This prohibition marks the formal distinction between magical and religious rites. It is the fact of prohibition itself which gives the spell its magical character."[4] In being unauthorised, it can also seem anti-social; hence R. Campbell Thompson's definition[5] of magic: "the difference between religion and magic is that, while the former is the worship for the good of the community, magic is the supernatural relation for the individual." There is also something alien or improper implied in such cults: "Magical

---

[1] *Matthew* 2:1–12. Tertullian first called them *'fere reges'* (nearly kings) c.200 AD; Origen decided there were three of them, and in the sixth century the names Gaspar, Melchior and Balthasar were settled on.

[2] *Etymologia* Bk.8 ch.9.

[3] "In a law of AD 318, Constantine the Great expressly permitted spells for the cure of illnesses and for preventing rains and hail from damaging harvests; for those using magic to harm others, however, he prescribed severe penalties." (BM exhibition text, 1995)

[4] Mauss, 1972, p.22. However, the "sacred things" which unite an established church are also "things set apart and forbidden," according to Durkheim (quoted Evans-Pritchard, 1965, p.p.57).

[5] 1908, p.xvii. Thus Evans-Pritchard, 1965, p.57, says (on behalf of Durkheim) "Magic has a clientele, not a church."

rites...are always considered unauthorised, abnormal, and, at the very least, not highly estimable."[1] They may explicitly be 'evil' – that is, intend harm to people, or contravene decency – or may involve evil means, such as reliance on demons. As such they represent the unacceptable side of supernatural action, though it must always be remembered that privileged intervention with the expected course of nature is an essential claim of Christianity itself, as in *Joshua* 10:12–13, when God assisted by making the sun and moon stand still.[2] That sort of 'magic' is common to Christianity and paganism at this period, and neither the Bible nor Christianity (at this period) denied for one moment that magic could work.[3]

The 'evil means' may be an important defining point. It is entirely possible that the 'hard' stance often taken on magic stems from the need of the early Christian Church to redefine and discredit demons (*daemones* in Latin, an acceptable part of Roman and Greek pagan belief). For demons did not necessarily imply evil in the classical world, rather they were the teeming invisible inhabitants of the sub-lunar sphere. To paraphrase the *Dictionnaire du Spiritualité* (Paris, 1957) on demons, they were considered, from Plato to Plutarch, as benevolent forces, suitable subjects for prayers and offerings; Plato defined their placement as intermediate between the realm of the gods and that of the mortals, and the role of demons followed on from this.

In Greek ideology, they became associated with the elements of earth, air, water and fire,[4] and so almost nature spirits or animistic phenomena, like the Roman *genius*.

> "...daemons, lesser divinities in the great chain of being, inhabiting upper regions this side of the moon, which goes back to Hesiod and Pythagoras but whose vogue at this period was derived from some mythical passages in Plato. Most people now believed in their reality. In the tradition of the daemonic sign that guided Socrates they were assimilated to the old Roman idea of an individual's *genius*. They were inspirers of prophecy. But chiefly they were the executives of the will of God... and conveyors to him of prayers from men."
>
> [Wilkinson, 1975, p.191]

---

[1] Mauss, 1972 p.24

[2] "Magicians believe that by words, spells, they can alter the world," (Evans-Pritchard, 1965, p.41, speaking as Freud). Such a definition would have to cover not only "poets... criminals... madmen," (*ibid.*) but legislators, scientists, news editors and the rest of us.

[3] For example, the pagan priest's attempt to immobilise Wilfrid and his crew (Eddius Stephanus' *Life of Wilfrid*, ch.13). Remember, the first law against magic that also queried its claims was not enacted in this country until the eighteenth century.

[4] Proclus fifth century AD via Cavendish, 1975, p.244

The discrediting of demons may owe something to Zoroastrian religion where *daevas* or evil supernatural entities are associated with the sublunary sphere surrounding the earth – i.e. that between earth and the moon – and increasing emphasis is laid on the confrontation of good and evil, with much that has to do with this world being evil (a point emphasised in Gnosticism). In Talmudic tradition there are the *sedim*, who eat drink multiply and die as men do, but have wings, foreknowledge of the future and can traverse the world as angels do.[1] To the Christian, though demon and angel had certain functional resemblances, it seemed safer (perhaps essential) to discredit and demote the demon; its quasi-inherent, independent power must seem incompatible with monotheism; and Mithraism an intolerable form of competition.[2] To Origen demons were inferior to and more evil than men, a step in the degradation of existence towards Satan. Despite this change in the image of demons, what Christians did not do was ignore them or pretend they did not exist or have no preternatural power. Thus Augustine of Hippo:

Daemonum ea est natura, ut aerii corporis sensu terrenorum corporum sensum facile praecedant; celeritate etiam propter eiusdem aerii corporis superiorem mobilitatem non solum cursus quorumlibet hominum vel ferarum, verum etiam volatus avium incomparabiliter vincant."

[Augustine of Hippo De *Divinatione Daemonum* (*Patrologia Latina* 40)]

It is the nature of daemons that they easily surpass the sensibility of terrestrial bodies with the sensibility of their aerial bodies; as also regards speed, for they beat outright not only the running of any man or beast, but even the flight of birds on account of the superior mobility of their aerial body.

"For Augustine believed in demons: a species of beings, superior to men, living forever, their bodies as active and subtle as the air, endowed with supernatural powers of perception; and, as fallen angels, the sworn enemies of the true happiness of the human race.... Thrust into the turbulence of the lower air, below the moon, these condemned prisoners, awaiting sentence in the Last Judgement, were always ready to swoop, like birds, upon the broken fragments of a frail and dissident humanity."

[Brown, 1967, p.311]

---

[1] Campbell Thompson, 1908, p.44

[2] Magic of that sort was also much too easily available: "A man has a pain in the head. A neighbour male or female will say to you, There is an enchanter here, there is a healer here, and a wizard somewhere. You say, I am a Christian, it is not lawful for me. And if he says to you, Why? Am I not a Christian? You should say, But I am one of the faithful." quoted by Jenkins, 1953, p.135, after Augustine *Sermo* 376.

Accredited with many powers like the ability to create illusions, demons seemed more than or other than human, and more precise legends soon developed to explain their origin within a Christian framework. According to Justin Martyr (and Tertullian) "demons are the offspring of angels who yielded to the embraces of earthly women."[1] In the apocryphal Bible book of *1 Enoch*, chapters 6–7, "two hundred angels of the order of Watchers, led by Azazel, came down to earth on Mount Hermon and took themselves wives..."[2] This led to the birth of giants, eventually destroyed, "but evils spirits issued from their corpses and have caused violence and trouble on earth ever since."[3] To Clement of Alexandria, demons were simply fallen angels; perhaps from a later wave of expulsions than that of Lucifer and his followers; nonetheless, in due course, all such fallen angels became Lucifer's subordinates,[4] and demons were attributed fanciful names from Jewish, Greek, Egyptian, Babylonian and Assyrian sources.[5] In Christian iconography, demons might be accorded feathered wings – as fallen angels – but they might also have talons, animal heads, sharp noses, hairy pelts,[6] – human forms debased by animal admixture. Thus the following description of evil spirits that tormented St Guthlac:

> *Wæron hie on onsyne egeslice 7 hæfdon micle heafdu, and lange sweoran, and mægere onsyne; wæron fulice and orfyrme on heora bearde; and hæfdan ruge earan, and woh neb, egeslice eagum, and ondrysenlice muðas; and heora teð wæron horses tuxum gelice...*

[Prose Life of Guthlac ch.5]

They were ghastly of aspect and had large heads and long necks, and narrow faces; they were foul and nasty in their beard(s); and had hairy ears and crooked noses, and horrible mouths; and their teeth were like horses' tusks...

In the Old English poem, *Solomon & Saturn 1*, demons are accorded the power to change shape, as well as great malevolence towards men:

> *Mæg simle se godes cwide   gumena gehwylcum*
> *ealra feonda gehwane   fleondne gebrengan*
> *ðurh mannes muð,   manfulra heap*
> *sweartne geswencan,   næfre hie ðæs syllice*
> *bleoum bregdað.   Æfter bancofan*

---

[1] *ibid.* p.73

[2] Quoted by Cavendish, 1975, p.187

[3] *ibid.* p.188; for full text of translation see Sparks, 1984; a similar legend is hinted at in *Genesis* 6:1–4.

[4] Cavendish, 1975, p.189

[5] *ibid.* 235–6

[6] Jordan 1983, pp.297–8 & illus. The modern fairy image is a mix of human and insect wings.

feðerhoman onfoð,   hwilum flotan gripað;
hwilum hie gewendað   in wyrmes lic
str[o]nges and sticoles,   stingeð nieten,
feldgongende   feoh gestrudeð.
Hwilum he on wætere   wicg gehnægeð,
hornum geheaweð,   oððæt him heortan blod,
famig flodes bæð,   foldan geseceð.
Hwilum he gefeterað   fæges mannes,
handa gehefegað,   ðonne he æt hilde sceall
wið lað werud   lifes tiligan;
awriteð he on his wæpne   wællnota heap,
bealwe bocstafas,   bill forscrifeð,
meces mærðo.   Forðon nænig man scile
oft orðances   ut abredan
wæpnes ecgge,   ðeah ðe him se wlite cweme,
ac symle he sceal singan,   ðonne he his sweord geteo,
Pater Noster,   and ðæt palmtreow
biddan mid blisse,   ðæt him bu gife
feorh and folme,   ðonne his feond cyme.

[*Solomon and Saturn 1*]

The word of God (i.e. The Paternoster) in the mouth of man – of any person – can always bring each and every fiend to flight, can torment that dark crowd of sinful entities – never can they again assume the same appearance. Over the skeleton they may put on a feathery surface, sometimes they assail ships, sometimes they take on a reptile body, strong and scaly, jab at animals and make the field-wandering cattle their prey. Sometimes at sea he will neigh like a horse, strike with his horns, until his heart's blood (and?) the frothing bath of currents (makes him) seek land again. Sometimes he binds a doomed person, incommodes his hands exactly when he has to defend his life against some fierce band of men in battle. He writes on his weapon a group of deadly symbols, evil letters, bewitching the blade and the glory of the sword. Therefore no one should thoughtlessly or frequently draw out his sharp-edged weapon – no matter how the fineness of it pleases him – unless he always (first) intone the Paternoster, whenever he draws his sword, and ask the palm-tree (? i.e. the Holy Cross) respectfully to give him both life and ?power, when his enemy comes.

93

Particularly vivid horror imagery is employed in detailing the variety of demons in the following bizarre passage from Saxo, when some travellers halt instinctively on coming to a haunted stretch of land:

> *Monstra quidem video celerem raptantia saltum*
>   *corpora nocturnis praecipitare locis.*
> *Bella gerit daemon, et iniquae dedita rixae*
>   *militat in mediis turba nefanda viis.*
> *Effigie spectanda truci portenta feruntur,*
>   *haecque hominum nulli rura patere sinunt.*
> *Agmina praecipiti per inane ruentia cursu*
>   *hac nos progressum sistere sede iubent;*
> *flectere lora monent sacrisque absistere campis*
>   *arvaque nos prohibent ulteriora sequi.*
> *Trux Lemurum chorus advehitur, praecepsque per auras*
>   *cursitat et vastos edit ad astra sonos.*
> *Accedunt Fauni Satyris, Panumque caterva*
>   *Manibus admixta militat ore fero;*
> *Silvanis coeunt Aquili, Larvaeque nocentes*
>   *cum Lamiis callem participare student.*
> *Saltu librantur Furiae, glomerantur iisdem*
>   *Fanae, quae Simis Fantua iuncta premit.*
> *Calcandus pediti trames terrore redundat,*
>   *tutis excelsi terga premantur equi.*

[Saxo Bk.2 ch.2]

For I see monstrous beings moving their bodies in some swift dance as they dash about the nocturnal scene. The demon-kind wage wars, and, dedicated to malicious trouble-making, battle on – a foul mob – in the open. The monstrosities come forward to be viewed with their ghastly faces, and will not allow mortals access to the open way. Armies of them dashing headlong on their mindless course force us to halt our progress in this spot; warn us to turn our reins and leave the awesome region; forbid us to go further into this land. A fierce band of ghosts advances, riding headlong on the wind, and issuing desolate cries to the stars. Then come fauns and satyrs, the troops of Pan, and join battle alongside the shades, with fierce mouth. *Aquili* join the rural crowd, and dangerous Larval spirits are keen to incorporate themselves in the procession, along with vampiric entities. The Furies arch and leap, and with them roll the *Fanae*, and the on-pressing half-ape *Fantua*. The very road resounds with the trampling terror of the throng: we are much safer high up on the backs of the horses!

Now in his vivid Latin couplets, Saxo not impossibly renders what in the original language could be the alliterative verse sections of saga-like narratives; and the dramatic passage above very ably corresponds to legends of Odin's

Wild Hunt elsewhere. But if so, the Latinisation is so thorough that the modern translator has a dilemma in returning the specialist Latin terms into English at all. Thus *fana* concern temple spirits or oracles, *fantua* are spirits that can possess humans, *aquili* are demons in the form of an eagle.[1] Moreover, the whole range of Latin terms could be derived from the work of Martianus Capella with perhaps the aid of Remigius' commentary[2] – so that it is hard to know whether we are dealing with authentic Germanic material or a Latinised fantasy upon some hint in the source.

In addition to visual horror and satanic links, the demon may have been feared for connotations with sexuality: "Wyrc sealfe wiþ ælfcynne 7 nihtgengan 7 þam mannum þe deofol midhæmð."[3] (Make an ointment against elf-kind and night-goers and those people who have sexual intercourse with the devil.) In other recipes 'night-goers' are found in the following contexts: "wið feondes costunge 7 nihtgengum" (against the devil's temptation and night-goers)[4] and "wið unhyrum nihtgengum 7 wið egeslicum gesyhðum 7 swefnum" (against monstrous night-goers and terrifying sights and dreams).[5] It once glosses the word *hyna*, which may be connected with German *Hüne* 'a giant'. In a monastic context, it may have seemed reasonable to attribute unprompted sexual arousal to the night visits of *succubus* (or *incubus*), forms of demons dedicated to sexual pleasure with humans, but potentially invisible. Was this seen as a more serious issue than actual physical illness?

The (evil) role of demons was well established in Christian lore before the conversion of Anglo-Saxon England, and was the obvious context in which to view (and discredit) pagan/magic practices; it could be used, after all, to cover every aspect of paganism: pagan gods were demons deceiving the unenlightened; so too elves and the like;[6] while prognostication, augury and even healing could be easily attributed to the agency of demons. As Boniface wrote to King Edwin: "The Psalmist says of such, 'All the heathen gods are devils; it is the Lord who made the heavens.'"[7]

---

[1] See Saxo, 1980, 2, note p.41

[2] *ibid.* as there pointed out

[3] *Leechbook* pt.3 item 61

[4] *Leechbook* pt.3 item 1

[5] de Vriend, 1984, p.30

[6] "When Christianity came, the elves of heathendom were equated with demons...." Bonser, 1953, p.159

[7] Quoted in Branston, 1974, p.54; the letter was written c.625 AD.

Magic in the Anglo-Saxon Period

The evidence for Anglo-Saxon magic is in large part literary and negative. Secular law-codes contain prohibitions[1], and a notable example is paragraph 30 in the Introduction to Alfred's *Laws*, arguably the most important public document of his reign. Otherwise, such brief notices as there are of witchcraft in the period are usually contained in Church regulations, which present a moral parallel to the more secular legislation of the King. The earliest and best-authenticated record is the Latin *Penitential of Theodore* (Archbishop of Canterbury d.669), believed to have been written down shortly after his death. This ought to reflect a situation in which official paganism had been dismantled, and only local belief survived.[2] Associated with Egbert, Archbishop of York in the eighth century, are a *Confessional* (with perhaps some early material) and a *Penitential* (with some debt to Frankish sources, and possibly Ælfric's involvement), both dating in their present form to c.1000 AD.[3] In these cases, references to the sort of practices introduced by Viking settlers are not impossible. Unfortunately, there are almost as many versions of these texts as manuscripts (plus translations into Old English); and because of some duplication of material, it is not easy to provide date limits for the practices objected to, nor always to be certain of their relevance to England itself. Confirmation from sources independent of each other is clearly desirable.

The sermons of Ælfric, at a time when a new insurge of pagan settlers was to be coped with, sometimes have references to magical practices. Of continental sources, the *Indiculus Superstitionum* is a list of chapter-headings preserved in the Vatican MS Palatinus 577, which summarises major superstitions to be countered; its origin may lie at Fulda in the eighth century. Grimm[4] identifies it as an appendix to Charlemagne's *Capitulary* of 743 AD and relates it to German-speaking Franks in the Netherlands. Laws of the Carolingian kings for their Germanic subjects are also admissible, I feel, especially as comparative or confirmatory evidence. Yet it is not only obvious sources that may indicate a 'foreign' colouring: Pope Gregory's concept of Anglo-Saxon paganism could have been influenced by reports from Gaul, where cults of idols persisted in the sixth century, including "wishing at wells," and "veneration of sacred stones or trees."[5]

Yet such is the available material, and it is from these sources we get initially a clear statement of the duty of the Church authorities to punish the worship of

---

[1] E.g. the Laws of Wihtred of Kent, of 695 AD, ch.12, of penalties for sacrificing to devils.

[2] Bede, in his commentary on Apocalypse, noted that the English had "cherished it [the seed of faith] only lukewarmly" since Gregory's day – via George H. Brown *Bede the Educator* (Jarrow Lecture, 1996)

[3] See Meaney 1989. p.13; further details in Frantzen, 1983, pp.7–72

[4] 4, 1888, pp.1739–40

[5] Dalton, 1927, 1, p.248; but in some opinions, this has little to do with Frankish (Germanic) belief, but rests on Romano-Celtic tradition – *ibid.* p.245. By the fifth century Celts in Gaul and Britain would be nominally Christian, however.

pagan gods (however loosely defined) and eradicate related magic practices. Thus Theodore's chapter 27 states:

> *Si quis immolat daemonibus in minimis I annum poeniteat... Si quis manducaverit vel biberit per ignorantiam juxta fanum, promittat quod deinceps nunquam reiteret, et XL dies in pane et aqua poeniteat.*
>
> [Thorpe, 1840, p.292]

> If anyone sacrifices to demons, let him do penance for at least one year... If anyone shall have eaten or drunk at a pagan shrine unknowingly, let him promise never to repeat the act, and do penance for 40 days on bread and water...

For those repeating the offence, or deliberately joining in demoniacal ceremonies, much stronger penances were ordained. But it is notable no specific cult is mentioned, only the general term 'demons', which could imply some uncertainty on what is to be countered, or indeed a lack of clearly defined single-god cults. Ritual feasting is stressed, and though the location given as a church-like edifice, remains of animal bones, it may be significant, are often associated with pagan human cemeteries as possible sites of sacrifice/feasting.

On the continent, the same duty was enforced in similar general terms:

> *Decrevimus ut secundum canones unusquisque episcopus in sua parrochia sollicitudinem adhibet, adiuvante gravione qui defensor ecclesiae est, ut populus Dei paganias non faciat, sed ut omnes spurcitias gentilitatis abiciat et respuat.*
>
> [*Capitulary of Carloman*, 742 AD, para.5, Pertz, 1835, p.17]

> We decree that, in accordance with the canons, each bishop in his own parish should, in pursuance of the duty that makes him a defender of the Church, ensure that he does not allow the people of God to be pagan, but should reject and cast out all the pollution of the gentiles [i.e. pagan beliefs and rites].

The objection here is to anything specifically non-Christian. 'Heathen' as a word is thought to be linked to 'heath', in the sense of a wild abode, much as 'pagan' comes from a Latin term denoting someone who lives in the remote countryside, and so someone out of the correct tide of behaviour and thought, someone following the old ways.[1] But are the practices objected to ones that actually took place, or are they a sort of fantasy of wrong-doing, or perhaps conventional formulas stated for the sake of reinforcing biblical convention such

---

[1] "Pagani... in locis agrestibus et pagis gentiles lucos idolaque statuerunt." Isidore *Etymologia* bk.8 ch.10 (Pagans are those who have established gentile groves and idols in rural places and villages.)

as *Deuteronomy* 17:3, where worshippers of the Sun or Moon are to be stoned to death?[1] A set of prohibitions might well contain traditional (i.e. anachronistic or irrelevant) material from respect for a revered source, even in conscious echo of what Classical authorities like Tacitus or Caesar reported of the pagan past in Germany, or indeed the false idols so typical of the enemies of Yahweh in the Old Testament.

> *And we forbeodað eornostlie ælcne hæðenscipe. Hæðenscipe byð, þæt man deofol-gyld weorðige, þæt is þæt man weorðige hæðene godas and sunnan oððe monan, fyr oððe flod, wæter-wyllas oððe stanas oððe æniges cynnes wudu-treowa, oððe wiccecræft lufige, oððe morðweorc gefremme on ænige wisan, oððe on blote oððe on fyrhte, oððe swylcra gedwimera ænig þing dreoge...*
>
> [*Laws*, 2 Cnut ch.5]

And we earnestly forbid any sort of heathenism. Heathenism it is when someone venerates an image of the devil, that is when someone worships heathen gods and the sun or moon, fire or water, springs or stones or any kind of tree, or loves witchcraft, or commits harmful acts in any fashion, either in a sacrifice or in divination, or takes any part in such impropriety...

It is hard not to feel that there is an element of fantasy, or at least a sort of legalistic cover-all insurance in such wide-ranging definitions. They represent what leading Churchmen *thought* was happening (by definition behind their backs), and the provisions may also have been cast in this form to cover all eventualities, as well as to seem knowledgeable; to dignify or maximise the problem to be tackled while at the same time seeming properly contemptuous of un-Christian activity.

Only slightly more specific is the following:

> *And we lærað þæt preosta gehwilc cristendom geornlice arære and ælcne hæðendom mid ealle adwæsce; and forbeode wilweorðunga and licwiglunga and hwata and galdra and manweorðunga and þa gemearr þe man drifð on mislicum gewiglungum and on friðsplottum and on ellenum and eac on oðrum mislicum treowum and on stanum and on manegum mislicum gedwimerum þe men on dreogað fela þæs þe hi na ne scoldon."*
>
> [*Canons* of Wulfstan]

And we instruct all priests to promote Christianity eagerly, and thoroughly obliterate any (trace of) heathenism; and we forbid the veneration of springs and magic involving dead bodies and omens and charms and the veneration

---

[1] Could worship of the sun only have meant observance of quarter-days like Midsummer's Day; and worship of the moon, rituals at times of eclipse? Or indeed, be imputed from the existence of Sunday and Monday in the pan-European calendar?

of human beings and the evil that people perpetrate through various spells and at common sanctuaries and near elder tress and also near various others (kinds of) trees and at stones and in all sorts of errors in which people persist the more they should not.

This would seem to imply some resistance to the Christian message among the Viking settlers. (Later penitentials may be aimed at coping with this new brand of subversion, but where earlier provisions are repeated, this cannot imply that the practice is still current: for tradition is essential to text at this time.) But whether new or old, the reference to the dead and worship of (unsaintly) humans in the above text I can only understand as relating to ancestral cults. The continuity of such practices, not openly but as a sort of specious Christianity, is suggested in *Indiculus Superstitionum* no.9 "De Sacrificio quod fit alicui sanctorum" (Of a (wrongful) sacrifice that is made to any saint) and no.18 "De Incertis Locis, que colunt pro sanctis." (Of unofficial places, which are revered as holy.)

The popular theme of worship of the inanimate occurs as early as Theodore (ch.27):

> *Si quis ad arbores, vel ad fontes, vel ad lapides, sive ad cancellos, vel ubicumque, excepto in æcclesia Dei, votum voverit, aut exsolverit, III annos cum pane et aqua poeniteat.*

> If anyone initiates or resolves a vow by trees or springs or stones or enclosures,[1] or anywhere except in a church of God, let him/her do penance for 3 years on bread and water.

And trees are specifically mentioned in Ælfric's sermon 'De Auguriis', but were they realistically venerated? We know that continental tribes revered trees, and one particular story reflects the Conversion on the continent:[2]

> *Se halga [Martin] towearp eac sum hæðengyld and wolde aheawan ænne heahne pinbeam, se wæs ær gehalgod þam heaðenum godum. Ða noldon ða hæðenan þam halgan geðafian þæt he swa halig treow æfre hynan sceolde; cwæð þeah heora an þæt he hit underfenge feallende to foldan, and hi hit forcurfon, gif he on God truwode þurh trumne geleafan. Þa geþafode Martinus þæt mid gebylde and wearð gebunden under ðam beame geset ðider ðe he bigde mid healicum bogum and næs him nan wen þæt he ahwar wende buton to ðam halgan swa swa he ahyld wæs. Hwæt ða ða heaðenan aheowon þæt treow mid ormæte blisse þæt hit brastliende sah to ðam*

---

[1] *Cancelli* can also mean boundaries. Elsewhere in ch.27, Theodore objects to feasting "in locis abhominandis gentilium" (in the abominable sites of pagans), without further specification.

[2] In Sulpicius Severus' *Vita*, ed. Migne *Patrologium Latinum* vol.20, 1845, col.167, of fourth century Gaul; Boniface is attributed with hewing down a similar tree, a sacred oak near Geismar in Hesse, in the 720s.

halgan were hetelice swiðe. Þa worhte he ongean ðam hreosendum treowe
þæs Hælendes rodetacn and hit ðærrihte ætstod, wende ða ongean, and
hreas underbæc, and forneah offeoll ða ðe hit ær forcurfon.

[Ælfric *Catholic Homilies* II, no.39 (St Martin)]

The holy Martin also pulled down some idol and wished to cut down a tall
pine tree that was formerly sacred to the heathen gods. The heathens did not
wish to allow the saint ever to bring low such a holy tree; but one of them
said that if he was willing to take the weight of the tree as it fell to the
ground, they would do the felling – if he believed that much in God, with
firm enough a faith. Then Martin submitted to that with courage and was
tied up and placed under the tree, on the side it naturally leaned towards
with its lofty boughs, and they never imagined it would incline anywhere
but where he was laid. Then he made the sign of the Saviour's cross against
the tottering tree, and it directly paused, then reversed, and fell backwards,
nigh on squashing them that did the hewing.

Other references to tree-worship come from the *Indiculus Superstitionum* no.6, "De
sacris silvarum quae nimidas vocant."[1] Evidence for such rites is lacking, as far as I
know, in England itself, though the later May-Pole could be cited; and to Phythian-
Adams[2] "It is… tempting to speculate whether at least those *hundredal* place-names
ending in *treow* (and often prefixed by a personal name) may indicate an association
between the pre-hundredal administrative meeting place and… an ancient
sanctuary." Whether these holy areas are related to communal assembly places or
shrines for veneration of a particular god or even a sort of pagan churchyard with
burials is unclear; compare the references to *cancelli* and *friðsplottas* above.

Accuracy of interpretation is not helped when alliteration becomes a factor in
compiling such lists:

Gif wiccan oððe wigleras, manswora oððe morðwyrhtan oððe fule, afylede,
abære horcwenan ahwar on lande wurðan agytene, ðonne fyse hi man of
earde 7 clænsie þa ðeode, oððe on earde forfare hy mid ealle, buton hig
geswican 7 þe deoppor gebetan.

If witches or wizards, perjurers or murderers or impure, corrupt, notorious
whores are discovered anywhere in the land, then one should drive them out
of the land and so cleanse the people, or let them perish entirely where they
are, unless they cease and the more effectively make atonement.

This provision must have been highly satisfactory, for it occurs not only in the
combined law-treaty (with special relevance for the Danelaw) known as *Edward &
Guthrum* (where it is ch.11), but is repeated in the Law-codes *6 Athelred* ch.7 and
2 Cnut ch.4.

---

[1] cf. Tacitus *Germania* ch.9 'They consecrate groves and woods…'
[2] 1975, pp.14–15

What is also confusing is the impression that many of the activities objected to were harmless or not unlike Christian equivalents, and that exception was being taken on grounds of competitive malice, or for lack of proper supervision and subordination to Church authority. What, after all, can be wrong with a little merry-making?

> *And we lærað þæt man geswice freols-dagum hæðenra leoda and deofles gamene...*
>
> [Canons of Edgar]

> And we instruct you to abandon the holidays of the heathen people and the pastimes of the devil.

Such holidays (holy i.e. lucky? days), condemned here as specifically giving credence or honour to the Devil (for any pagan entity), or perhaps as calendar-based feasts, show a blithe unawareness of the role of Christmas itself as a legacy of the midwinter solstice (the Saturnalia of the Romans, the Sol Invicta celebrations of the Mithraists[1]).

Of similar observations, the *Indiculus Superstitionum* no.21 objects to shouting 'vince luna!' (let the moon win) during an eclipse, and no.22 mentions the use of horns and snails (*cocleis* – small curling musical instruments?), presumably to produce a cacophony to influence the weather or the passage of an eclipse. In seventh century Gaul, "shouting during eclipses of the moon" was denounced in sermons.[2] So too in the *Penitential of Theodore*, ch.27, it is laid down,

> *Qui student exercere quando luna obscuratur, ut clamoribus suis ac maleficiis sacrilegio usu eum defendere confidunt, v annos poeniteant.*

> Whoever thinks to exert themselves when the moon is obscured, as though they hope to defend it with their shouts or sorceries in some sacrilegious rite, let them do penance for 5 years.

---

[1] See Wilkinson, 1975, p.191, where a polite note is added on *Sun*-day. Also Ling, 1968, 180–82.

[2] Dalton, 1927, vol.1, p.248. In the nineteenth century, orchard ceremonies were "accompanied by gun-shots – perhaps a latter-day relic of the use of noise to keep evil spirits at bay." (Phythian-Adams, 1975, p.15)

Does this confirm the suspicion that the sports of Anglo-Saxon tradition were condemned from some (pagan) religious association? Bonser[1] notes one version of the *Canons of Edgar* as demanding that "on feast days heathen songs and devils' games be abstained from." And Ælfric is stern about the activities in the week preceding Easter:

> *Forwel fela sind þe wyllað on ðisum dagum drincan oð speowðan and fracodlice him betwynan sacian; ac ðillice ne magon singan þone lofsang 'þes is se dæg ðe Drihten worhte'. Him andwyrt þærrihte Drihten, 'Ge sind þeostru, and na leoht.'*
> [Ælfric *Catholic Homilies*, II, 'Alius Sermo de Die Paschae']

> Very many there are who are pleased on these days to drink to spewing and wickedly fight (or compete?) among themselves; but such cannot sing the hymn 'This is the day the Lord wrought'. Them God answers straight out: 'You are darkness and not light.'

Antipathy of this kind may also have stemmed from the Christian opposition to physical display and indulgence in pleasure. Thus the young St Cuthbert is warned to stop fooling about in a divinely-inspired reproach put into the mouth of a desperate 3-year-old child. It proves a sobering lesson, and Cuthbert was not thereafter found with the other lads "twisting themselves about in all kinds of contortions in the excitement of the game."[2] (Or in the words of the older, less decorous *Anonymous Life*, indulging "in a variety of games and tricks; some of them stood naked, with their heads turned down unnaturally towards the ground, their legs stretched out and their feet lifted up and pointing skywards."[3])

And in the Old English version of *Gregory's Dialogues*,[4] there is the grotesquely grim story of some travelling jester who unwittingly crossed a saint:

> *Þa þa he com to þæs forecwedenan Fortunates beode, þa ær ðon þe he Gode þone lofsang asægde (swaswa sume men gewuniaþ þæt hi singað mid hergendlicum cræfte ær hi etan), þa stod þær semninga sum man mid anum apan 7 bæd him metes 7 sloh cymbalan. Þa sona se halga wer wæs forhycgende þæt glig 7 eorringa þus cwæð: 'Walawa! dead sceall beon þes erming! Ic com to þisses gereordes mysan, 7 nu git ic na minne muþ to Godes herenysse ne ontynde 7 he com mid apan 7 slog cymbalan!' Þa get he togeecte þas word 7 cwæð þus, 'Gangað ge nu 7 for Godes lufan syllað him mete 7 drync 7 witað ge hwæþre þæt he dead bið unfyrn.'*

> When he had come to the aforementioned Fortunatus' table, before he managed to say his praise to God – for some men are used to sing with praiseful skill

[1] 1963, p.124
[2] Bede prose *Vita* ch.1, trans. Webb
[3] ch.3, trans. Colgrave 1940, p.65
[4] Bk.1 ch.9

before they eat – there suddenly appeared a man with an ape, and asked him for food, and clashed his cymbals. Straightaway the holy man was contemptuous of such levity and wrathfully said, 'Alas! this wretch will die! I come to this board's refreshment, and have not even yet opened my mouth in praise of God, and he turns up with an ape and bangs his cymbals!' Further he added these word and spoke thus: 'Take him away and for love of God give him some meat and drink, and watch and see if he is soon dead or not.'

After this unpropitious welcome, the jester receives some food and is about to carry it out the door with him, when a big stone falls from above, hits him on the head, and, as feared, he is killed. Nor should the extraordinary nature of the story blind us to the reality that narrator and audience alike would be on the side of the saints; and give a satisfied nod, no doubt, as the stone whizzes down.[1]

What to the modern taste seems fairly innocent sport often had a sinister overtone to Christianity, either because of a distrust of physical pleasure, or because such festivals and festivity were seen as honouring non-Christian forces. Another area of doubtful political correctness was womankind.

Women's needs and especially the problems of childbirth must have been a practical and ethical difficulty for the Church. There was little that medical science could do to help with the processes of procreation or parturition, and no great Christian sympathy for or understanding of such processes. A celibate life was the ideal; though one of the advantages of Christianity over Mithraism was that it did not exclude women from communion. So it was politic to focus women's attention too on Christianity, beyond the recognised duty of making provision for female monastic institutions. Thus the *Indiculus Superstitionum* no.19 deals with "De petendo, quod boni vocant sanctae Mariae" (of seeking [elsewhere] what decent people ask of Holy Mary) – suggesting both that the Virgin Mary played a special role within the Church, perhaps related to motherhood, and that that area of need was not being adequately covered.

To return to the texts:

> *Si quis pro sanitate filioli, per foramen terrae exierit, illudque spinis post se concludit, XL dies in pane et aqua poeniteat.*
> [*Penitential of Theodore* c.27]

If anyone, for the health of their baby son, should pass through a hole in the ground, and close it behind with thorns, let such do penance for 40 days on bread and water.

---

[1] In case it might seem that I imply that ill-temper is a Christian failing, please recall the incident during Baldur's funeral in the *Prose Edda* when Thor ill-naturedly kicks the dwarf Litr into a fire.

Wifman beo þæs ylcan wyrðe gif heo tilað hire cilde mid ænigum wiccecræfte, oðõe æt wega gelæton þurh þa eorðan tihð. Eala, þæt ys mycel hæðenscype!

[*Penitential of pseudo-Egbert*]

Let a woman be worthy of the same (penalty) if she tries to cure her child with any witchcraft, or at crossroads draws (it) through the earth. Alas, that is terrible heathenism!

The meaning is far from clear here; *tilað* would imply 'encouraging' a child, i.e. bringing on an overdue birth, or seeking to restore the health of one already born. In either case, the aim is ultimately the welfare of the child, with which some sympathy might be expected. Moving underground or perhaps drawing or passing a child through the earth is also an obscure image, and in the Latin it reads more like a venture of the parent into perhaps some animal den – or an access opening into a burial mound or prehistoric chamber? (Christian relics were doubtless kept in underground crypts such as that at Hexham, but no pagan parallel to that is known, though Mithraic temples could be below ground level.) Or it might indicate some act intended to improve a weak or deformed baby by bringing it into contact with special soil; for crossroads may have been associated with pagan deities[1] as later they were a place for gibbets and the burial of suicides. Or earth here may be associated with graves, not in some deliberately perverse rite, but in the sense of seeking help from ancestors at a burial site, and it is not impossible that the Christian horror expressed in this prohibition relates to the soil belonging to a grave, and so implying a kind of worship of the dead. By comparison, particles of dust from on or near a saint's tomb, steeped in water, produced a perfectly acceptable Christian remedy: "The *potio de pulvere sepulchri* was perhaps the best known panacea of the Dark Ages."[2] And the use of soil from an ?unsaintly grave is specified in the Old English *Charm for Delayed Birth* (below, pt 2 no.11), in a text that has some Christian components.

Ælfric in his homily *De Auguriis*,[3] repeats the warning against rites at crossroads, and adds, "Sume hi acwellað heora cild ærðam þe hi acennede beon, oðõe æfter acennednysse þæt hi cuðe ne beon, ne heora manfulla forligr ameldod ne wurðe." (Some of them kill their children before they are born, or after birth,

---

[1] In Ælfric's sermon *De Falsis Diis*, crossroads are connected with Odin, but perhaps as an attribute of the Roman equivalent, Mercury; otherwise in Roman superstition such sites were associated with Hecate as goddess of the crossroads (Cavendish, 1975, p.98); a man killing an enemy at a crossroads and dedicating him as a human sacrifice to Odin is mentioned in one Icelandic case (see Turville-Petre, 1964, p.53), so the association could have a Germanic validity. Curiously William of Malmesbury has King Alfred hanging gold armlets up at crossroads: "per publicos aggeres, ubi semitae in quadrivium finduntur, armillas aureas juberet suspendi" [Bk.2, para.122] (at public mounds, where paths split in a crossroads, he would order golden armlets to be hung up).

[2] Dalton, 1927, vol.1, p.257 n.1

[3] *Lives of Saints* Bk.1 no.17

that they may not be discovered, nor their wicked adultery be betrayed. – trans. Skeat.)[1] Such crude attempts at controlling the life process may have been condemned as a sort of (in)human(e) sacrifice, or (like suicide) as a denial of life as a gift of God, a misappropriation of divine destiny into private hands.

There are other specific transgressions committed by women:

Si qua mulier filium suum vel filiam super tectum pro sanitate posuerit, vel in fornace, VII annos poieniteat.

[*Penitential of Theodore* ch.27]

If a woman places her son or daughter on the roof or in an oven, let her do penance for 7 years.

Wif gif heo set hire dohtor ofer hus oððe on ofen for þam ðe heo wylle hig feferadle gehælan: fæste heo VII winter.

[*Confessional of Egbert* ch.33]

If a woman puts her daughter on the roof or in an oven because she wishes to cure it of a feverish sickness, let her fast 7 years.

Again, the intention seems purely good, but perhaps the uncomfortable locations named had some significance in relation to pagan ritual now lost to us, concerning hearth or the main supporting house pillars or the sun (at some specific time of year?). Thus *Indiculus Superstitionum* no.17 deals "De observatione pagana in foco vel in inchoatione rei alicuius." (On the pagan rite at the hearth or in the inception of any matter.) Or would this refer to foundation ceremonies?

Could there be some concept here of life as deriving from or being comparable to fire, with cremation the reciprocal ritual at death? Certain types of fire may have had special significance (*Indiculus Superstitionum* no.15, "De igne fricato de ligno" i.e. fire obtained by friction from wood,[2] or the hearth may have gained significance as the centre of the home.[3] Meaney[4] asks whether the move might

---

[1] In a rogation homily – no.4 in Bazire & Cross, 1989, p.63 – a special sixth zone of hell, filled with hell-hounds, is accorded to any woman who has killed her own child or betrayed her husband.

[2] Grimm 1883, 2, 607 records *not-fiur*, connected with OHG *hniotan* 'to rub, shake, thump'; the Capitulary of Carloman (Pertz, 1835, p.17) prohibits "illos sacrilegos ignes, quos nied fyr vocant," (those sacrilegious fires which they call *niedfyr*). In England, Phythian-Adams (1975, p.14) notes the different folk uses of fire including 'bone-fires' (for cremation?) and a 'need-fire', mentioned in 1268; but the first mention I can locate in the *OED* is in sixteenth century Scotland, a typical seventeenth century Scottish reference being "for the curing of cattell." Grön, 1953, p.147, suggests that *Nothfeuer* implied "the use of smoke for expelling the demons of diseases." An extensive article on *Notfeuer* is included in Hoffman-Krayer & Bächtold-Stäubli, 1934–5, vol.6, cols.1138-1151.

[3] cf. French words like *feu, foyer* < *focus*, 'a fireplace'

[4] 1989 p.21

have "a purely practical purpose," i.e. to sweat out a fever, but it has to said that without a theoretical knowledge of disease, any practical cures would be arrived at by chance, and the high penalty exacted here is strongly suggestive of some perceived pagan element.

Another area of presumably female interest is the magic of lovers:

> *Gif hwa wiccige ymbe æniges mannes lufe and him on æte sylle oððe on drince oððe on æniges cynnes gealdorcræftum, þæt hyra lufu for þon þe mare beon scyle, gif hit læwede do, fæste healf gear.*

[Penitential of pseudo-Egbert]

If someone lays an enchantment upon any one's affections and gives him something in food or drink or by any other kind of spell, to make her love (i.e. love of her?) greater – if a lay person do this, let [them] fast half a year.

The sex of the grammar is not entirely clear, as pronouns (and even Old English *mann*, which refers to a person of either sex) can be ambiguous; but apparently it is a woman administering the potion – the reverse might be just as likely (as in the well-known later example of Shakespeare's *A Midsummer Night's Dream*). The penalty rises in the following more explicit case:

> *Mulier quae semen viri cum cibo suo miscuerit, et id sumserit, ut masculo carior sit, III annos jejunet.*

[Confessional of Egbert ch.29]

A woman who mixes the semen of a man with her food, and consumes it, in order to make herself more cherished by the man, let her fast 3 years;

– and at a lesser tariff:

> *Mulier si sanguinem viri sui pro aliquo remedio gustaverit, XL dies jejeunet.*

[Confessional of Egbert ch.31]

If a woman tastes of the blood of her husband for any kind of remedy, let her fast 40 days.

As a general prohibition, this is found in Wulfstan's *Canons of Edgar:*

> *And riht is þæt ænig cristen man blod ne þycge*

[Fowler, 1972, ch.53]

It is proper that no Christian person taste blood.

The association is presumably between blood and pagan sacrifice. Other provisions overtly attest the seriousness with which the Church regarded any ritual involving the dead:

Qui grana arserit ubi mortuus est homo, pro sanitate viventium et domus, V annos in pane et aqua poeniteat.

[*Penitential of Theodore* ch.27]

Quicunque grana combusserit in loco ubi mortuus est homo, pro sanitate viventium et domus, V annos jejunet.

[*Confessional of Egbert* ch.32]

Anyone who has burned grain for the health of the living or the benefit of his home, for 5 years let him fast on bread and water.

Swa hwylc man swa corn bærne on þære stowe þær man dead wære lyfigendum mannum to hæle, and on his huse: fæste V winter.

[*Penitential of pseudo-Egbert*]

Any man that burns grain in a place where someone died, or in his own house, to benefit the living – let him fast 5 years.

The versions vary somewhat: the Latin original makes it more a family ritual, I think. Are we to imply some sort of offering to or invocation of ancestral powers, contrary to the neutral status of the dead in Christianity and God as the sole source of proper power? "Sacrificia mortuorum" (sacrifices to the dead) are the first item to be condemned as pagan in Carloman's Capitulary of 742,[1] and it is notable that burnt corn has been found at certain Anglo-Saxon cemeteries,[2] which might be taken as a symbol of conveying food to another dimension rather than as a gesture of dismissal or exorcism.[3]

There is little in the above that would seem today anything more than weird superstition or aberrant personal bad taste, depending on exactly how reticent the texts have been about the background to the various practices; but in the context of a possible revival of paganism in England in the ninth to tenth centuries, such prohibitions must have seemed worth maintaining and enlarging on. It is notable that they centre on transgressions by women; that they concern solutions outside the Church ambit and have a possible political dimension; that links to the ancestral dead could well be present e.g. in siting rituals at graves, or relating them to the home; and that no specific pagan god is ever formally mentioned, suggesting that magic may belong to a different stratum, even that of low-key private superstitions.[4]

---

[1] para.5, Pertz, 1835, p.17

[2] Meaney 1964, p.18

[3] This is, as far as I am aware, the sole example of archaeology confirming the Penitentials.

[4] Here Margaret Murray *The Witch-Cult in Western Europe* (1921) which argued for survival of pagan fertility cult from Anglo-Saxon times to seventeenth century is relevant – as discussed in Merrifield, 1987, p160. – and also how "inert conservatism of

But just occasionally an exceptional case would occur that demonstrated witchcraft at its foulest:

...7 þæt land æt Ægeleswyrðe headde an wyduwe 7 hire sunu ær forwyrt forþanþe hi drifon serne stacan on Ælsie Wulfstanes feder 7 þæt wearð æreafe 7 man teh þæt morð forð of hire inclifan. þa nam man þæt wif 7 adrencte hi ætt Lundene bricge 7 hire sunu ætberst 7 werð utlah 7 þæt land eode þam kynge to handa...

[Robertson, 1939, p.68]

...and that estate at Ailworth a widow and her son had previously forfeited because they drove an iron ?nail into (?an image of) Ælfsige, Wulfstan's father, and that was discovered and they brought that thing of death (?deadly image) out of her room. Then they took the woman and drowned her at the London bridge[1] but her son escaped and became an outlaw and the estate passed into the hands of the King...

The charter[2] in which this note occurs is not specifically dated, but apparently mid tenth century; the estate perhaps near Peterborough, an area not uninfluenced by Viking settlement, though the victims at least do not bear Viking names.

It is conventionally translated as referring to a manikin or victim-doll of some kind, into which an iron nail or pin has been driven, causing pains (or worse) in the corresponding part of the victim's body, or it is just possible that this accusation relates to causing some sort of accident to occur; but relevant also is "Gif hwa drife stacan on ænigne man: fæste III gear."[3] (If anyone drive a stake through a person, let him fast 3 years.) Here again, a 'straightforward' violent assault with a weapon is clearly not involved; either a form of magic upon a manikin is implied or just possibly the reference is to driving a stake through a dead body to lay an uneasy spirit (with the heart, as in Aristotle, targeted as the centre of intelligence?). This is specified in another case, Saxo's account of the mortal career of the supposed god Odin, who is so troublesome even when laid in the ground that "the citizens... disinterred the body, decapitated it and impaled it through the breast with a sharp stake; that was the way the people cured the problem."[4]

In the Ailsworth case, the discovery of the crime by evidence in the woman's inner chamber suggests something small-scale like a wax image, nor is this sort of activity at all the preserve of later witchcraft.[5] It is noted in Roman times, as in Ovid,[6] and is

---

ritual behaviour ensured the continuance of similar basic practices through many changes of belief." Merrifield, 1987, p.194

[1] According to Davies, 1989, p.51, a bridge where Ermine Street crossed the Nene.

[2] Robertson, 1939, no.37

[3] *Penitential of pseudo-Egbert*

[4] Trans. Fisher, Saxo, 1979, 1, p.26

[5] For references see Brand, 1849 pp.10–12 and notes; earlier references are provided in Grimm, 1883, pp.1092–3

[6] *Heroides*, Letter vi, line 91

perhaps a universal method of obtaining power and influence over another person in fantasy (directly, be it noted, and not through the mediation of a god).[1]

One last, even more obscure reference comes in a charter[2] as part of a list of bounds...

> ...*of Hafoles beorhge on þonne wyte wege, on þæt sclæde, of þam sclæde on Echilde hlæwe – a þa smye wicce – of Echilde hlæwe on hengestes earas...*

> from Hafol's barrow to the ?white roadway, to the gully, from the gully to Echild's (?burial) mound – (there) ever still ?ponders the witch – from Echild's mound to Hengest's ?lands...

– that is, taking *smye* to be a form of the verb *smean* 'to meditate', as though Echild's mound was somewhere to gain inspiration, as seekers in Viking lands are said to have done; but the alternative verb, *smugan* 'to creep' cannot be ruled out.

Women As Seeresses

Though *wicca* can be male or female as a word, Alfred names especially women as encouragers of witchery in his *Laws*:[3] "Ða fæmnan þe gewuniað onfon gealdor-cræftigan 7 scin-læcan 7 wiccan, ne læt þu þa libban." (The women who are accustomed to receive (?harbour, ?support, ?give credence to) spell-workers and mirage-dealers and witches – do not allow them to live.) – after *Exodus* 22:18,[4] except that the provision is specifically aimed at women, and seems so phrased as to deal with (or target?) the patrons as much as the practitioners of harmful magic.

Meaney[5] asks whether the many amulets found in women's graves may signify woman's role as the healer in the family, and concludes that the Church was concerned with excluding them from extending such a role: in the pagan period it may have been that women "had had more independence of action, and a more responsible position within both sacred and secular society than they were allowed under the Judaeo-Christian ethic."[6] The accusation of witchcraft could thus become a political (gender) tool. I would not presume to comment on the source of the magicness of womankind; but it may not be entirely a misimpression deriving from the Christian state's reaction to the less favoured sex, for we have some

---

[1] See further Frazer, 1993, pp.13–14, 38

[2] Sawyer, 1966, no.648, issued in 957 AD by Kind Eadwig to New Minster, Winchester, and perhaps relating to Heighton in Sussex; Sawyer notes that Dorothy Whitelock expressed some reservations about its text.

[3] Intro. sect.30 (between prohibitions on seduction and buggery)

[4] *Exodus* 22:18: "Maleficos non patieris vivere." (You shall not allow sorcerers to live); cf. *Leviticus* 20:27 rendered in Old English "Se man þe bega wiccecræft, swelte he deaðe." (the person who practices witchcraft, let him/her die the death) – by stoning apparently.

[5] 1989, p10

[6] *ibid.* p.30

evidence of a long tradition of women as seeresses, a quasi-priestly, quasi-shamanistic role which would have involved tribal as well as personal concerns, apparently in divination as much as healing.

Curiously, though Bates' *Way of Wyrd* (1983) portrays such shamanistic rites in the expected context of healing,[1] his central figures are male; the Lacnunga MS.[2] he claims as inspiration is a compilation of fairly standard recipes, relatively low-key and practical, with some admittedly important verse charms – but even they show only the slightest hint of spirit-world travel.[3] Conversely, in later Scandinavian accounts, the special woman is likelier to deal in prophecy than healing – could this be a way – in the post-Christian era – to deny her a sympathetic role?

As early as Tacitus we have the statement, "Indeed they believe that there is in women some divine spark of foreknowledge and they do not despise their advice or neglect their answers,"[4] which is early evidence of a long association between women and the supernatural. But in stressing the art of divination, was he thinking of Graeco-Romano parallels like the Delphic Sibyl?[5] Perhaps he even wished to highlight the (for him) unusual case of women being accorded a role at all in matters like serious debate?[6]

Now all such contacts with an other-world depend on a linking up with (usually invisible) friendly forces, which could indeed be specifically ancestral:[7] they might act to counter some threat or avert some misluck, repair some misadventure, or give advice on how to act; but in general, I would assume Germanic divination to be not so much a matter of trance as of chance selection among physical objects, or a reading of physical events, conducted in a conscious state. A matter, in short, of augury rather than prophecy.

In Saxo, the healing role is emphasised in one encounter: Hading is innocently at table when he is almost challenged to take a trip to the other world by a casual gesture:

---

[1] So Glosecki (1989, p.3) defines a shaman as "a tribal doctor – sometimes just a seer, but typically a healer."
[2] BL Harley 585, c.1000 AD
[3] Possibly in '*Wið Dweorh*' (below, pt.2 no.9)
[4] Tacitus *Germania* ch.8 trans. Fyfe
[5] On such see Fontenrose, 1959, 1980, p.416
[6] A horse was, I believe, at one point given membership of the Roman Senate, but never a woman.
[7] 'Family shamanism' is noted as being considered more archaic than 'professional' shamanism, Glosecki, 1989, pp.42–3, 103.

'As he was dining, a woman beside a brazier, bearing stalks of hemlock, was seen to raise her head from the ground and, extending the lap of her garment, seemed to be asking in what part of the world such fresh plants might have sprung up during the winter season.'

[trans. Fisher, Saxo, 1979, 1, p.30]

But relevant also is Meaney's discussion of the vocabulary of women as seeresses/witches in her 1989 article pp.14–18, for terms like *hell-rune* indicate woman as oracle or augerer; there is also material collected in Grimm;[1] and challenging monographs like Stone's (1994) on *seiðr*. A particular emphasis on prophecy is placed in the detailed description of a consultation from the Saga of Eric the Red: during a famine in Greenland an approach is made to a *seidkona* (woman practising *seiðr*), who receives them in very ornate formal costume:

'...she wore a blue mantle fastened with straps and adorned with stones all the way down to the hem. She had a necklace of glass beads. On her head she wore a black lambskin hood lined with white cat's-fur... On her feet were hairy calfskin shoes with long thick laces which had large tin buttons on the ends. She wore catskin gloves, with the white fur inside.'

[trans. Magnusson & Pálsson, 1965, pp. 81–2]

She is given a meal of animal hearts. Next day other women are procured to make a special chant (*vardlokur*) in a circle round a dais, where the *völva* sits, in order to attract spirits who will enable her to prophecy. The chant worked so well, that "many spirits had been drawn there now who thought it lovely to lend ear."[2] She was able to give an assurance that the famine would end soon; and gave predictions to many assembled there, "and little indeed of what she said failed to come about."[3]

Now there are certainly elements here of the primitive; but the preoccupation with predictions of the future seems more the concern of a logical, fixed-world Christian ambit; to them a mapped-out future existed and special access to the knowledge of it would give someone distinct advantage when it came to sensible planning ahead. So, in the Icelandic *Landnama-bok*:

'Of the two rivals Eanwind and Eric, Eanwind cast the hallowed chips to know when Eric was going to set out to take possession of the dale; and [so] Eanwind was the quicker of the two...'

[trans. Vigfusson & Powell, 1883, 1, 411]

This, however, is a rather cynical approach, a bit of pre-technological espionage for personal profit; perhaps that is how men approach magic. Divination may or may not have been a special role of woman in Anglo-Saxon England, but the

---

[1] 1883, I, 94–8, 396–400
[2] Jones, 1961, p.136
[3] *ibid.* p.137. See also Derolez, 1962, pp.214–5.

process – to my understanding – lacks a clear deistic setting. Bear in mind, that with an emphasis on male descent, and military and probably political power a male concern (if not monopoly), the pagan Anglo-Saxons themselves subordinated womankind to some degree; pair-bonding does not necessarily imply equality, and there is some ambiguity in cases like Nanna's death by grief at the funeral of her husband Baldur in the *Prose Edda*, when compared to the enforced burial of the 'favourite wife' with her dead husband among Norsemen in Russia.[1] Viewed as the arts of the less politically empowered sex, could magic and healing and augury be counter-talents in some balance of roles?

But such roles tend to be encouraged by the dominant partner. Thus Trimalchio in pre-Christian Rome concludes a story of witchery with the comment, "Give me Credit, I beseech ye, Women are craftier than we are, play their Tricks by Night, and turn every thing Topsy-turvy."[2] And similar generalised blame is apparent in the following item, drawn attention to by Meaney:

> *Viþ wif gemædlan: geberge on neaht nestig rædices moran; þy dæge ne*
> *mæg þe se gemædla sceþþan."*   *[Leechbook pt.3 item 57]*

> Against a woman's spell, after fasting for a night eat the root of a radish; on
> that day the spell will not have power to harm you.[3]

This aptly illustrates several points: witchcraft might often be attributed to a woman; the effectiveness of magic was not denied in a Christian world; and that the Christian compilers of such manuscript recipes saw themselves as providing an alternative and more effective service – in much the same line of work.

Amulets and Oddments

Ornamental items may also have a magical function, and in Latin the words *ligamen* (something that is tied or bound on) or *phylacterium* (a written charm suspended in like a locket round the neck) are used to describe such practices. Against these the *Penitential of Theodore* (ch.27) issues a prohibition: "Non licet clericos vel laicos, magos aut incantatores, existere aut facere philacteria, quae animarum suarum vincula comprobentur." (It is not allowed for clerics or lay people to credit or make phylacteries, which forge chains for their own souls.)[4] This, however, must be understood of pagan or illicit charms of an unauthorised kind, for collecting Church relics, even by lay people, was encouraged – King Alfred apparently included[5] – and Augustine of Hippo distinguished between

---

[1] Foote & Wilson, 1970, p.412; see also Ellis Davidson, 1969, p.43.

[2] Petronius' *Satyricon*, trans. J. Burnaby (1694)

[3] Trans. Meaney 1989 pp.26–7

[4] For similar opposition by Bede see the *Life of Cuthbert* ed. Colgrave, 1940, ch.9 or p.184; and cf. *The Capitulary of Carloman* (Pertz, 1835, p.17) against "sortilegos vel divinos, sive filacteria et auguria, sive incantationes…"

[5] See Asser's *Vita* ch.71

allowable and evil: "amulets worn to placate demons must go; but ear-rings worn to please human men could stay."[1]

Small items of 'jewellery', found in Anglo-Saxon graves are often supposed to have significance beyond the ordinary, though this is hard to pinpoint. Perhaps fossil belemnites (rather torpedo-shaped, and thought to resemble a thunder-bolt) may have been esteemed as a protection against thunder;[2] jet may also have been considered a protection against thunder, or perhaps snakes.[3] Similar superstitions may have attached to fossil echinoderms (sea-urchins).[4] It is hard to see, however, why people should need a protection *against* a god like Thor, who might be rash, but was not a personified agency of destruction. Apart from symbols like the hammer of Thor,[5] or perhaps the spear of Woden,[6] it is usually difficult to associate an object with a known deity, suggesting that the role of such ornaments, if special, belongs to the world of personal magic not that of the major divinities.

Finds in graves include fossils, quartz balls, amethyst, a boar's tusk, cowrie shells, and much more.[7] Were they purely ornamental, or of other personal (e.g. sentimental) value to the deceased, or could they have formed symbols important to the burial process or be valid clues to some belief in mystical protection or positive luck the individual trusted to in the world of the living? Similar strange collections of objects were typically included in many Bronze Age burial urns: "oursins pétrifiés, coquilles, griffes d'oiseau, queues de serpent, dents de cheval, cailloux, petits morceaux d'ambre et de pyrite de fer, etc."[8] – so the practice has many centuries of justification behind it; and can be paralleled in other cultures:

> 'Instead of sacred places the [American] Indians venerated the medicine-bundles, which were in effect portable shrines. The Indians believed that they contained relics of the first ancestors, or sacred objects given by the gods to protect man and bring good fortune.'[9]

Small personal collections could be contained in pyxides, "little cylindrical bronze boxes,"[10] worn suspended from a woman's waist, containing scraps of thread, cloth, herbs, etc. These are unlikely to be practical odds and ends, but could have a

---

[1] Brown, 1967, p.266

[2] See Ellis Davidson, 1969, p.71; Meaney, 1989.

[3] See Kitson, 1989

[4] Ellis Davidson, 1969, p.71, where a sea-urchin broach with goats might relate to Thor; similarly the 'chalk heart' mentioned by Horne, 1933?

[5] His hammer (as inverted cross or 'T') came to parallel the Christian protective cross, and inspire the same sense of power – as one hero comments, 'I fear no supernatural power but that of the god Thor' – "Thor deo excepto" (Saxo Bk.2 ch.2).

[6] Ellis Davidson, 1969, pp.36–7

[7] Wilson, 1992, p.97–123; Horne, 1933

[8] Derolez, 1962, p.164

[9] Burland, 1965, p.87

[10] Meaney, 1989, pp.9–10

relic-like role (and indeed sometimes carry Christian motifs). "Could they …have been symbolic of woman's role as the healer in the family?"[1] Low again in obvious prestige, but perhaps of a similar purpose, are small bags of assorted odds and ends found in women's graves – possible protective or magical items? Meaney[2] suggests they might constitute a rag-tag assemblage of the sort that would be useful in divination; and if this is, as I suppose, primarily a process dependent on chance, then a 'random' selection of objects to start with might indeed be propitious. Their importance, if rather vaguely, is affirmed in *Eirik's Saga*, where it is noted of a seeress that "round her middle she wore a belt made of touchwood, and on it was a big skin pouch in which she kept those charms of hers which she needed for her magic."[3]

Lastly, and perhaps in a class on their own, are the crystal balls "worn by women from the waist on a long band."[4] In this country these have been found in a fifth century Kent context, but also later and elsewhere e.g. the Rhineland. Meaney considers this too early for use in clairvoyance (which is attested in the fourteenth century and onwards,[5]) – rather they "may have been used to make fire"[6] or as curing stones, which could be dipped into water that would then be drunk. To the mystical, they might even suggest radio sets.[7]

Beyond the physical evidence, it is worth considering whether Anglo-Saxon personal names in -*stan* (stone) may have originally implied a sort of talisman, to induce some transfer of power to the holder of the name. The intention would seem to be a positive not a defensive one and those names with war elements may aim to attract qualities rather than protect against harm e.g. *Wigstan* (war-), *Ordstan* (battle-front-), *Ecgstan* (blade-), *Sigestan* (victory-); the same sympathetic bond may apply to *Ælfstan* (elf-) and *Wulfstan* (wolf-), possibly also to *Thurstan* (?Thor- or giant-) and *Birnstan* (fire-). Of general good omen are *Helmstan* (protection-), *Eahlstan* (temple-), *Weohstan/Weoxtan* (idol-), *Heahstan* (tall-, prominent-), *Fryþestan* (safety-), *Leofstan* (dear-), *Cynestan* (royal-), *Wærstan* (trust-), *Eadstan* (blessed-) and *Athelstan* (noble-).[8] Old English *stan* can imply a large standing stone, but also something quite small and perhaps ornamental, as in *gimstan* (gemstone) or the word *windelstan* (that glosses Latin *coclea* 'snail'), or *popelstan* (pebble). The popularity of this class of personal name and its potential non-Christian components offer an intriguing parallel to the frequent small objects turned up in graves.

---

[1] *ibid.* p.10

[2] *ibid.* pp.10–12

[3] Jones, 1961, p.134

[4] Meaney, 1989, p.9

[5] *ibid.* p.9

[6] *ibid.* p.9 – recalling Weston, 1913, on the Holy Grail

[7] "The radio has been with us since the dawn of time." Robert Aickman, *The Wine-Dark Sea*, 1990, p.44.

[8] Other names in this class I cannot pretend to analyse e.g. *Ceolstan, Beanstan*.

THE WORLD OF SCIENCE

For the period we are studying, magic is arguably indistinguishable in terms of its credibility from (applied) science. To us, with hindsight and more knowledge of experimental method, theory and proof, magic seems a dislocation of cause and effect, a pretend science, a sort of delusion. But it must be considered also as a practical line of action, in the light of how the material world was then understood (including cause and effect); something designed to steer events into the right channel, to bring about a desired end, and it would be hard to deny that we place a similar trust in science today, as though we want to be assured of our own power and ability to cope (at the risk of demonstrating how to destroy).

The linkage between the theoretical and magical, the scientific and the religious and the practical, cannot be better illustrated than in the study of the heavens and the calendar.

Astronomy and Astrology

The division between astronomy and astrology and the view of one as respectable and the other as a sham is a relatively modern one. Thus Ptolemy (Claudius Ptolemaus, an Alexandrian Greek of the second century AD) wrote not only four books on observational astronomy (the *Tetrabiblos*) but also a parallel set on what we would call astrology. The distinction appears to be one not of critical force but of disciplinary analysis, much as we might distinguish between 'pure' and 'applied' mathematics. The classical Greeks, if anyone, might have been expected to reject astrology as irrational. But on the contrary they warmly welcomed it as rational, and as proof of the interdependence of the whole universe.[1] As one commentator[2] cheekily puts it: "It seems that it was not only Livy's boring old Romans who were riddled with superstition, but the exciting enlightened Greeks as well."

Astronomy and Astrology were first distinguished in moral judgement by Isidore of Seville (560–636) in his *Etymologia* Bk 3: "astronomia est astrorum lex" (astronomy is the law of the stars) – he saw it as derived from the Egyptians (ch.24) – whereas astrology is "navitatis observatio" (the observation of birth-signs) and derived from the Chaldeans (ch.25).

---

[1] A tenet of the Stoics, see Tester, 1978, p.18

[2] Morrison, 1981, p.111

Inter Astronomiam autem et Astrologiam aliquid differt. Astronomia caeli conversionem, ortus, obitus motusque siderum continet, vel qua ex causa ita vocentur. Astrologia vero partim naturalis, partim superstitiosa est.

[*Etymologia* Bk.3 ch.27]

Between astronomy and astrology there is some difference. Astronomy concerns the revolving of the heavens, the rising, setting and motion of heavenly bodies, and how they come about. Astrology though is partly scientific, partly superstitious.

It is doubtless the possible role of demons in astrology that made Isidore suspicious of that side of the science of the heavens – that is, a judgement by religious orthodoxy, not by reason; it was part of the process of recollating Christian and Roman ideas, by which some were accepted into or modified for the new religion, some rejected. Yet astrology remained popular, even within the Church, where the link between stars and men seemed entirely probable in a carefully designed universe with a future established or at least evident to God, and so in some sense fixed.

In Tester's summary: "Hard astrology is that which assumes or accepts a firm determinism, so that sufficient knowledge and expertise should allow firm predictions to be made of events and actions which are 'written in the stars' and so must happen. Soft astrology allows for the moral freedom of man, and its attitude is summed up in the maxim, 'the stars incline, they do not compel'."[1] Only in the second case can we "modify our behaviour in the light of the knowledge we gain from astrology."[2]

Behind determinism, of course, lies an external directing force, most often visualised as God in control, with the potential for extra-human knowledge of the future: "Hence it is written: 'Show the things that are to come hereafter, and we shall know that we are gods.'"[3] A God who created everything and who could not be limited by time (part of His own creation), must know the future, and so in turn the future should have a fixed and predictable nature, since it is complete in the mind of God. That is, unless human freewill was introduced as a deliberate random element: "two kinds of effects escape the causality of heavenly bodies... all effects that occur accidentally...[and] acts of the free-will"[4]

What was the role of the planets and stars? They must have some purpose, it seemed, up in the sky, doubtless a very special and serious one. *Genesis* ch.1 suggests all the heavenly bodies were created "to give light upon the earth," (verse 15) but a more general explanation is also given: "let them be for signs, and for seasons, and for days, and years." (verse 14) In this sense they are already

---

[1] Tester, 1987, p.2; cf. discussion of such issues throughout *Romeo & Juliet*
[2] Tester, 1987, p.3
[3] *Isaiah* 41, 23 via Aquinas p.192
[4] Aquinas p.202

something more than practical illumination, they have a symbolic role as indicators of time, and perhaps much else. Certainly other Mediterranean mythologies had comparably ambitious ideas.

As early as the second millennium BC the Mesopotamians had begun to put their observed knowledge of the heavens to practical use, as witnessed by "a vast bulk of omen-literature.... These omens are taken from stars, sun, moon and planets, eclipses, clouds, thunder and earthquakes. They clearly presuppose that there is some relationship between what happens in the sky and what happens on earth, though they do not suggest that the relationship is one of cause and effect."[1]

This observation of prodigy, as omen, remained a prime role of astronomy and is reflected in important state texts even at much later periods such as the Roman *Annales Maximi*, brief notices of major events, written on a whitened board and displayed at the official residence of the Pontifex Maximus, and apparently used in one of the earliest Christian lists of dates, the work of the so-called 'Chronographer of the Year 354'.[2]

The public and monumental role of such early annals made for brevity and an emphasis on the unusual and therefore significant (reflecting the religious and astrological origins of such compilations). A typical entry might be the strike of lightning on a statue,[3] or matters like grain shortages, eclipses, the names of dictators if appointed, special religious acts and what were perceived as important political events.[4] So stereotyped could such entries become that Aulus Gellius (second century AD) was moved to comment, "It is demeaning for a historian to interrupt his narrative because some trivial prodigy occurred, and because an owl was seen sitting on the roof of the Capitolium."[5] What is equally odd is that medieval chronicles, such as the *Anglo-Saxon Chronicle*, still reflected the same conciseness of style[6] and preoccupation with the marvellous.

For example, in the *Parker Chronicle* (Chronicle A) we have a preponderance of: notes of main dates of kings and major secular events (e.g. battles), main dates of bishops and select ecclesiastical events (e.g. the progress of the Conversion) – such events together with the acts of the leaders of society were seen as the shapers of history, and continue to be so viewed; but there are also astronomical notes e.g. 664 "Her sunne aþiestrode... þy ilcan geare wæs micel mancuealm" (The Sun was eclipsed... in the same year was a great plague); 671 "Her wæs micle fugla wæl" (Here occurred a great mortality of birds); 678 "Her oþiewde cometa se steorra, 7 Wilfriþ biscop wæs adrifen of his biscepdome from Ecgferþe

---

[1] *ibid.* p.13
[2] For further details see Finnegan, 1964, 93–5
[3] Frier, 1979, p.56, where Horatius Cocles was the victim.
[4] *ibid.* p.91
[5] Quoted *ibid.* p.221
[6] Other explanations are not much space left in columns in Easter Table lists, or a crude stage of the written use of Old English.

cyninge" (Here the star called a comet appeared, and Bishop Wilfrid was driven from his see by King Ecgferth); 734 "Her wæs se mona swelce he wære mid blode begotan, 7 ferdon forþ Tatwine 7 Bieda" (Here was the moon suffused as with blood, and Tatwin and Bede died).

A particularly vivid example is found in the *Anglo-Saxon Chronicle* for 793 AD, (in versions D,E and F, but not A, suggesting a non-West Saxon origin for the entry):

> In this year harsh omens were appearing throughout the land of the Northumbrians, that severely frightened the people: there were extraordinary flashes of lightnings and fiery dragons were seen flying in the sky. Quickly after these signs followed a great famine, and later still in the same year... the attacks of the heathen destroyed God's church on the Island of Lindisfarne with looting and slaughter.

Arguably, if you consider the average news bulletin put out by contemporary television or radio (and especially a newspaper headline), it will show much the same kind of concerns, with natural or man-made disasters in first rank, political personalities and issues (including scandals) second, and strange individual fortunes a useful (humorous) closing contrast – do we still identify with or react to a standard 'range' of conventionally important, sometimes mysterious events? Whether we have a universal or a culturally inherited sense of the sensational, in all these cases, special phenomena (and their interpretation) are considered to be dramatically significant for humans.

In the past, in astrological terms, this supposed influence showed either that the heavens in some way mirrored or prefigured events on earth, or that the stars and planets were themselves gods and so exhibited a mind-like policy that directed or influenced human events.

For the earlier period of Mesopotamian astrology, we are told that "Usually... the heavenly bodies are not overtly treated as manifestations of the divine," so that "there is no indication of the thought that a god is, if not actually visible in the form of the celestial body, at least active behind it and manipulating its appearance to give a direct message."[1] Omens are objective rather than deistic or personal and "represented not a god's decision upon a situation but rather a recognized correlation between past and future phenomena."[2]

This seems to have changed, perhaps in the Babylonian period (even with the influence of Mithraism?) to a closer connection between gods and planets, until "They assumed that changes in the heavenly bodies, manifestations of the gods, portended changes on earth."[3] The more mobile bodies, the planets, in particular, became closely associated with individual divinities, and their position or juxtaposition an indication of the divine disposition. Babylonian deities seem to

---

[1] Saggs, 1978, p.136

[2] *ibid.* p.132

[3] Mercer, 1957, p.81

have been associated with both cities and heavenly bodies, and the implication is that there was a development from the plain observation of data and prodigies to an interpretation of the skies as direct evidence of (regional) divine intention.

The question continued to be debated in Roman times. "Should we assume that these bodies that go around in their courses have souls or not? For if they have no souls, they offer nothing but heat or cold," noted Plotinus,[1] (the Alexandrian Greek philosopher teaching in Rome in the third century AD; he also objected to determinism on the grounds that the soul was immaterial and so above the physical world and its laws[2]). Origen, in the first half of the third century AD "who was perhaps as much a Platonist as a Christian, believed, like Philo, that the stars are rational (or spiritual) beings that take an interest in humans and foretell many things, although they do not cause events to happen."[3]

Theoretical Greek astronomy as we know and admire it seems to have begun with figures like Eudoxus in the fourth century BC, but not to have flourished until the third to second centuries BC.[4] Previous to this the Greeks (Hellenes) are not known to have had any cult of stars or planets, for which descriptive names alone existed (i.e. they did not originally attribute planets the names of deities). It seems likely therefore that the Greeks accepted the rudiments of astronomy and astrology together from Babylonian sources at some time in the centuries before Christ.[5] They then proceeded to attribute the planets god-names after established Babylonian attributes: e.g. Aphrodite paralleled Ishtar.[6] The full Babylonian-Roman list of equivalents is Marduk (Jupiter), Ishtar (Venus), Ninib (Saturn), Nergal (Mars), Nebo (Mercury).[7]

By the second century BC a standard order for the planets had been assumed, with the Earth at the centre of the solar system;[8] it ran: Earth, Moon, Mercury,[9] Venus,[10] Sun, Mars,[1] Jupiter, Saturn.[2] (Uranus can be spotted with the naked eye,

---

[1] Via Luck, 1985, p.356
[2] Tester, 1987, p.53
[3] Luck, 1985, p.315
[4] Tester, 1987, p.11
[5] McIntosh, 1969, p.19, suggests third century BC, but North, 1989, p.247, on the contrary implies Chaldean astrology only peaked in the first century BC and may have owed its source to the Greeks.
[6] McIntosh, 1969, pp.16–17
[7] Mercer, 1957, p.82
[8] A heliocentric system was proposed by Aristarchus (early third century BC) but refuted by Aristotle (Tester, 1987, p.6).
[9] "much more difficult to spot since it stays so close to the sun" – Tester, 1987, p.4; it is only rarely visible (e.g. before sunrise near autumn equinox, after sunset at spring equinox) – *ibid.* p.9.
[10] Known also as Lucifer (the morning star) and Hesperus/Vesper (the evening star) – Tester, 1987, p.9

but wasn't.[3]) Clearly, the planets, as more mobile than the stars, would permit more definite and varied assumptions to be made about events on earth and human destiny and so play a large part in astrology. "The Babylonians were aware of the distinction between stars and planets. To them the stars formed a background against which the planets moved. The background itself moved in a yearly cycle, but the patterns on it never changed."[4]

The way was thus opened in the West for viewing the skies as material not only for useful (mathematical) study but also as important predictive or defining forces; and the two are by no means incompatible, for better knowledge of the behaviour of the heavenly bodies implies better understanding of their influence. In Graeco-Roman terms, Stoic philosophy would provide some backing for astrological principles: "their creed, insisting that fate ruled all things, and that a common law and sympathy bound everything in the universe into one whole, clearly allowed for divination, the perception of the workings of that law, of fate, through signs, including signs in the heavens."[5] The planets, by this theory of interconnection, became associated with specific plants, colours, stones, metals, parts and humours of the body. In turn, Christians by no means scorned this sort of study. Aquinas records a variety of views: that of Dionysius who affirmed that heavenly bodies are the cause of what takes place in the world[6] – and others who believed the stars signify rather than cause the things foretold by means of their observation.[7] Or perhaps they were a map of events, put there to guide or warn us? Augustine of Hippo typified the Magis' star not as something governing or causing Christ's birth, "but a servant bearing witness to it."[8] Or were they straightforward physical bodies, possessing an entirely natural influence on our characters and futures by physical (one might almost say chemical) means?

The Sun might be taken to prove the case that celestial bodies had a physical effect on life on earth. "The seasons changed with the movements of the Sun, therefore, they [the Babylonians] argued, the other heavenly bodies must surely exercise a similar influence."[9] It was no great leap to the assumption that this effect might be more than just heat and light, and similarly that the night sky might also

---

[1] Mars is reddish, visible for 18 months, then invisible for 4–6 months: has observed irregular motion.

[2] Saturn is slowest in terms of visible motion: "Its slowness suggested age, and age no doubt wisdom and power, and it also suggested great remoteness, and so coldness and mystery" – Tester, 1987, p.9

[3] Tester, 1987, p.4

[4] McIntosh, 1969, p.5

[5] Tester, 1987, p.32

[6] *Div.Nom.*iv via Aquinas p.200

[7] Aquinas, p.201

[8] quoted by Tester, 1987, p.111

[9] McIntosh, 1969, p.5

have a measurable effect on human life. Thus among the Greeks, Aristotle gave the Sun a causative role,[1] and more clearly so Ptolemy, in an almost physical sense:

'A certain power... emanates from the aether, causing changes in the sublunar elements, and in plants and animals. Effluence from the Sun and Moon – especially the Moon, by virtue of her proximity[2] – affects things animate and inanimate, while the planets and stars also have their effects. If a man knows accurately the *movements* of these celestial bodies, and their *natures* (perhaps not their essential but at least their potentially effective qualities), and if he can deduce scientifically the qualities resulting from a *combination* of the factors, why should he not judge both the weather and human character?'

[Ptolemy *Tetrabiblos*, I,2 qu. North, 1989, p.248]

This 'influence' or flowing of power was accepted by Christian Anglo-Saxons;[3] thus Ælfric's "It is perfectly natural that all earthly entities should be more perfect during the waxing than the waning moon." [see page 238 no.33] We cannot from this deduce that "Moon-worship is reflected in two charms... where instructions are given to boil herbs in water 'when the moon is waning'."[4]

Into this already crowded theoretical debate, the influence of Mithraism made itself felt in the West from the second century BC to the third century AD. Mithras was a prominent solar deity, associated with the Persians and the fire-worshipping darkness-opposing duality of Zoroastrianism, and it centred interest on the formation of character by heavenly influence at the point of an individual's birth rather than on general omens. Skilful mapping of the heavens permitted the construction of a horoscope, or time-specific chart of the night sky, which could indicate what was happening of importance now, or about to happen (if positions of the stars could be projected forward), especially in combination with knowledge about the aspect of the sky in the past at the time of the subject's birth. The basis for this direct link between the skies and the human was as follows: "Another cult [i.e. Mithraism] held that the soul had originally descended to earth through the planetary spheres, gaining from each one a different earthly quality. After death it had to re-ascend through the spheres, shedding these qualities and arriving at the outermost sphere in its pristine state of purity."[5] The Greeks' practice of placing dead heroes among the stars, called *catasterism* (translation to the stars), may well reflect the Mithraic idea of the soul

---

[1] North, 1989, pp.243–4

[2] Means, 1993, p.24, traces the descent of the belief in the influence of the moon from Alexandrian writers through the second to fifth centuries AD in Latin writers like Vetius Valens and Firmicus Marturnus.

[3] And even by some modern folk; thus Bede's assertion of the influence of the moon on humans (*De Temporum Ratione* ch.27) is defended by Stevens, 1985, p.11, on the basis that "at full moon 'the crazies come out!'" (his exclamation mark)

[4] Branston, 1974, p.50

[5] McIntosh, 1969, p.38

returning to its divine origin.[1] Quite probably, the modern practice of the seven-day week (with days named after planets which were named after gods), and details of the zodiac were also Mithraic influence on Greek and Roman thought.[2] Latin texts that passed to Anglo-Saxon England, representing something of this complex tradition, include Manilius' poem on astronomy (by the ninth century),[3] and Martianus Capella's *De Astronomia* (book 8 of his *De Nuptiis Philologiae et Mercurii*) by the tenth century.

The Calendar

Some such Classical picture of the universe, with earth (round?) at the centre and planets (including the Sun) revolving around it against a fixed background of stars is affirmed in Alfred's version of Boethius. [see page 238 no.32] Independent Old English names for some constellations [see the Rune Poem, pt.2 no.21] imply a pre-existing study of the night-sky, but to what end is not clear. The only hints are contained in calendar survivals, and here by the very nature of the records the predominating influence is Christian and Classical.

A useful subdivision of the solar year was provided by the zodiac, which both linked day and night conveniently and was more regular (since invented) than the lunar month, which it served to characterise. The zodiac divides the year according to which constellation is present at the western horizon just after sunset. It is an overlaying, as it were, of Sun on stars, and the 'circuit' the Sun appears to make against the astral 'background' is neatly repeated each solar year. (The Zodiac was apparently standardised by the end of fifth century BC,[4] and may provided a further proof of Greek borrowing, in astrological matters, from the Babylonians,[5] and indeed of the important role Zoroastrianism/Mithraism played in shaping both sciences.[6])

[1] And cf. Daniel 12:2–3 "And many of them that sleep in the dust of the earth shall awake, some to everlasting life, and some to shame and everlasting contempt. And they that be wise shall shine as the brightness of the firmament; and they that turn many to righteousness as the stars for ever and ever." Such images are specifically given a Persian origin – Ling, 1968, p.120.
[2] See below, on calendar
[3] Ogilvy, 1967, p.197
[4] Tester, 1987, p.14
[5] Tester, 1987, pp.15–16; Mercer, 1957, p.83 ascribes the concept of constellations to the Babylonians.
[6] Tester, 1987, p.104

The use of the Zodiac of course depended on easily recognisable and clearly named constellations, familiar to us still today (*Aries*, the ram, *Taurus*, the bull, etc.). These names do not seem to have been arrived at from imaginative fantasies of gazing at stars, but rather to have been a superimposition upon star clusters of commonly appreciated concepts, "taken from existing mythological symbols to which the shapes of the groups of stars were adjusted."[1] Originally these signs were accorded extra identity in terms of attribution to day (e.g. Aries) and night (e.g. Taurus), light and dark alternating through the Zodiac. Only later were the signs linked to planets.

Possible alternative Germanic constellations are hinted at in the entry for 'NG' in the Old English *Rune Poem*. But the Zodiac was adopted in its Classical form. Here is Ælfric's Old English version of the signs (*Old English De Temporibus Anni*, 4.1-4.16)

Þære sunnan gear is þæt heo beyrne ðone micelan circul Zodiacum 7 gecume under ælc þære twelf tacna. Ælce monað heo yrnð under an ðæra tacna.

The year of the sun consists of it travelling the great circle of the Zodiac and passing under each of the twelve signs. Each month it runs through one of the signs.

An ðære tacna is gehaten Aries þæt is Ramm.
The first of the signs is called Aries, that is the Ram.

Oðer, Taurus, þæt is fearr.
The second, Taurus, that is the Bull.

Ðridda, Gemini, þæt sind getwisan.
The third, Gemini, which are the Twins.

Feorða, Cancer, þæt is Crabba.
The fourth, Cancer, that is the Crab.

Fifta, Leo.
The fifith, Leo (the lion).

Sixta, Uirgo, þæt is mæden.
The sixth, Virgo, that is the Maiden.

Seofoða, Libra, þæt is pund oþþe wæge.
The seventh, Libra, that is weights or scales.

---

[1] McIntosh, 1969, p.7

Eahteoðe is Scorpius, þæt is ðrowend[1].
The eighth is Scorpio, that is the scorpion.

Nigoðe is Sagittarius, þæt is Scytta.
The ninth is Sagittarius, that is the Shooter.

Teoðe is Capricornus, þæt is buccan horn oððe bucca.
The tenth is Capricorn, which is the goat's horn, or the Goat.

Endlyfte is Aquarius, þæt is wætergyte oþþe se ðe wæter gyt.
The eleventh is Aquarius, that is the pouring of water, or he that pours water.

Twelfte is Pisces, þæt sind fixas.
The twelfth is Pisces, which are Fish.

...Ælc ðære twelf tacna hylt his monað, 7 þonne seo sunne hi hæfð ealle underurnen ðonne bið an gear agan.

Each of the twelve signs represents a month, and when the sun has run through them all, then a year has passed.[2]

While Ælfric notes the similarity of length between a zodiacal sign and a month, the latter is based on the cycle of the moon (Old English *monað* 'month' being derived from *món* 'moon' and meaning the space from one new moon to the next). But "The basic difficulty in these calculations was that the lengths of the solar year, the lunar month and the day are incommensurable. No number of days can make an exact number of lunar months or solar years, and no number of lunar months can make an exact number of solar years."[3] The simplest solution might have been to abandon the lunar month, but the moon remained of perceptible importance, visually in the sky, in astrological terms, and as a definition of Christian Easter (for the Jewish Pass-Over was a lunar festival). Attempts had therefore to be made to reconcile sun and moon, and many of these had already been worked out by Greek astronomers to whom the challenge of harmonising the sun and the moon appealed at a mathematical level. Thus there was the Metonic Cycle of 19 years (19 solar years = 235 lunar months) developed in the fifth century BC, or the Pythagorean Great Year of 59 solar years; or the (fourth century BC) Callipic[4] Cycle of 76 solar years (i.e. 4 Metonic Cycles less one day).[5]

The question became of importance in the seventh century when Irish and Anglo-Saxon methods of calculating Easter came into conflict, along with many

---

[1] Attested elsewhere as the Old English for 'scorpion', but literally meaning 'suffering' or the 'suffering one'.

[2] In Bede, *De Temporum Ratione* ch.16, the months are given as April, Aries, and so forth, to March, Pisces.

[3] Crombie, 1961, p.20

[4] Named after the devisor, Callipus

[5] North, 1989, p.94; see further Stevens, 1992.

other tenets such as the celibacy of monks, the style of tonsure, asceticism, freedom of movement, and the comparative authority of bishops and abbots. This was the background for Bede's treatise *De Temporibus* in ca.703 AD, a brief re-statement of the realities of time, as then seen, underlying the calculations of the disputed festival.

Perhaps this early experience of the problem of months is why Bede paid special attention to them in his *De Temporum Ratione*, devoting ch.15 to a study of the Anglo-Saxon month names. His list has the following equivalents, sometimes with additional explanation:

January (and December) – *Giuli* (Yule)

Feburary – *Solmonath* (*mensis placentarum*, seemingly referring to cakes, which they offered their gods then; Skeat, 1889, suggests "*Sol* means simply *mire*, or *mud*.")

March – *Hredmonath* (after the goddess Hreda; Skeat 1889: "I do not quite see why it may not mean simply 'fierce-month'.")

April – *Eosturmonath* (after the presumed goddess Eostre)

May – *Thrimilchi* (because they could milk thrice a day in this month)

Iunius – Lida ('blandus sive navigabilis' – re calm weather for voyages; from Old English lithe 'mild', "so that June and July are the mild, or warm months." Skeat, 1889)

July – likewise *Lida*

[an intercalary month could be inserted here – also unsurprisingly called *Lida*]

August – *Weodmonath* (on account of the weeds which then proliferate)

September – *Halegmonath* ('mensis sacrorum' – month of rituals or sacrifices)

October – *Winterfilleth* (after the full moon, which was taken as the start of winter)

November – *Blodmonath* ('mensis immolationum' – the month of sacrifices (*blot*, in compounds often *blod-*), in which that livestock which was to be killed was offered to the gods.[1] ...and so back to Yule.

The New Year, he says, was celebrated on the 25th December, which they called *Modranect* ("id est matrum noctem" – that is Mothers' Night) perhaps due to ceremonies, part of the vigils they held then. These Mother-figures could be divine,[2] but as *matronae* were more prominent in Roman belief than Germanic; and Phythian-Adams[3] links the festival to the Feast of the Nativity, as the pre-eminent celebration of Christian motherhood.

---

[1] Bonser, 1963, p.140, ties this in with the annual animal cull in the farming world.
[2] See Derolez, 1962, pp.140–44
[3] 1975, p.27

Fascinating evidence, but it will be noted there is a certain *un*monthly ring to all this: two supermonths or seasons, Yule and Lida spoil the sequence literally from the start; while remaining names either come from a specific festival within the month, or are loose agricultural descriptions of a type not met again until the French Revolution decreed poetic descriptive names to celebrate their own cultural independence. While the Anglo-Saxons would be well aware of the activities of the moon, it must be possible that Bede's list is an attempt to recreate a native calendar – for either the Anglo-Saxons would have adapted the Roman week and the Julian calendar months together, or had some other (incompatible?) system of their own.[1] Bede's list seems therefore more useful in terms of providing information on the main festivals: autumn seemed the most important ritual season, with Mid-winter and Easter major (sun-based) festivals.

Practically, a more modest division of time than the month was useful in organising human affairs. This unit we call the week, but its duration was not necessarily seven days: the early Romans had an eight-day week, the eighth being a market-day;[2] it is from Judaeo-Christian religion that the familiar seven-day week derived, with its Sunday a sort of Sabbath or day of rest.

> 'The seven-day week is of Semitic origin. Traces of it are to be found among Chaldean, Egyptian and even Greek records... but it was among the Jews that the seven-day week was fully developed and it is from them that its observance has spread over, and now so largely dominates the civilised world.'
>
> [Philip, 1921, p.29]

But this convenient seven-day cycle was also common in the East, known to Mithraic theory, where it reflected the seven visible major celestial lights, from Sun to Saturn. Their prior claim to the planetary week is demonstrated e.g. by an inscription of the 'days of the God' in the modern week-order at Pompeii in the first century AD.[3] This system of naming days after the planets was linked to the Mithraic concept[4] of the soul descending at birth and reascending at death through the spheres of the planets (which is why there is no 'Earthday'?); and was most likely popularised in advance of Christianity by the spread of Mithraism through the Roman army, so that when the Christian week took its place or rather confirmed its use, the days of the week were already and remained planetary. The fourth century poet Ausonius makes the following observation:

---

[1] The opening of Wihtred's *Laws* specify the date as 'the sixth day of Rugern' – the month of the rye harvest? Did the need for a Julian-type calendar exist in pre-Christian England?

[2] Finegan, 1964, p.75; Michels, 1967, pp.191–2, finds evidence for an early Roman nine-day week.

[3] Finegan, 1964, pp.15–16

[4] See Griffiths, 1989

*Nomina, quae septem vertentibus apta diebus
annus habet, totidem errantes fecere planetae…*

[*Eclogue* 8]

The names which the year has accorded to the seven recurring days are derived from the same number of wandering planets.[1]

Our modern Tuesday (Tiw, Mars), Wednesday (Woden, Mercury), Thursday (Thunor, Jupiter) and Friday (Frig(a), Venus) and basically the vernacular equivalents of the established planet names, as the inclusion of a Saturday, Sunday and Monday shows; but whether they were established among Germanic tribes prior to the settlement in England or even the conversion to Christianity[2] is not clear. It is not impossible that the Church sought out vernacular equivalents for the sake of calendar convenience (after all, no objection to use of the term 'Easter' seems to have been raised). Thus we need to think carefully about Stenton's assertion that "the cult of the fertility goddess Frig is sufficiently proved by the occurrence of her name in the Old English *Frigedæg…*"[3] It is indeed the existence of Old English forms at all of these gods' names that provides the main evidence of their assumed worship: but the equation of Tiw to Mars and Woden to Mercury is problematic. In later texts it is Woden/Odin who is portrayed as a god of war.[4] Are *þunor* (thunder) and *frig* (love)[5] any more than common noun equivalents for Jupiter and Venus? – 'Thunder-day' and 'Love-day'? Is the equivalence at the level of gods, or planets, or of convenient words?

The division of the day, that is of the hours of sunlight, involved a further set of problems. Though our concept 'hour' is based on the Roman *hora*, that unit of time might actually vary in order to fill the longer or shorter 'day' of the varying seasons. The sub-division of the day was only of practical import in the monastic context, where it was desirable to have some means of determining when the various church services during the day should commence. This problem was eventually solved (for church and then for factory) by mechanical clocks, but simpler methods of time measurement were available to the Anglo-Saxons, and

---

[1] That the days of the week bear names "which we immediately perceive to be the names of what the ancients held to be the 7 planets" was affirmed in modern times, but not developed, in an article signed 'J.C.H.' in *The Philological Museum*, 1832, p.1.

[2] In Old English, the earliest reference would seem to be a mention of *Monanæfen* (Eve of Monday) in Wihtred's *Laws* (ch.9) at the end of the seventh century, in the context of observing the Sabbath.

[3] 1947, p.98. The German *Dienstag* for Tuesday and *Mittwoch* for Wednesday do not imply the irrelevance of Tiw or Woden on the continent.

[4] 'Wodanum sculptare sicut nostri Martem solent' – Vigfusson & Powell, 1883, 1, 402–3, quoting Adam of Bremen: "They portray Woden as we would Mars."

[5] See *frig(u)* in Bosworth & Toller. However, an alternative source is proposed for the modern colloquial 'frigging' (see Jonathan Green *Slang Down the Ages*, 1993, p.239).

Ward[1] gives a summary of such devices, some aimed at measuring absolute time, some giving divisions according to the sun.

As well as the candles in lanterns, mentioned as a project of King Alfred's by Asser,[2] each candle burning (ideally) for four hours, there were water-clocks and sundials. Water-clocks of this period consisted of a cistern of water and a bronze bowl some 6–10" in diameter with a small hole in its base. Placed dry upon the water, this would gradually fill and eventually sink, giving a measure of time. Sundials would have been commoner, and were, typically, engraved on a stone in the south-facing wall of a church, with a horizontal gnomon, and lines radiating from it: "a horizontal line for sunrise and sunset, a vertical one for midday, and two intermediate lines, which were drawn at about 45°."[3] This gave a very approximate division of the day, which may have been sufficient to assess the intervals between the divine services that punctuated the monastic day.

One text (*Records of Sundials,* Cockayne, 1866, pp.218–221), gives apparent measurements for the shadows thrown by a gnomon of perhaps six foot, but whether this was original experimentation or not is doubtful: Jones[4] is content to comment, "The Northumbrians were studying shadows seriously and conscientiously, but certainly not accurately."

---

[1] 1947, pp.16–17

[2] *Vita* ch.104

[3] Ward, 1947, p.17

[4] 1943, p.127; Stevens, 1985, is pleased to credit Bede with a gain in accuracy (p.17) over Pliny of 30 seconds while excusing (p.16) his "broad degree of imprecision in the date of the vernal equinox." The measurement of shadows is dealt with by Stevens, *ibid.* pp.9–10, but as a means of determining latitude, not as a measurement of time, which would be tricky with only a vertical gnomon.

DIVINATION

Divination, or gaining information about the (likely) future and the outcome of events, implies, as already noted in the case of astrology, some fixity about what is going to happen, comparable to the fixity of the past. This in turn could imply an abstract concept like 'fate', or an omnipotent deity to whom all time was known, and who had shaped the future of the world as easily as he had created the universe to begin with, and who might reveal, directly or indirectly, something of His plan. It might alternately depend on some universal interconnectedness that made the various parts of creation act in unison, of their own accord. In the modern world, it is most usually an analysis of the past in order to provide a useful trend or pattern that enables someone to say what is likely to occur in the future,[1] and, of course, if you know what you want the future to turn out as, then it is relatively easy to take the decisions you believe will bring that end about. But (especially at unpredictable crises) it is tempting to consult or borrow knowledge from the Power that is responsible for the shaping of all events. It seems incredible to us now that heads of state like William the Conqueror and Queen Elizabeth I actively consulted astrologers, but of course it is exactly because the stakes are so high that even the most practical and capable person may like to take account of any possibility, and especially so in troubled or uncertain times.

If such prediction is to be taken seriously, a formal theory of the process is desirable to lend credence to it all. A test of the reliability of prediction does not seem to have occurred to anyone as a useful precaution. (Perhaps it would have seemed sacrilegious.) The effort was put instead into arriving at a convincing theory of how it worked. Thus the Stoics supposed that "Any event on earth, even a trivial one, could reflect or foreshadow the intentions of the gods because the universe is a living organism, a whole, and what happens in one part of it might be caused by a happening in some distant part."[2] Accordingly, "Divination was possible because there was at least a part of a cosmic soul in everything."[3] And this could involve consulting factors as subtle as the behaviour of eddies in water currents.[4]

Whether this Cosmic Soul became in due course the Holy Ghost of the Christians is a matter of debate. There was a limit to which Christianity could

---

[1] This sort of augury is flagrantly practised by Local Councils, whose County Structure Plans apparently identify practical statistical trends for the future; but their forecasts are in some sense policy and serve to bring about what they claim is needed.

[2] Luck, 1985, p.230

[3] *ibid.* p.253

[4] The Chronicle of the Monastery of Abingdon records a case in the tenth century where a land dispute was settled by observing the course taken a by a shield floated down a river. See Herbert, 1994, p.17. And let us not forget the butterfly of Chaos Theory.

challenge the accumulated knowledge of the Classical world, and prediction of the future was largely common ground. Prophecies were an established part of the history and practice of the new Church, a demonstration of the power of the Hebraic and then the Christian God; it became therefore a matter of detail – with Christians attributing this power of prediction to access to God's purpose, instead of to demons. And so augury by selecting a word or passage in a Bible on a church altar (*Sortes Biblicae*) was reported in use in Gaul in the Merovingian age, by saints and princes alike.[1]

Ivo in his *De Divinationibus et Incantationibus*[2] (c.1100 AD) claimed the authority of Augustine of Hippo (*In Psalmo XXX*) to adjudge "Sors non est aliquid mali, sed res in dubitandi humana, divinam indicans voluntatem." (Divination is not anything to do with evil, but a human concern with the doubtful, and a means of indicating the divine will.) Indeed the desire to find out about the future seems entirely respectable. "Should not the people seek of their God, a vision for the living and the dead?" (*Isaiah* 8:19)

Aquinas concurred in his high medieval summary: "It would seem that divination is not a sin. Divination is derived from something *divine:* and things that are divine pertain to holiness rather than to sin. Therefore it seems that divination is not a sin."[3]

Augustine of Hippo himself did not contest that demons possessed the power of prediction, for after commenting on their incorporeality and speed of movement, he says:

Quibus duabus rebus quantum ad acrium corpus attinet praediti, hoc est, acrimonia sensus et celeritate motus, multa ante cognita praenuntiant vel nuntiant, quae homines pro sensus terreni tarditate mirentur.

[De Divinatione Daemonum (Patrologia Latina vol. 40)]

Which two considerations so contribute to the aforesaid sensitivity of body, that is the faculties of sharpness of the sense and speed of motion, that they can predict or inform (us) of many things which they know about (before we do), which men marvel at on account of their own terrestrial slowness of perception.

The questioning of demons might not be a sin in itself: Jesus did so (*Mark* 5:9) and Saul's interrogation of the dead Samuel in *1 Kings* 28:8 might also be quoted. But having explained the operation of demons in divination, Augustine of Hippo is far from recommending them. In Aquinas' summary: "Hence Augustine says (*Gen. ad Lit.* ii.17):... 'Thus a good Christian should beware of astrologers, and of all

---

[1] Dalton, 1927, vol.1 p.251
[2] *Patrologia Latina*, vol. 161
[3] Aquinas, p.191

impious diviners, especially of those who tell the truth, lest his soul become the dupe of the demons and by making a compact of partnership with them enmesh itself in their fellowship.'"[1]

Divination without demons was less perilous, for:

> "Augustine says (*Conf.*iv.3): 'Those astrologers whom they call mathematicians, I consulted without scruple; because they seemed to use no sacrifice, nor to pray to any spirit for their divinations; which art, however, Christian and true piety rejects and condemns.'"
>
> [Aquinas, p.201]

A good deal of Christian opinion did reject the whole concept of divination, presumably on the basis of *Deuteronomy* 18:10 which says: "There shall not be found among you any one that...useth divination, or an observer of times..." In the third century, Origen objected on the grounds that demons were definitely involved:

> "Origen says in his *Peri Archon* [sixteenth homily on the Book of Numbers]: 'There is an operation of the demons in the administering of fore–knowledge, comprised, seemingly, under the head of certain arts exercised by those who have enslaved themselves to the demons, by means of lots, omens, or the observance of shadows. I doubt not that all these things are done by the operation of the demons.'"
>
> [Aquinas p.194]

Isidore in Bk 8 ch.9 of his *Etymologia* had the same strong objection:

> *Sortilegi sunt qui sub nomine fictae religionis per quasdam, quas sanctorum sortes vocant, divinationis scientiam profitentur, aut quarumque scripturam inspectione futura promittunt... In quibus omnibus ars daemonum est ex quadam pestifera societate hominum et angelorum malorum exorta.*
>
> [Isidore *Etymologia* Bk.8 ch.9]

Which I tentatively translate:

> Diviners are those who under the name of false religion (and) through certain artifices which they call 'the lottery of the saints' pretend to knowledge of divination or who issue it in writing for future view... In all which matters the art of demons is involved which arises from the most dangerous association of men and evil angels.

---

[1] *ibid.* p.204

With which preparation, we may take a longer excerpt on the techniques of divination from Aquinas:

> 'When demons are expressly involved, they are wont to foretell the future in many ways... Sometimes they offer themselves to human sight and hearing... Sometimes they make use of dreams, and this is called *divination by dreams*; sometimes they employ apparitions or utterances of the dead, and this species is called *necromancy*, for as Isidore observes (*Etym.*viii)... *after certain incantations and the sprinkling of blood, the dead seem to come to life, to divine and to answer questions.* Sometimes they foretell the future through living men, as in the case of those who are possessed: this is divination by *pythons*, of whom Isidore says that *pythons are so called from Pythius Apollo, who was said to be the inventor of divination.* Sometimes they foretell the future by means of shapes or signs which appear in inanimate beings. If these signs appear in some earthly body such as wood, iron or polished stone, it is called *geomancy*, if in water *hydromancy*, if in the air *aeromancy*, if in fire *pyromancy,* if in the entrails of animals sacrificed on the altars of demons, *aruspicy.*
> The divination which is practised without express invocation of the demons is of two kinds. The first is when, with a view to obtain knowledge of the future, we take observations in the disposition of certain things. If one endeavour to know the future by observing the position and movements of the stars, this belongs to *astrologers*... If one observe the movements and cries of birds or of any animals, or the sneezing of men, or the sudden movements of limbs, this belongs in general to *augury*...
>
> To this second species of divination, which is without express invocation of the demons, belongs that which is practised by observing certain things done seriously by men in the research of the occult, whether by drawing lots, which is called *geomancy*... or by holding out several unequal sticks and noting who takes the greater or the lesser: or by throwing dice, and observing who throws the highest score; or by observing what catches the eye when one opens a book, all of which are named *sortilege.*
>
> Accordingly it is clear that there are three kinds of divination. The first is when the demons are invoked openly, this comes under the head of *necromancy*; the second is merely an observation of the disposition or movement of some other being, and this belongs to *augury*; while the third consists in doing something in order to discover the occult; and this belongs to *sortilege.*[1]'

---

[1] *ibid.* pp.196–8

In their pagan form, such practices were prohibited in Anglo–Saxon England, as in *Theodore's Penitential* ch.27:

> *Qui divinationes expetunt, et more gentilium subsequuntur, aut in domos suas hujusmodi homines introducunt, exquirendi aliquid arte malefica, aut expiandi causa, isti, si de clero sunt, abjiciantur...*

Those that consult divinations and use them in the pagan manner, or that permit people of that kind into their houses to seek some knowledge by the evil art, or for the sake of averting some omen, they, if clergy, shall be expelled [from the Church]...

> *Si quis mathematicus est, id est, per invocationem daemonum hominis mentem converterit, v annos poeniteat, i in pane et aqua.*

If anyone is a wizard,[1] that is seeks to control someone's mind through the invoking of demons, let him do penance for 5 years, one on bread and water.

> *Qui observat divinos, vel praecantatores, philacteria etiam diabolica, et somnia, vel herbas... si clericus est, v annos poeniteat, laicus ii annos poeniteat.*

Whoever employs diviners or predicters, and devilish talismans, and dreams, or herbs... if a cleric, let him do penance 5 years, if a layman, 3 years.

[Thorpe, 1840, p.293]

In the same century, on the continent, Carloman's Capitulary of 742 AD forbade: "sive sortilegos vel divinos, sive filacteria et auguria, sive incantatione...."[2] (both lot–casting and divination, talismans and auguries and spells...) – while in newly–conquered Saxony, Charlemagne's Capitulary of 797 AD tackled the problem this way: "Divinos et sortilegos ecclesiis et sacerdotibus dare constituimus."[3] (We enact that diviners and lot–casters be handed over to the Church and its priests (for punishment).)

And the question becomes relevant again when the Vikings have entered England, for Ælfric notes of the 21st of March, that when "the earth also makes known by her plants which then return to life.... now foolish men practice manifold divinations on this day."[4]

---

[1] *mathematicus* would seem to mean astrologer, but is used also of a wizard or enchanter e.g. in Saxo (1980, 2, p.29).

[2] Pertz, 1835, p.17

[3] *ibid.* 1835, p.49

[4] *Catholic Homilies*, Thorpe, 1, *The Octaves & Circumcision*

Dreams

The use of dreams in divination is based on the assumption that the information they contain derives from an external source, and therefore has objective value. During sleep the soul of the dreamer was conceived to be somehow loosened from the body. "Swa eac ure gast bið swiðe wide farende urum unwillum... þonne we slapað" (So too our soul is travelling very widely without our conscious knowledge – when we sleep – *Old English Boethius* ch.34). Presumably the soul in this state found itself better able to receive communications from spiritual entities. God himself might choose to make contact in this way e.g. *Numbers* 12:6 – "...If there be a prophet among you, I the Lord will make myself known unto him in a vision, and will speak unto him in a dream...." So too in *Job* 33:15–16: "By a dream in a vision by night, when deep sleep falleth upon men, and they are sleeping in their beds, then He [God] openeth the ears of men, and teaching instructeth them in what they are to learn." In *Genesis* 31:11 (telling Jacob to leave Laban) and *Matthew* 1:20 (telling Joseph to marry Mary), the messenger is an angel.

To the Roman world, the conveyors of dreams were demons: "...we know from Cicero (*Div.*1.64) how Posidonius explained dreams that came true: in sleep the human soul communicated either with the gods directly or with an 'immortal soul' (i.e. one of the many demons that throng the air beneath the moon). These divine beings know the future, and they often share their knowledge with human souls when they are not encumbered by the body."[1] (In this context it is to be remembered that demons were not intrinsically evil forces to the Romans, but neutral supernatural forces.)

The information received in a dream might be a straightforward injunction or warning, or a more indirect communication, through some sort of symbolism, which necessitated interpretation to make sense.[2] In the Old Testament, Joseph and Daniel are famous interpreters of dreams; so it is rather surprising to find in *Deuteronomy* 28:10 the stricture: "Neither let there be found among you any one that... observeth dreams." This prohibition does not seem to have dimmed Jewish or Christian enthusiasm for dream study at all; and two notable cases are preserved in Old English poems, in *Daniel* lines 538 on, and Constantine's dream in *Elene* 69 on; and as well as these, the famous contemporary example of Caedmon the cowherd of Whitby related in Bede's *Ecclesiastical History* Bk.4 ch.22.

---

[1] Luck, 1985, p.231

[2] The Old Norse poem 'Baldur's Dream' shows confidence in dream significance, though Odin needs help to interpret it.

There are also a number of Old English texts designed to assist in interpreting dreams. These seem to go back to Classical models, and Cockayne[1] notes the strong Greek and Judaic interest in the matter. A major individual figure in this science was Artemidorus in the late second century AD, who developed a complex system of symbological interpretation which must have impressed his contemporaries.

> "Symbolism is the key to understanding the dream mechanism, according to Artemidorus. Some of the symbols are fairly obvious. An abyss means impending danger; a blossoming tree, happiness and prosperity... In a sense, Artemidorus already anticipates the Freudian concepts of wish fulfilment and wish substitution; thus he says that the dreamer, if he is in love with a woman, will not see the object of his passion in his dreams, but he will see, for example, a horse, a mirror, a ship, the sea, or a woman's garment..."

> [Luck 1985 p.237]

His work was not entirely speculative, for Artemidorus seems to have deduced some dream 'meanings' by checking up on what happened to his dreamers afterwards. But in general, surviving interpretations seem arbitrary and fanciful, if only from a process of long and perhaps inaccurate transmission. Let us start with a fairly straightforward Old English example:

> Þonne him þince þæt he spiwe þæt byð swa hwæt swa he ana wiste þæt hit weorðæð yppe.

> [*De Somniorum Eventu*]

If he dreams that he is vomiting, then what he only knew will become public.

That simple a symbolism is usually lacking in Old English texts; many examples are at best traditional and now seem quite inexplicable, as two moons symbolising joy; an eagle can variously symbolise joy or honour or death[2] – indeed it is not surprising that we end up with the popular modern superstition that dreams represent the reverse of what they seem to say.

One fourth century AD Christian, Synesius, attempted to counter superstitious trust in dreams by seeing them as human–generated, and if anything practical or creative: – "the soul is lucid and mobile only when the body is asleep."[3] But this optimistic reassessment did not leave much impress on the Anglo–Saxons. To them all dreams were significant, but not necessarily benevolent or accurate phenomena. Thus a note of warning was sounded by Ælfric in his *Life of Swithun*: "Now it is to be accepted that we should not believe too seriously in dreams

---

[1] 1866, p.x

[2] See texts below, pt.2 no.25, p.221 and no.27, p.226

[3] Per Luck, 1985, p.239

because they are not all from God: some dreams are indeed from God, as we read of in books, but some are from the devil to deceive us in order to destroy the soul." – a problem familiar to us from Shakespeare's *Macbeth*. St Thomas Aquinas also concurs: "Sometimes however it is due to the action of demons that certain images appear to persons in their sleep..."[1] – not the neutral demons of Roman belief but opponents of God by this time.

Following on from this confused tradition, the attitude of the modern Western world to dreams is strangely ambivalent. We reject any prophetic significance (unless we are acutely superstitious) but cling to the idea that dreams are significant nonetheless – in Freud's system, of the internal functions of the individual mind, that is of the subconscious. To regard them as random constructs, it seems, is as unacceptable now as then.

Lots

A particular form of divination, of enduring popularity, was the casting of lots. In this a number of alternative pieces are presented blind to the selector, and a decision of some kind achieved according to the result. This can be a Yes/No alternative, or the picking–out of an individual from among a group ('getting the short straw') or some other direct answer dependent on chance.

The simplicity (democracy?) of the process has long made it attractive,[2] and Christians approved of the method as indicating the will of God rather than random chance, with the added attraction that the procedure seemed to preclude intervention by demons. Thus Augustine of Hippo, in a comment on *Psalm* 30:16 said "It is not wrong to cast lots, for it is a means of ascertaining the divine will when a man is in doubt."[3]

That it was an acceptable procedure on the Christian Western frontier seems clear from a reference in the *Laws* of the Frisians[4] that lots were kept in areliquary on the altar, one of which was marked with a cross, and used to determine guilt or innocence. *The Penitential of Theodore* (ch.27) nonetheless takes exception to some practices of this kind, perhaps because they were likely to take place outside the rules of the Church (or perhaps because it existed as some established pagan usage seeming to parody the allowable form?):

---

[1] Aquinas, p.206

[2] For example, the Old Saxons are said to have chosen their leader in time of war by lots – Bede *Ecclesiastical History* Bk.5, ch.10; in medieval England lots were used to portion out parish fields – see Elliott, 1959, p.42.

[3] Per Aquinas, p.209

[4] *Lex Frisionum tit.*14, 2 per Saupe p.20

Si quis sortes habuerit, quas Sanctorum contra rationem vocant, vel aliquas sortes habuerit, vel qualicunque malo ingenio sortitus fuerit, vel divinaverit, III annos poeniteat, I in pane et aqua.

[Thorpe, 1840, p.292]

If anyone practices the lots which are reckoned disrespectful to the Saints, or indeed any kind of lots, or lots are cast under some evil influence, or if anyone makes divination, let them do penance for three years, one on bread and water.

Which is much in agreement with the proverb, "Ne sec ðu þurh hlytas hu ðe geweorþan scyle." (Do not seek by lots (to discover) what will happen to you.) Yet there was considerable precedent for the use of lots in the Bible. Saul drew lots in *1 Samuel* 14:42 to determine guilt among many; Jonah was revealed as the cause of a storm in *Jonah* 1:7; Zacharias' duties in the Temple were determined by lot (*Luke* 1:9); and the Apostles elected Matthias by lot, *Acts* 1:26 – to give a few examples. Among these there could be no more dramatic case than that of Jonah, seeking to avoid God's errand to preach to Ninevah:

Ac sona swa he wæs in agan on þæt scip, þa geræste he hine on anum ende, and þa sona swa þa men þe on scipe wæron ut on ðære sæs dypan gesegled hæfdon, þa onsende God micelne ren and strangne wind and grimme ysta on þa sæ, swa þæt þæt scip ne mihte naðor ne forð swymman ne underbæc, for ungehyrsumnysse þæs witegan þe Ionas wæs haten. Þa forðan ondredon þa scipmen him swiðe þearle, hluton þa heom betweonum for hwilces heora gyltum him swa getimod wære, and þa behluton hi hit sona to Ionam þam witegan and he his nan þing nyste. Þa wundredon hi sona þæt þæt se hlot ofer þone Godes þegen gefeoll; awrehton hine þa of slæpe and rehton hit him eall; and he geþafode þæt hine man wearp ut on sæ...

[Rogation Homily 2, Bazire & Cross, 1989, p.20]

As soon as he (Jonah) had gone on board the ship, he set himself to sleep at one end, and as soon as the men that were on the ship had sailed out onto deep water, then God sent a great storm of rain and a strong gale and terrible waves upon the sea, so that the ship could neither make progress forwards nor backwards, all on account of the disobedience of the prophet called Jonah. Then because the crew feared him greatly, they drew lots among themselves over whose fault it was this was happening to them and the lot straight away indicated Jonah – he knew nothing of what they were doing. They marvelled at once that the lot should fall upon a servant of God; they aroused him from sleep and told him all about it; and he allowed them to cast him into the sea...

In this version, lots seem to have been resorted to to avoid some other sort of confrontation: an objective impersonal judgement, as it were, when no one is volunteering, and a hierarchical decision would be inappropriate. (Comparably, at *Andreas* lines 1099–1107, lots are cast to select a victim for a cannibal sacrifice.)

The usefulness of such a decision process may have been appreciated long before Christianity brought stories as vivid as these to Anglo–Saxon attention.

In the Germanic world, Tacitus noted that 'No people attach more importance to auspices and the decision of the lot.'[1] Saxo recorded the process itself: 'They also knew how to draw lots: three bits of wood, white on one side, black on the other were used for this, and when thrown into the lap, the white meant good and the dark evil fortune;'[2] a set of *astragali* or sheep's ankle bones of c.500 AD, found at Caistor–by–Norwich,[3] one of which has runic markings, may have served for divination as much as for gambling.

Regarding the disputed word *unhlitme* in *Beowulf* line 1129, Vickrey[4] seems to me to risk an anachronism when he asserts that "An important function of the ancient Germanic casting of lots was to ascertain the will of the powers which ruled man's fate." For it must remain doubtful whether the drawing of lots, in pre–Christian ideology, implied a guiding hand from a deity or depended on chance as revelation.

Perhaps significantly, the word 'lot' (in Old English, *hlot, hlet, hlyt*) seems to shift in meaning with Christian influence, coming to mean something like 'ordained future' in the opening of *Andreas* (line 6) – compare the modern sense of 'allotted' – or in the following anecdote of the hereafter, something more like 'control, disposal'. (The passage is somewhat restored, but supported by a Latin version and a parallel Old English passage)

> *And he þær geseah eac sumne þara manna þe he ær gewundode þa hwile þe he lifigende wæs – and se man lifde þa gyt – and to gewitnesse his yfela he wæs þider gelæded; and sio wund wæs open and þæt blod wæs stemende, and he wæs cegende his agenre stefne and hefiestu edwit cweðende, and he stælde þas blodes gyte swiðe wælhreowlice, and he tealode and heapode micel meniu synna on hine; and þa ealdan feond trumedon and sædon þæt he wære hira gewealdes and hira hlytes.*
>
> [*Letter from Wynfrið*, Sisam 1953, p.216]

And he saw there also a man whom he had wounded when he was living – and that man still lived – and had been brought there as witness to his crimes; and the wound was open and the blood issuing from it, and he was calling out in his own voice and reproaching him most gravely, and charged him remorselessly with the spilling of blood. And the ancient demons confirmed it all and said that he (the accused) would soon be in their power and at their disposal.

---

[1] *Germania*, ch.10 trans. Fyfe

[2] Trans. Christiansen, 1981, Saxo, 2, p.496 (Bk.14)

[3] Crawford, 1963, p.104

[4] 1977, p.92

Runes

The belief that Odin 'crucified' himself to achieve knowledge of runes is interesting as a myth, but it is a little disconcerting to find Kemble[1] and even Elliott[2] taking at face value the idea that runes had primarily a magical role. Surviving early examples indicate use in standard inscriptions, to attest ownership, for monumental display, and the like, and though this may be an accident of survival, there is no reason to doubt that the appeal of runes (as of any alphabet to any people) was essentially practical. Like any such well–known series of symbols (e.g. numbers or playing–cards), it can be used for divination and magic, and that potential may have been inherent in runes from their first adoption: but it cannot be satisfactory to put the magical associations first.   An alphabet is the name of any system of writing containing approximately two dozen letters, which analyses sound to enable writing down of speech with the fewest number of component signs. If each spoken syllable has a separate sign (as in Ancient Egyptian, Japanese, etc.) then many dozens of 'letters' will be needed; if each word has its own individual sign (as in Chinese), then many thousands are going to be needed.[3] The alphabet was therefore something of a revolution in communication, for it meant that reading could be mastered with relatively little training as opposed to being the preserve of a specially educated elite who needed to devote their whole career to this one art.[4] The invention is believed to have taken place the once, perhaps in Phoenicia in about the thirteenth century BC, and from that all Western (and perhaps Eastern) alphabetical systems developed.

But the Phoenician/Semitic alphabet had another bonus. A letter had a shape which was symbolic of an object whose name began with the sound represented by the object. For example, *aleph* or *alf* (their name for the letter 'a') looked rather like the modern V (or an inverted 'A' perhaps) which could be taken as two horns sticking up in the air; and the letter–name meant 'ox'. *Bet(h)*, a rather square letter to start with, had the meaning 'house'. *Delt* or *daleth*, a triangular letter, had the

---

[1] 1991, pp.20–21

[2] 1959, p.2: "Communication among people remained a secondary function of runic writing throughout its long history; much more common was the use of runes to invoke higher powers to affect and influence the loves and fortunes of men." So the runic 'alphabet' "came to be primarily an instrument of magic." (*ibid.*) These comments were revised in the second edition. For similar material see introduction to Taylor & Auden, 1973.

[3] Allegedly 80,000, of which however only 9,000 are in common use – Diringer, 1968, 1, 13

[4] "Thanks to the simplicity of the alphabet, writing has become very common; it is no longer a more or less exclusive domain of the priestly or other privileged classes." (Diringer, 1968, 1, p.13) Arguably through the medium of bad hand–writing, differing upper and lower case forms, and a grotesque tradition of spelling (let alone professional jargon) we have restored much of the elitism and mystery.

meaning 'door', appropriate to the shape of a tent–flap, and so on.[1] In such a system, an alphabet was virtually self–explanatory, and the task of remembering the letter–value greatly facilitated. When the letter–shapes were transferred to (and transformed into) Greek and Latin, this convenient aide–memoir disappeared, and classical letter names (like 'alpha', 'beta', etc.) are no longer meaningful but in effect arbitrary labels, like our 'bee', 'eff', 'aitch', and so on. How much simpler it would be for us, if when we said 'A is for Apple', the letter 'A' looked like an apple! Now, without suggesting that any sense of the Semitic scheme was known in the medieval period, this is a concept relevant to rune–names, I believe, and a mnemonic system that might have been independently arrived at then for similar practical ends.

The similarity of rune–shapes to classical Greek and Latin letters is obvious (with apologies to the creative originality of Woden). Which exact classical alphabet served as its model has long been debated, however. Some rune shapes recall a particular section of the Greek alphabet, others the Latin, still others the Etruscan or North Italic forms.[2] No one alphabet however seems to give a complete source. This problem largely resolves itself when we recall the medium upon which writing was placed.[3] The stone of classical inscriptions can take straight or curved lines in any direction, though the serif is necessary to provide a neat end to a groove. An even more flexible series of shapes is possible with a pen on parchment or papyrus. Wood, however, is different, especially if we try to write upon the grained surface (e.g. a plank). Here, a line coinciding with the grain becomes lost, for the eye can hardly distinguish it from the background lines making the pattern of the grain direction. It follows that curved strokes are better, and straight lines (to be visible) can only be cut at right angles or diagonal to the grain.[4] And this is exactly what we have in runes. In no rune are strokes permitted that form a right angle (except the G–rune whose X shape proves the point, for the strokes are both diagonal). Given this simple premise, the transformation of F into ᚠ and H into ᚺ becomes a function of transferring a Latin alphabet to a context of inscribing on wood. Other letters may vary in order to avoid confusion, e.g. P cannot be like runic W or R, N cannot be like runic H (or vice versa).

---

[1] See Diringer, 1968, vol.1 pp.167–9

[2] See Morris, 1988, for summary

[3] Though many surviving runic inscriptions are on metal or stone, this does not preclude arguments based on wood, examples of which will have perished. "This use is abundantly evident from some 600 runic inscriptions on wooden sticks ('bills of lading', messages, love–letters, etc.) excavated in recent years at Bryggen in Bergen, Norway…" Moltke, 1985, p.32; a touching example is given by Elliott, 1989, p.92: 12 runes which read *'ost min kis mik'* (my darling, kiss me).

[4] "On évitait systématiquement les traits horizontaux et les lignes courtes." Derolez, 1962, p.173

ᚠ	ᚢ	ᚦ	ᚩ	ᚱ	ᚳ	ᚷ
f	*u*	*þ(th)*	*o*	*r*	*c(k)*	*g*
feoh	*ur*	*þorn*	*os*	*rad*	*cen*	*giefu*
ᚹ	ᚻ	ᚾ	ᛁ	ᚼ	ᛇ	ᛈ
w	*h*	*n*	*i*	*g(j)*	*?*	*p*
wynn	*hagol*	*nied*	*is*	*gear*	*eoh*	*peorð*
ᛉ	ᛋ	ᛏ	ᛒ	ᛖ	ᛗ	ᛚ
x	*s*	*t*	*b*	*e*	*m*	*l*
eolh	*sigel*	*Tiw*	*beorc*	*eoh*	*mann*	*lagu*
ᛝ	ᛞ	ᛟ	ᚪ	ᚫ	ᛠ	ᛤ
ng	*d*	*œ*	*a*	*æ*	*y*	*ea*
Ing	*dæg*	*eþel*	*ac*	*æsc*	*yr*	*ear*

Rune shapes accompanying Hickes' printing of the Old English Rune Poem

We need no longer strive to place the origin of runes back in the centuries BC in order to account for a particular letter shape borrowing from Greek, or before the second century AD to account for similarities to Etruscan, for the Germanic alphabet was a creative adaptation to a particular medium, not a direct facsimile of its exemplar. And this means that the first use of runes could be dated to any time up to the first archaeological evidence, that is up to as late as the fourth century AD.[1] A late date would further help account for the patchy evidence of rune distribution: Page[2] outlines a dissemination in England through East Anglia (sixth century) to South and North in seventh century, as though one particular division of Anglians brought them to this country.[3]

Having adapted an alphabet, the Germanic peoples also chose to name the letters. More than one author[4] has hoped to trace the origin of these names back to words of (pagan) divine significance, compatible with their supposed original use for magic; but when we look at those rune–names common to the Old English and Norwegian and Icelandic, we find (perhaps disappointingly) the most everyday of concepts: 'wealth' (F), 'riding' (R), 'generosity' (G), 'hail' (H), 'ice' (I), 'birch–

---

[1] The two earliest surviving runic inscriptions are on the Vadstena bracteate of c.300 AD and the Kylver (Gotland) Stone of c.400 AD; the last recorded spontaneous use of runes was in Denmark, 1745 AD, according to Moltke, 1985, pp.503–4.

[2] 1973, p.34

[3] Bammesberger, 1991, p.406, suggests that special Old English rune forms were developed by c.600 AD.

[4] Polomé, 1991, Schneider, 1956

tree' (B) – on a par, I suggest, with the simple A is for Apple syndrome. There is no certainty that the more exciting names in the Scandinavian Rune poems e.g. Norwegian/Icelandic *þurs* ('giant') for 'th', are any more authentic than the Old English forms: they could be a gesture of later paganism or indulgent antiquarianism. An apparent exception in the Old English context, *os* for 'o', is interesting, for 'os' is meaningless on its own,[1] while the same name is used in the later Icelandic and Norwegian poems and given the meaning of 'a god' in Icelandic but a 'river–mouth' in Norwegian. Further, the equation *os* = 'god' is not expected in Icelandic, for the Gothic version of the word was *ans–*, giving the Old Norse *áss,* plural *Æsir.*[2] The change from long 'a' to long 'o' can be accounted for in Old English, but is not appropriate to the Scandinavian forms. Meanwhile, *Tyr* for 't', though close to Tiw, is even closer to the Norse form, *Tír*, and in the Old English poem represents a 'tacn' or heavenly sign (planet), while *Ing* for 'ng' is specified as a 'hero' (*hæle*), perhaps a legendary figure, but of uncertain status in the supernatural world. These examples are tantalising, and a non–Christian connotation to some rune–names cannot be ruled out; but antique material does not of itself guarantee an early date. Arguably there is no consistent pagan voice in the names, and in some cases no consistent names at all. The variety, not only between English and continental rune–names, but in some cases of the name of a single rune in Old English,[3] is a big barrier to any theory of originally divinely–sanctioned rune–names: would not such have all survived or all been suppressed? It is difficult to be certain on this point, but I find the search for originally mystical rune–names unrewarding, and prefer to think of those we have as practical tags.

Seeking to use extant rune names to predict anything, it is surprising (to me) how difficult it is to arrange the 'words' into a message. Simple indicators like 'yes/no', 'now/later', 'good/bad' are lacking, for the rune–names are not instructions. Rather they seem to be a selection of terms from the natural world (e.g. trees, animals), the weather (e.g. day, hail), and moral concepts (e.g. generosity), resulting in an easy–to–pronounce commonly–used and hard–to–confuse word in most cases.[4] But if not conveying great inspiration, how did the rune–names come about? This also is impossible to say, from lack of evidence of early forms, but in at least a few cases, the rune–name seems to reflect the shape of

---

[1] Although occurring as a word–name element; see Jente, 1921, p.66, and above p.53.

[2] cf. Old English gen. pl. *esa.* See A. Campbell *Old English Grammar* (Oxford, 1959), p.47.

[3] The 'signatures' of the poet Cynewulf are relevant here; see also Hacikyan, 1973; Elliott 1991, p.246, n.15, asserts that "single runes do not stand for any words except their traditional names." I respectfully ask, what traditional names?

[4] cf. Diringer, 1968, 1, p.167: "…the Semitic names of the letters refer mainly to everyday objects." On the pronunciation of Old English rune names, *ur* and *yr* sound alike, but are related signs also; *iar* and *ear* present a difficulty, but the remaining vowel names are distinctive.

the rune – rather as in the alphabet's ultimate origins, and this seems a more hopeful line to explore.

I am not suggesting that the shape was modelled on the name, but rather that it is not impossible that some names could have been selected to fit the shapes. A strong case, for example, can be made out in relation to the name 'thorn' for the 'th' rune (þ) – remembering that on wood the loop of the letter would have a pointed form (Þ), seeming very much like a rose or other thorn on a stem. The enigmatic *os*, with its apparent (Latinised) meaning 'mouth', may perhaps owe something to the pair of curved horizontal lines – a little like lips? 'S', if for *segel* ('sail'), as I propose, at least in the context of the Old English *Rune Poem*, may bear some resemblance to a mast, especially if spliced from two pieces of wood;[1] *Eolhxsecg* ('bulrush') for 'eo', with its three upper points, is arguably plant–like. Does the shape of the mysterious P–rune suggest a dice–cup, a container in which dice could be shaken before throwing?[2] It surely explains Greinberger's conjecture (1921) of 'throat, gullet' for the P–rune name. Does the shape of *iar* lend some credence to its interpretation[3] as a four–legged animal with a long tail; and the *ing* rune suggest the pattern of stars in the constellation Boötes?[4] Of the M–shaped 'E' rune, with its accompanying name *eh* 'horse', Pollington[5] notes "the rune's shape may represent the legs and bent back of the creature." (By origin, the shape itself will be an E rotated through 90 degrees.) Later, in Middle English parlance, *yogh* ('yoke') becomes the name of ȝ (g or y), and clearly demonstrates the shape of the piece of wood designed to keep two oxen in parallel. There is not the consistency here that would suggest a motive for all the rune–names (at least as we know them), but it may help account for some later names or modifications of names, or simply for the names selected for use in certain stanzas in the Old English *Rune Poem*; and the suggestion is that that poem is ornamental or educational in purpose, not mystical or primeval.

This exposition of the practical nature of runes may seem to founder on Tacitus' evidence. In chapter 10 of his *Germania* we learn of the method of casting lots:

> ...*Virgam frugiferae arbori decisam in surculos amputant eosque notis quibusdam discretos super candidam vestem temere ac fortuito spargunt. Mox, si publice consultetur, sacerdos civitatis, sin privatim, ipse pater familiae, precatus deos caelumque suspiciens ter singulos tollit, sublatos secundum impressam ante notam interpretatur.*

---

[1] The 's' rune in Cotton MS Domitian A.ix f.10 is glossed by the Latin 'velum', but this is dismissed by Sisam (1953, p.18) as "the work of an ill–informed Elizabethan antiquary." The only evidence for this value therefore remains the context of the verse in the *Rune Poem*.
[2] See Bauschatz, 1982, p.70 and material there.
[3] Osborn & Longland, 1980
[4] Osborn, 1980
[5] 1995, p.22

Having cut a wand from a fruitful (or fruit–bearing, nut–bearing?) tree, they slice it into slips, and mark these with different signs and strew them at random on a white cloth. Then the official priest, if it is to be public consultation, or the father of the family if is to be private, calls upon the gods, and looking up into the sky, chooses three pieces, one at a time, and interprets them according to the symbol previously placed thereon.

Two comments are relevant. First, that the raising of eyes may not be so much an indication of seeking help from the gods, as an averting of gaze to ensure the selection is random. Second, rather importantly, Tacitus' Latin uses only the word *notis, notam* ('symbol(s)') of the supposed runes, not *litteris* ('letters'). Of course, Tacitus may not have had detailed knowledge of the ritual or the exact form of the signs, but his choice of terms at least leaves it open what exactly is involved.

Did Tacitus in fact fill out his information in accordance with similar rites in Roman augury? – Cicero's "sortes in robore insculptas priscarum litterarum notis," (lots inscribed on oak with symbols of antique letters) and Servius' picture of the Sibyl giving interpretations "litterarum ut per unam litteram significet aliquid," (of letters, so that one concept is signified by one letter).[1] This might in turn incline us to see, with him, a more sophisticated system of divination than was the case. "But Tacitus's writing is too early; runes do not appear to have been in wide use until the third century after Christ... Yet, these markings seem to suggest a scoring of a related but prerunic type."[2]

The so–called Kitzbühel rune find[3] does not, to my mind, provide the missing runic or pre–runic signs Tacitus may have known, but are more like Roman numerals scratched on bits of wood, perhaps as gaming pieces, or work tallies.[4] In fact, an imaginative, quasi–pictorial set of (simple) symbols was already known in prehistoric Scandinavia, but whether as pictograms or with any meaning at all attached – let alone for divination – is hard to say. There are examples and some discussion in Elliott 1989, pp.84–5.

To add to the uncertainty, while there are indications of familiarity with the use of lots in Anglo–Saxon texts, to establish a decision or indicate a person, there is no one example of runes being named as used for lots or for the purpose of divination, though *tan–hlyta* (diviner by lots made of wood) occurs once as a gloss for the Latin *sortilegus*. The Vikings may have come to use them thus,[5] but even this is not specified:

'When Hakon came east off Gothland, then he cast the hallowed chips, and the answer was that he should have good–luck to fight at day–break.'

[Vigfusson & Powell, 1883, 1, p.412]

[1] Per Schneider, 1955, pp.46–7
[2] Bauschatz, 1982, p.68
[3] Altheim & Trautmann–Nehring, 1943
[4] See Pittioni, 1954, p.88
[5] See possible examples in Vigfusson & Powell, 1883, 1, 411–12

Are these simple lots, giving a yes–or–no answer, or runes providing a fuller more active message? It is surprisingly difficult to settle this point.

But if their role in divination is so doubtful, where does our overwhelming sense of runes as magical ware come from? Largely from later Scandinavian sources, but not exclusively so. An early tomb inscription of perhaps the seventh century in Sweden attests to the supposed power of runes as follows (in Derolez' French version) –

> *Prédiction de malheur. Moi, maître de la série de runes, cachai ici de puissantes runes. De perversité [périsse] sans repos, d'une mort mystérieuse, celui qui viole cette [tombe/monument].*
>
> [Derolez, 1962, p.176]

> Warning of ill–luck. I, master of the set of runes, have hidden here some powerful runes. Of his own perversity shall perish, without rest, by a mysterious death, he that violates this monument.

And Bede has an early story, which suggests a magical (but not a divinatory) role for runes – a story designed perhaps to show how superstitious the Mercians were compared to the (more advanced and Christian) Northumbrians:

> 'Beda, relating the adventures of a Saxon [sc.Northumbrian] nobleman, made prisoner in the battle between Ecgfrith of Northumberland and Aethilred of Mercia, A.D.679, and whose bonds fell off whenever his brother, who supposed him dead, celebrated mass for his soul, – adds that his captor believed the miracle to be caused by his having magical Runes: *'Interea comes qui eum tenebat, mirari et interrogare coepit quare ligari non posset; an forte literas solutorias, de qualibus fabulae ferunt, apud se haberet, propter quas ligari non posset.'*[1] The Saxon translation[2] renders *Literas solutarias, by alysendlice Rune.'*
>
> [*Ecclesiastical History*, Bk.4 ch.20 via Kemble, 1991, pp.21–2]

Note the plural forms *literas, rune*, however. If a simple single rune were capable of achieving this end, there would hardly be any point in tying anyone up at all – it is the combination of a number of runes that is involved, implying special knowledge of how to apply them rather than any power inherent in the individual rune as such. The Bede example seems confirmed, both in terms of rune use and complexity of procedure in the following stanza from the *Hávamál* (The Words of the High One) stanza 139:

---

[1] 'Meanwhile the officer who held him began to marvel and enquire why he could not be bound; did he perhaps have about him the letters of unbinding, of which sort of thing stories are told, and on account of which he could not be tied up?'

[2] Ælfric retells the story in his *Catholic Homilies*, 2, 'Hortatorius Sermo', using *runstafum* where the Old English Bede has *alysendlice rune*.

I know a fourth (spell): if I am tied, I chant it and free myself; the fetters will fall from my feet, the bonds from my hands.

Perhaps this was what Odin should be credited with – not runes themselves, but the potential of formulas based on runes to make magic? (Spiesberger[1] conjectures that these rune combinations would be drawn as an involved conjoined single pattern, adding a visual mystique to the process.) In the poem, *Sigrdrifumál*, stanzas 8 and 10, rune combinations are used for healing purposes.[2]

In the sagas of the Northmen there are many references to runes used in spells, and specifically in 'black' magic. In *Grettir's Saga*, when his enemies can make no progress against him, witchcraft is resorted to. An old woman with a valid grudge against Grettir prepares a tree–stump found washed up by having a patch on it smoothed for her work and inscribes runes on it, smearing them with her blood, while chanting spells. Then she walks *widershins* round the trunk before launching it back into the sea. It drifts to the island where Grettir is making his defence and firewood is scarce, and in a moment of carelessness Grettir himself takes a swing at it with an axe; the blade glances off the wood and cuts his own leg, initiating an infection that so weakens him that a later attack by his enemies leads to him being easily overcome and killed.

A more grotesque sending occurs in the story of Thorleif the Earl's poet (from the *Flateyjárbók*), where a stump of wood is reanimated by inserting a human heart in it, during various incantations, and sent off to commit a revenge murder.

In a more sportive example, Saxo talks of the god Oller (Ull) as "such a cunning magician that instead of sailing in a ship he was able to cross the seas on a bone which he had engraved with fearful charms."[3] The implication is that while ordinary bone–runners sufficed for skating on ice, a pair prepared with suitable magic – runes? – could do the same for water.

Would such inscriptions have had the same effect in the Roman alphabet? Perhaps there grew a feeling that these traditional alternative letters were more potent than Latin ones, indeed were almost constituting a challenge to the European supremacy of Latin rituals and invocations. But in general a lot of the power seems to come from the right ritual – from the correct combination of signs, the colouring with blood, from their use by a skilled witch, etc. Runes remain basically a neutral medium (again, like any letters) – the magic, or the will to do magic with them, comes from elsewhere.

---

[1] 1955, pp.110–111

[2] Per Grön, 1953, p.149

[3] Trans. Fisher, Saxo, 1979, 1, p.79

Runes

ᚠᛁᛋᚳ · ᚠᛚᚩᛞᚢ · ᚪᚻᚩᚠ · ᚩᚾ ·
f i s c   f l o d u   a h o f   o n

(line cont.) ᚠᛖᚱᚷᛖᚾ · ᛒᛖᚱᛁᚷ ·
    f e r g e n   b e r i g

ᚹᚪᚱᚦ · ᚷᚪᛋᚱᛁᚳ · ᚷᚱᚩᚱᚾ · ᚦᚫᚱ ·
w a r ð   g a s r i c   g r o r n   þæ r

(line cont.) ᚻᛖ · ᚩᚾ · ᚷᚱᛖᚢᛏ · ᚷᛁᛋᚹᚩᛗ ·
    h e   on   g r e u t   g i s w o m

ᛗᚱᚠᛏᛟᚾ · ᛒᚠᛏ. (solution to riddle?)

fisc flodu ahof on fergen–berig
warþ gasric grorn þær he on greut giswom

Bill Griffiths

Inscription from the Franks Casket (8th century Northumbrian)

147

THE ANIMAL WORLD

Anglo-Saxons undoubtedly hunted,[1] herded, bred, utilised and ate animals of many kinds, but it is unlikely they excluded them from religious significance and a measure of respect as life-forms with quite the man-centred aloofness of Christianity.[2] For it was a distinctive tenet of the new religion that man (with a soul) was the purpose of God's creation,[3] while the animal (without a soul) was something quite separate and inferior.

> 'And God blessed Noah and his sons, and said unto them, 'Be fruitful, and multiply, and replenish the earth. And the fear of you and the dread of you shall be upon every beast of the earth, and upon every fowl of the air, upon all that moveth upon the earth, and upon all the fishes of the sea; into your hand are they delivered. Every moving thing that liveth shall be meat for you; even as the green herb have I given you all things.'
>
> [*Genesis* 9:1–3]

The animals were a separate, exploitable class, with no claim on mankind any more; indeed their inclusion in the Ark meant they were indebted for their very existence to human resourcefulness. Ælfric makes the situation clear in his *Catholic Homily* Bk 1 no.1, when after summarising the process of creation, he comments,

> *ac he ne sealde nanum nytene ne nanum fisce nane sawle, ac heora blod is heora lif and swa hraðe swa hi beoð deade, swa beoð hi mid ealle geendode."*

> But He [God] gave no beast or fish a soul, but their life is their blood and once they are dead they are finished with.

– I cannot reproduce the forceful triple negative of the Old English, but it could hardly be more emphatic in the original.

---

[1] Note the badger-hunting as a sport implicit in *Riddle* 15; and reference to an aurochs in the *Rune Poem*.

[2] A strand of Christian animal presentation was the Physiologus or Bestiary, a sort of manual of animals real and mythical in which "facts of natural history collected from Pliny were mixed with entirely mythical legends to illustrate some point of Christian teaching." (Crombie, 1961, p.16) This collection may have originated in second century AD Alexandria, and was translated into Latin in the fifth century. Its often idealised portraits underline the Christo-functional attitude to the animal world.

[3] And the human in turn was to be accorded a goal and a mode of life defined by divine revelation.

Plato in his *Timaeus* had put it rather more tactfully – that the soul has three parts: rational, irascible, and appetitive – true humanness consists in the rational part, the 'man within man', achieving mastery over the lower forces. King Alfred in his *Metres*, (translating and adapting Boethius) considered (unlike Ælfric) that animals do have a life-force or soul, certainly, but an inferior or partial one, using Plato's scale:

> I have just said that the soul is three-fold in each person, because all wise men say that one aspect of each soul is irascibility, a second desire; the third is of a better kind than those two – rationality: that is no shameful ability because no creature possesses it but man. All sorts of beings have the other two: every animal has desires as well as irascibility. But men have conquered the whole earth because they possess, what the others lack, that attribute of reasoning.
>
> [*Metre* 20, 176–203]

While rationality is not 'shameful' (*scandlic* in Old English), the implication is clearly that animal existence is, given that we are taking man as the criterion.

A revealing and lyrical passage in the life of Cuthbert[1] gives us a sense of the new relationship between man and animals:

> *Þa dyde Cuthbehtus swa his gewuna wæs,*
> *sang his gebedu on sælicere yðe, standende oð þone swyran*
> *and syððan his cneowa on ðam ceosle gebigde,*
> *astrehtum handbredum to heofonlicum rodore.*
> *Efne ða comon twegen seolas of sælicum grunde*
> *and hi mid heora flyse his fet drygdon*
> *and mid heora blæde his leoma beðedon,*
> *and siððan mid gebeacne his bletsunge bædon,*
> *licgende æt his foton on fealwum ceosle.*
> *Þa Cuðberhtus ða sælican nytenu on sund asend mid soðre bletsunge,*
> *and on merigenlicere tide mynster gesohte.*
>
> [Ælfric *Catholic Homilies* 2nd series, no.10]

Then did Cuthbert according to his practice, and sang his prayers amid the sea's waves, standing in the water up to his neck, and then bent his knees on the sand, with his palms stretched out to the heavens. Just then came two seals from the sea's depths and dried his feet with their fur and warmed his limbs with their breath, and then by sign asked his blessing, lying at his feet on the yellow sand. Then Cuthbert sent the sea-creatures back to the water with a proper blessing, and himself returned to the monastery at daybreak.

---

[1] Might this reflect a Celtic tradition of sensitivity to nature? I am thinking of examples like the Irish epigram to a blackbird (Jackson, 1971, no.71) of perhaps the eighth–ninth century.

This is both affectingly told, touching in its concept, and yet ultimately patronising in the casual way the animal is subordinate to the human – in this instance fulfilling the role of combined towel and hot air dryer. Yet most animal encounters lack even this imperialistic charm: thus when St Neot mislays a shoe:

> *An fox, þe is geapest ealra deora, þær arn geond dunen 7 denen wunderlice beseonde mid egen hider 7 þider, 7 færinge becom to þære stowe, þære se halge wer his fet geðwoh, 7 þone scoh gelæhte, 7 ætfaren þohte.*
>
> [Warner, 1917]

A fox, that is the most cunning of all animals, was running over hills and denes, excellently observing this way and that with his eyes, and suddenly he came to the place where the holy man had washed his feet, and he caught up the shoe and intended to run off with it.

A servant, sent to recover the shoe, observes the fox, and prays to God for assistance:

> *Gesænde þa slæp on þone fox, swa þat he his lif alet, habbende þa þwanges of þan sco on his fracede muðe.*

He (God) then sent sleep upon the fox, so that he gave up his life, having the thongs of the shoe in his wicked mouth.

Yet a number of *fox*-based Old English plant-names (*foxes clate, foxes clife, foxes fot*, and *foxes glofa*) indicate a more affectionate (even whimsical) view of the animal. Not so the many unkindnesses with animals that typify the *Medicina ex Quadrupedis*, Classical in source, that appealed to one Anglo-Saxon translator.[1]

With Christianity, as it were, the animal was cast forth from the serious world: but can we speculate as to its status in a pre-Christian England? Animals often form a decorative feature on helmets, but it is hard to know why – as tribal 'totems' or as invocations of a particular power? Among the best known as symbols are the wolf, the bear, and the boar; they may have some connection with the great gods (the wolf and bear – via berserker – with Odin, the boar with Frey, as in the *Prose Edda*) but as servants rather than embodiments of the god or the god's power. What more clearly links them is their common character as wild beasts of ferocious type, somewhat higher in the chain of predators than even man himself, and perhaps commanding awe or respect for that reason. In Old English personal names only compounds of *earn* ('eagle'), *hun* ('bear-cub') and *wulf* ('wolf') occur, again conveying energy, power and combativeness. (These

---

[1] A mild example is: 'For sleep, lay a wolf's head under the pillow.' de Vriend, 1984, p.262; we also find that the lungs of a hare, bound to human eyes, relieves soreness (ch.5, item 2); a pierced wolf's eye laid on a human eye relieves glaucoma (ch.10, item 4); or that drawing the teeth from a live badger (while invoking God's name) provides a charm to be worn against any evil (ch.1, item 2).

characteristic qualities are speculative; the pagan emotional response to animals was surely more complex than a hierarchical reaction of fear/contempt.)

But to assume that the animal goes beyond this, and the Germanic individual saw himself (less probably herself?) as possessing an animal double, or *fylgja*, almost an external soul, opinions explored by Arthur Wachsler[1] and Turville-Petre,[2] seems less certain. A *fylgja* has been defined as "a personification of the essential nature or power of an individual or family. It often appeared in the form of an animal whose nature corresponded to the name or character of the individual it represented."[3] A human assuming animal qualities[4] and even animal shape is supposed in Germanic lore; but, for example, when Odin is accorded the power of travelling like an eagle, fish, beast or dragon in spirit, while asleep,[5] this seems closer to the Christian model of the soul as wandering abroad during sleep – compare the bird-like persona taken on in the *Seafarer*, lines 58–60:

> *forþon nu min hyge hweorfeð   ofer hreþerlocan,*
> *min modsefa   mid mereflode*
> *ofer hwæles eþel   hweorfeð wide.*

therefore my mind now poises over the body, my spirit travels wide over the whale's domain...

Transformation of man into animal occurs also in the Classical tradition: thus men's souls punished or trapped in an animal body is a theme of Boethius' account of Circe (Alfred's *Metre* 26); on the one hand, the account celebrates the continuity of mind in man-changed-into-animal (hardly a consolation for the victim) as demonstrating the immortal invulnerability of the soul to magic, while at the same time claiming that Ulysses' crew were changed into animals according to their existing propensities, which seems more like a sort of judgement:

> *Sume hi to wulfum wurdon,   ne meahton þonne word forðbringan,*
> *ac hio þragmælum   ðioton ongunnon.*
> *Sume wæron eaforas,   a grymetedon*
> *ðonne hi sares hwæt   siofian scioldon.*
> *Þa þe leon wæron   ongunnon laðlice*
> *yrrenga ryn   a ðonne hi sceoldon*
> *clipian for corðre.   Cnihtas wurdon,*
> *ealde ge giunge,   ealle forhwerfde*

---

[1] 1985, pp.382–3

[2] 1964, pp.228–30

[3] *The Saga of Gunnlaug*, ed/trans Foote & Quirk, 1957, note p.42. A rare human example is that of Bothvar Biarki, said to send out an emanation in the form of a fighting bear while himself remaining whole if inactive elsewhere – see Ellis Davidson, 1964, p.68.

[4] To Glosecki (1989, p.201) the process is one of borrowing, e.g. Beowulf of the bear, in some characteristics.

[5] Snorri via Ellis Davidson, 1969, p.46

> *to sumum diore   swelcum he æror*
> *on his lifdagum   gelicost wæs.*   [*Metre 26, 79–88*]

Some were become wolves, and could not manage to speak a word, but sporadically set to howling. Some were boars (and) always grunted when they would have expressed something of their suffering. Those that were lions began to roar angrily and horribly whenever they intended to speak in company. The crew, both old and young, had each been changed to that sort of animal that he was most like before, during his life.

Here the point seems to be a quasi-reincarnatory situation, in which the animal suits the deserts of the man's soul.[1] In the Germanic pagan relationship, the emphasis seems the other way round, as though the human is seeking to define himself after the model of an animal ideal – as though we can more confidently define our vague quality of 'humanness' in externalities.

Animal-element names in this case would imply a borrowing or recording of desirable qualities – a compliment or an expression of good luck. That this need for super-human fortitude becomes most important in situations of great emotion such as battle, may be one explanation of the belief that human could actually transform into animal. Such a power is initially attributed to giants and gods: "Both these types, being dextrous in deceiving the eye, were clever at counterfeiting different shapes for themselves and others, and concealing their true appearance under false guises"[2] – note the implication that no true metamorphosis takes place, but it is all a matter of power over the minds of the beholders. Harthgrepa, a lady suitor of Hading, and of giant descent, explains the art as follows: "I become huge to fright the fierce, but small to lie with men."[3] And it is not only gods that are attributed with shape-changing powers: Sigmund and his son change into wolves,[4] Siward of Northumbria is associated with a white bear;[5] and there is something bear-like about Beowulf's great strength and wrestling style of combat, as well as his name.

Conversely, a human who encountered an exceptional animal might tend to imbue it with human status, or recognise in it the metamorphosis of a god. Thus in Norse legend, Loki unwittingly shoots an otter who was in fact the son of a powerful entity who exacts a considerable settlement from the gods. The shape-transformation sometimes becomes apparent at death, when animal reverts to its true form. Saxo, Bk.5,[6] includes a story of human shape-changers who assume the

---

[1] Campbell Thompson (1908, p.4) mentions a curious Jewish belief in an underworld 'farm' where human souls passed into animals under the control of a necessarily sinister underworld herdsman.

[2] Trans. Fisher, Saxo, 1979, 1, p.22

[3] Trans. Fisher, *ibid.* Bk.1 ch.6

[4] Ellis Davidson, 1964, p.68

[5] *Genealogists' Magazine*, vol.15 no.10, June 1967, p.365

[6] 1980, 1, p.157

form of 'sea-cows'; when trapped and killed, they resume human form, but retain the animal head. Another late legend, concerning the certainly blameless Ælfthryth (step-mother of Edward the Martyr), in the *Liber Eliensis*, accuses her of shape-changing, into the guise of a mare.[1] By later centuries, this ability had clearly become a source of reproach and insult.

Possible man-like behaviour by animals could make this fallacy more credible: thus the bear, capable of walking on its hind legs like a human, or the social co-operation of the wolf, or the courage and anger of the boar. To quote Wachsler:[2] "The supernatural and manlike qualities of the bear are attested also in the Norse belief in lycanthropy. Men who had the gift of shape-changing frequently changed into animals, often appearing as bears as well as wolves. Indeed, in many of the primitive northern cultures, it appears the most common animal forms taken by shape-shifters are the wolf, the bear and the wild-boar, these being the most admired and feared animals of the region." Perhaps they were also perceived as the most man-like, though another aspect of the wolf, its 'cowardice' and underhand cunning led to the animal becoming synonymous in Old English with an outlaw or criminal. Another Christian transformation of concept as with 'elf'? Curiously, a passage in a homily by Wulfstan[3] gives us the first glimpse of a werewolf:

Þonne moton þa hyrdas beon swyðe wacore and geornlice clypigende, þe wið þone þeodsceaðan folce sceolon scyldan: þæt syndan bisceopas and mæssepreostas, þe godcunde heorda bewarian and bewerian sceolon mid wislican laran, þæt se wodfreca werewulf to swyðe ne slite ne to fela ne abite of godcunde heorde.

[Wulfstan, *Homily on Ezekial*]

Then should the herdsmen be watchful and ever calling out, who aim to protect the people from some harm: those are bishops and priests, who ought to watch over and guard the divine flock with wise words, so that the dangerous werewolf neither rend too much of nor eat too many of the divine flock.

Berserkers, possibly named after bears,[4] are the most famous case: they are associated with animal rage, that of bear or of wolf (hence the epithet 'wolf-coats' in *Hrafnsmál*[5]), either donning the skin of such an animal or believing themselves transformed. Though Ellis Davidson gives examples of such super-ordinary

---

[1] See Davies, 1989, pp.47–9

[2] 1985, p.383

[3] Quoted by Jente, 1921, p.143

[4] *Bjorn* (bear) is both the name of one known berserk, and forms a common element in berserk names – see Saxo, 1980, 2, p.95, note.

[5] The *Erbyggja Saga* has the less flattering simile "like mad dogs." (ch.25)

warriors from Tacitus,[1] beserkers are more obviously associated with ninth century Norway and thereafter, and with the cult of Odin.

A graphic description of such a transformation is given by Saxo.[2] Taunted about his chances of success in battle...

> 'Harthben, possessed by immediate transports of rage, took hard bites out of the rim of his shield, gulped down fiery coals into his entrails without a qualm, ran the gauntlet of crackling flames and finally went completely and savagely berserk...'

– attacking friend and foe alike!

A similar picture is recorded by Snorri in the *Ynglinga Saga* ch.6:

> 'His [i.e. Odin's] own men went without byrnies, and were mad as dogs or wolves, and bit on their shields, and were as strong as bears or bulls; menfolk they slew, and neither fire nor steel would deal with them: and this is what is called Bareserks-gang.'
>
> [trans. Morris & Magnússon, 1893, pp.17–18]

A surely less aggressive and perhaps deliberately playful custom is aluded to in *Theodore's Penitential* ch.27:

> *Si quis in Kalendas Januarii in cervulo aut vetula vadit, id est, in ferarum habitus se communicant,[3] et vestiuntur pellibus pecudum, et assumunt capita bestiarum; qui vero taliter in ferinas species se transformant, III annos poeniteant; quia hoc daemoniacum est.* [Thorpe, 1840, p.293]

> If anyone at the turn of the year goes about like a young stag or calf, that is, if people get together in the disguise of wild animals, and dress themsevles with the pelts of animals, and put on the masks of beasts, as though to transform themselves into those wild species, let them do penance for three years, for this is a demoniac thing.

Derolez associates such practies with Yule rather than the New Year: "Dans les coutumes populaires nordiques relatives à l'époque du jul, les travestissements jouent un rôle important: hommes et jeunes gens se déguisent, entre autres en animaux... Cette coutume existe encore ailleurs: les personnes qui se sont déguisées parcourent les villages, font beaucoup de bruit et inventent toutes sortes de taquineries."[4] The practice was noted in seventh century Gaul (was this perhaps

---

[1] Her 1964, pp.67–9

[2] 1979, trans. Fisher, 2, p.206, from Bk.7

[3] For *commutant*, Thorpe queries, in his edition.

[4] Derolez, 1962, p.198

its source in Theodore?[1]), in the form of mumming and dances, with people disguised as stags or oxen, on New Years Day.[2]

Beyond the realm of personal identification, animals also clearly had a significant role in religion and augury. Saupe refers to Charlemagne's *Capitulary* of 797 AD as containing prohibitions against the veneration of animals; the *Indiculus Superstitionum* no.16 is "De cerebro animalium" (Concerning the brain of animals) – suggesting some sort of cultic eating perhaps, or perhaps a form of augury by the organs of sacrificed animals. Derolez presumes a sequence of ritual killing, offering and feasting: "Certains morceaux de la victime étaient réservés aux dieux, par exemple la tête."[3] The eating of animals, as a sort of feast associated with animal sacrifice is specified in Bede's *Ecclesiastical History* Bk.1 ch.30, where oxen are mentioned; in a remarkable passage, Pope Gregory advised Abbot Mellitus:

> *Et quia boves solent in sacrificio daemonum multos occidere, debet eis etiam hac de re aliqua sollemnitas immutari; ut die dedicationis, uel natalicii sanctorum martyrum, quorum illic reliquiae ponuntur, tabernacula sibi circa easdem ecclesias, quae ex fanis commutatae sunt, de ramis arborum faciant, et religiosis conuiuiis sollemnitatem celebrent; nec diabolo iam animalia immolent, et ad laudem Dei in esu suo animalia occidant, et donatori omnium de satietate sua gratias referant...*

> And as they are accustomed to killing many oxen as a sacrifice to demons, let them change this into something solemn and proper: for example, on the day of dedication, or on the nativities of the holy martyrs, whose relics are deposited there, let them construct shelters from tree-branches round the outside of those churches that were converted from use as pagan shrines, and let them celebrate the solemn occasion with pious feasts; but do not let them continue to sacrifice animals to the devil – rather they should kill the animals for food in praise of God, and give thanks to the Bestower of Everything for their abundance...

This indulgence may have led, unwittingly, to later license, for Stubbs in the sixteenth century made scathing comment on the character of early or mid summer festivities surrounding the Lord of Misrule, when a company with "Hobby-horses, dragons & other Antiques, togither with their baudie Pipers and thundering Drummers" moved round church and churchyard "where they have commonly their Sommer-hauees [?enclosures], arbors, & banqueting houses set vp, wherein they feast, banquet & daunce al that day & (peraduenture) all the night too."[4] Not to mention the tradition of a boar's head at Christmas....

---

[1] However, there may be a parallel tradition in this country; such disguise as 'guizers' is still common in East Durham at the New Year, at fancy-dress parties.
[2] Dalton, 1927, 1, p.248; Hatt, 1970, pp.134–5, emphasises the role of the stag in Gallic Celtic beliefs.
[3] Derolez, 1962, p.187
[4] Quoted by Phythian-Adams, 1975, p.23

A sterner policy is exhibited in Carloman's *Capitulary* of 742 AD when a ban was placed on "hostias immolatitias, quas stulti homines iuxta ecclesias ritu pagano faciunt" (burned animal offerings, which deluded people make according to some pagan rite, near churches).

Ox skulls found at Yeavering, Northumbria, and a cache of a thousand ox skulls found buried at Harrow Hill (Sussex)[1] point to similar rituals. Human burials have been found including goat's head, ox skull and pig's head[2] – also sometimes animal bones have been found in human cremations, presumably as sacrificial additions.[3] Further afield animal sacrifices have been found accompanying burials in Denmark.[4] But are we dealing with sacrificial feasts at a centre of worship for some pagan god, or rites associated with burials (special sites that only become associated with 'god' and formal religion in the Christian era)?

There are notes of even stranger rituals. Horse skulls have been found under threshing-floors, and it is speculated whether these had an acoustic role in some pre-Christian ritual.[5] Animal skulls have been recovered from under doorways[6] – part of a continuing tradition of sacrifice associated with building projects? Equally bizarre, it was thought that "to raise the head or the skull of a dead horse on a pole was a means of threatening an opponent, felt to possess magic potency."[7] In later examples, animals were hanged alongside felons (to shame the latter?).[8] In all these, it is clear what is being sacrificed, but not to whom or exactly why.

In auguries, animals played a particularly notable role. Tacitus[9] refers to divination via the neighs and snorts of sacred horses, observed by priest and leader during sacred processions – and otherwise the horses were kept in a special grove for this use only – which may account for the taboo about horses mentioned in Bede *Ecclesiastical History* Bk.3 ch.13 broken by the priest Coifi, when he mounts the sacred animal on his crusade of destruction. The *Indiculus Superstitionum* no.13 expresses doubt "De auguriis vel avium vel equorum vel bovum stercora vel sternutationibus" (about auguries from bees or horses or by the dung or snorting of oxen). Saxo[10] gives a form of augury linked to horses and spears. In these cases we are likely to have records of divination via particularly favoured animals, dedicated in some special way, but it seems that ordinary animals played a role too in popular superstitions.

---

[1] Owen, 1981, p.45

[2] *ibid.* pp.45–7

[3] *ibid.* p.87

[4] See Ellis Davidson, 1964, p.134

[5] Merrifield, 1987, p.125

[6] *ibid.* pp.117–9; and for further examples of foundation sacrifices see de Jubainville, 1905.

[7] Saxo, 1980, 2, p.76 , note on Bk.5 and compare *Egil's Saga* ch.57

[8] Saxo, 1980, 2, p.137, note

[9] *Germania* ch.10

[10] Bk.14 – Christiansen, Saxo, 1981, 2, p.496

Of the typical person, we learn from Saxo that "before setting out on various other sorts of business, they would determine the success of what they intended by whatever animal they met first."[1] Brockie[2] of nineteenth century Co. Durham (though transformed into a mining district) recorded that if a worker met a woman or a hare on the way to work, he would turn back. Many similar customs are given in Brand's *Observations on the Popular Antiquities of Great Britain:*[3] for example, to meet a hare on the way is bad luck and a warning to turn back, but a wolf or a sow could indicate good fortune. These are, as it were, shadows of beliefs, indicating the durable emotional base of many superstitions.[4]

This popular regard for animal warnings is not without its Judaeo-Christian dimension. The passage *Jeremiah* 8:7 "The kite in the air hath known her time; the turtle [i.e. dove], the swallow, and the stork have observed the time of their coming," is taken as indicating that there is a sort of natural knowledge in animals from which we can benefit. And for the Christian "natural knowledge is infallible and comes from God."[5] But the new religion also wished to distance itself from paganish customs, and so kept open the option to make light of such practices. Understandable, perhaps, but at the same time, some quality of a universal bond between man and animal at a non-food level was discarded also.

> *Eall swa gelice se ðe gelyfð wiglungum*
> *oððe be fugelum oððe be fnorum*
> *oððe be horsum oððe be hundum*
> *ne bið he na cristen ac bið forcuð wiðersaca.*
>
> [Ælfric *Lives of Saints* Bk.1, no.17 (*De Auguriis*)]

So likewise he who trusteth in auguries, either from birds, or from sneezings, either from horses, or from dogs, he is no Christian, but is an infamous apostate. [trans. W. Skeat]

May I be permitted to quote a slightly caustic eastern comment on such affairs? –

> 'The cry of jackals or of birds is understood with ease;
> Yea, but the word of men, O king, is darker far than these!'
>
> [trans. J. G. Jones[6]]

---

[1] *ibid.*

[2] 1886, p.30

[3] 1849, vol.3, pp.201–3

[4] Receiving a third light from a match was deemed unlucky by youngsters in Harrow, Middlesex, in the 1970s as I recall, though the origin of this seemingly lay in the trench conditions of World War I.

[5] Aquinas p.207

[6] J. G. Jones *Tales and Teachings of the Buddha: The Jataka Stories in relation to the Pali Canon* (1979), p.111

THE ROLE OF LITERATURE

Having suggested that the gods are not strictly great gods, that magic and superstition play much the same role as science, that fate implies the accidental, and runes are essentially alphabetical and functional, the reader may feel a little cheated of an authentic role for the magical in the Anglo-Saxon period. But if there is one area where magic (as assumed power of mind) has been underestimated, it seems to me it is the realm of poetry, and that the verse charms hold some important pointers to the origins of Old English literature. For, as Grimm says, "Poetry borders... closely on divination, the Romans *vates* is alike songster and soothsayer, and soothsaying was certainly a priestly function."[1] Similarly, Glosecki (after Frank): "Germanic verse kept its primeval associations with sympathetic magic – with the effective power of the rhythmic word."[2] Storms[3] may insist that "The literary value of the charms is very small," but this is to judge from a criterion of poetic achievement as elaborate workmanship or refined cultural thought, and fails to take into account that simplicity may have its own standards, a validity in social or religious context rather than in an intellectual or entertainment one.

Technically, magic is capable of accounting for two features of Old English verse: repetition and alliteration. Repetition, of lines, phrases, formulae, may be considered typical of oral verse, where it assists structure and memory, but surely its basis is also emphatic, the assertion of word-importance, indicating the assumed power of statement over event. Repetition of line or phrase is a feature of the *Nine Herbs Charms*, but in its purest form it builds up into chains of echoic lines, with a chant-like effect, as in the 'nine poisons' section, very close to an incantation, that is, an accumulation of power as well as sound. Lists are a feature of several Old English poems, as demonstrations of knowledge or an almost legalistic coverage of eventualities: poems like *Widsith* and *Deor* are catalogues; literary creations, too,[4] but ones that go back to or replicate the roots of knowledge and oral memory, implying always the specialness of that knowledge or set of words. Laws can have set diction in the same way, to reinforce and lend majesty or mystery to their content; and the thunderous lists in Wulfstan's *Sermo Lupi* (and many another Anglo-Saxon homily) invite attention and credence through a technique any pagan enchanter would have been proud of. The genealogy may be

---

[1] Grimm, 1900, 1, p.94

[2] 1989, p.89

[3] 1948, p.125

[4] But not, I think, necessarily derived, in form, from the Graeco-Roman encyclopaedic tradition, as suggested by Howe, 1985, p.16.

included here too: for there an alliterative linking can be apparent also,[1] reflecting the process of a handing on of identity in a culture that may not have had fixed theories explaining birth as the attainment of a soul.

Alliteration is common to all the Germanic verse-forms, and is an effective way of organising words in patterns, for the purpose of remembering, or giving aural pleasure, but also of imparting special energy. For the pattern rehearsed by the arranger of the words seems to have its own validity, as though this is what it is sensible and right for the words to do, revealing through the arrangement their inner power and potential. Words in alliterating pairs, or sets of three or four, are the basis of the verse technique; and though we are used to a four-stress Old English verse line,[2] yet alliterating word-pairs remain also a common technique, in lists, in emphatic passages in homilies, in everyday and legalistic formulas. They become part of the resource of the literary creator, though a large number of Old English poems remain anonymous, as though not concerned with innovating or demonstrating individual skill.

The social context of words and ideas can always change;[3] magic and science can become blurred together when they simply mean a hierarchy of information; but the apparently casual 'magic' of imparting pattern to words (and so to our perception of much else) is part of a process of regulation between human and external world that may serve to establish an equilibrium more important than we like to admit. It is no coincidence, I would argue, that the techniques of alliteration and repetition are found prominently in texts devoted to demonstrating knowledge and achieving confidence in healing, as a symbol of benevolent aim and safe outcome. There could be no clearer declaration of 'magical' intent, a purpose shared by Christian and pagan, by scientist and sorcerer, by 'dark ages' and the enlightened present alike.

---

[1] Searle, 1897, p.xiv, examples *Sige-* names reoccurring in the kings of Essex, and Eormen- forms in a Kentish family. Woolf, 1939, treats the subject in some detail, noting that name "repetition sets in among the Burgundians, the Goths, and the Merovingians several centuries before it is found in England," (p.246), and that grandparent-grandson may be linked by identical names e.g. in eleventh century England (pp.256–7). The Wessex genealogy in the Chronicle 597 has alliterative poetic form, though it must be unlikely children were ever named to assist bardic technique.

[2] As a convention or 'rule', by which verse passes to a conscious and neutral 'civilised' medium

[3] Is the pursuit of a single all-embracing theory of language unproductive?

SOURCES

ALTHEIM, F. & E. TRAUTMANN-NEHRING *Kimbern und Runen* (Berlin, 1943)

ST THOMAS AQUINAS *The Summa Theologica*, Question XCV per M. J. Weller, *Sortilege of Allotment: A poem found* (1991)

ARNOLD, CHRIS 'Wealth and social structure: A matter of life and death' pp.81-142 in *Anglo-Saxon Cemeteries 1979* ed. P. Rahtz, 1980.

ARNTZ, HELMUT 'Runen und Runennamen' *Anglia* 67-68 (1944) pp.172–250.

ASTON, MICHAEL *Interpreting the Landscape: Landscape archaeology in local studies* (1985)

AUDEN, W. H. & LOUIS MACNEICE *Letters from Iceland* (1937)

BAMMESBERGER, ALFRED 'Ingvaeonic Sound Changes and the Anglo-Frisian Runes' pp.389–406 in *Old English Runes and their Continental Background* ed. A Bammesberger (Heidelberg, 1991)

BASSETT, STEVE 'In Search of the Origins of Anglo-Saxon Kingdoms' pp.3-27 in *The Origins of Anglo-Saxon Kingdoms* ed. Steve Bassett (Leicester, 1989)

BATES, BRIAN *The Way of Wyrd: Tales of an Anglo-Saxon Sorcerer* (1983)

BAUSCHATZ, PAUL C. *The Well and the Tree: World and time in early Germanic culture* (Amherst, Mass., 1982)

BAZIRE, JOYCE & JAMES E. CROSS (eds.) *Eleven Old English Rogationtide Homilies* (1989)

BONSER, W. 'General Medical Practice in Anglo-Saxon England' pp.154-163 (vol.1) in *Science Medicine and History: Essays in honour of Charles Singer* ed. E. A. Underwood (2 vols., Oxford, 1953)

— *The Medical Background of ASE* (1963)

BOSWORTH, J. & T. N. TOLLER *An Anglo-Saxon Dictionary* (2 vols., Oxford, 1898, 1921)

BRAEKMAN, WILLY L. 'Notes on Old English Charms' *Neophilologus* 64 (1980) pp.461–9

[re Nine Herbs Charm]

BRAND, JOHN *Observations on the Popular Antiquities of Great Britain*, vol.3 (1849)

BRANSTON, BRIAN *The Lost Gods of England* (1957, 1974)

BRIGGS, KATHARINE M. (ed.) *A Dictionary of British Folk-Tales in the English Language* Part B *Folk Legends* vol.1 (1971)

— *The Vanishing People: A study of traditional fairy beliefs* (1978)

BROCKIE, WILLIAM *Legends & Superstitions of the County of Durham* (Sunderland, 1886)

BRODEUR, A. G. (trans.) *Prose Edda by Snorri Sturluson* (New York, 1929)

BROWN, PETER *Augustine of Hippo: A biography* (1967)

BUCKMAN, ROBERT & KARL SABBAGH *Magic or Medicine?* (1993)

BURLAND, COTTIE *North American Indian Mythology* (1965)

CAMERON, M. L *Anglo-Saxon Medicine* (Cambridge Studies in Anglo-Saxon England no.7, 1993)

CAMPBELL THOMPSON, R. *Semitic Magic: Its origins and development* (1908)

CAVENDISH, RICHARD *The Powers of Evil in Western Religion, Magic and Folk Belief* (1975)

COCKAYNE, O. (ad./trans.) *Leechdoms, Wortcunning and Starcraft of Early England* (3 vols., Rolls Series, 1864-6)

[vol.1 includes the *Herbarium of pseudo-Apuleius*, the *Medicina de Quadrupedis*, and some short items e.g. some metrical charms; vol.2 is based on BL MS Royal 12 D.xvii: pt.1 recipes, pt.2 *Bald's Leechbook* proper, on internal disorders, pt.3 further recipes, some with charm element; vol.3 includes the *Lacnunga* (MS Harley 585), the *Peri Didaxeon*, and many small items such as prognostics.]

COLGRAVE, BERTRAM (ed. and trans.) *Two Lives of St Cuthbert: A life by an anonymous monk of Lindisfarne and Bede's prose life: text, translation and notes* (Cambridge, 1940)

— **& R. A. B. Mynors** (ed. and trans.) *Bede's History of the English People* (Oxford, 1969) [Latin & English text]

COPLEY, GORDON *Early Place-Names of the Anglian Regions of England* (British Archaeological Reports, British series, no.185, 1988)

CRAWFORD, JANE 'Evidences for Witchcraft in Anglo-Saxon England' *Medium Ævum* 32 (1963) pp.99-116

CRAWFORD, J. S. (ed.) *Byrhtferth's Manual* (Early English Text Society, ordinary series 177, 1929)

CROMBIE, A. C. *Augustine to Galileo* (2 vols., 1952, 2nd edition 1961) [here, vol.1 used]

DALTON, O. M. (ed.) *Gregory of Tours: History of the Franks* (2 vols., Oxford, 1927)

DAVIES, ANTHONY 'Witchcraft in Anglo-Saxon England: Five case histories' pp.41-56 in *Superstitions and Popular Medicine in Anglo-Saxon England* ed. D. G. Scragg, (Manchester, 1989)

DAVIS, CRAIG R. 'Cultural assimilation in Anglo-Saxo royal genealogies'; *Anglo-Saxon England* 21 (1992) pp.23–36

DEROLEZ, RENÉ *Runica Manuscripta* (1954)

— *Les Dieux et la Religion des Germains* trans. F. Cunen (Paris, 1962)

DICKINS, BRUCE (ed./trans.) *Runic and Heroic Poems of the Old Teutonic Peoples* (Cambridge, 1915)

DIRINGER, DAVID *The Alphabet* (2 vols., 1968)

DOBBIE, E. V. K. (ed.) *The Anglo-Saxon Minor Poems* (New York, 1942) [includes Old English verse charms & *Rune Poem*]

DODGSON, JOHN McNEAL 'The significance of the distribution of the English placenames in *-ingas*, *-inga-* in south-east England' *Medieval Archaeology* 10 (1966) pp.1–29

EKWALL, E. *English Place-names in* -ing (1923; 2nd edn., Lund, 1962)

ELIADE, MIRCEA *Shamanism: Archaic techniques of ecstasy* trans. W. R. Trask (1989)

ELLIOTT, RALPH W. V. *Runes: An introduction* (Manchester, 1959, 2nd edn. 1989)

— 'Coming back to Cynewulf' pp.231-247 in *Old English Runes and their Continental Background* ed. A Bammesberger (Heidelberg, 1991)

ELLIS, HILDA R. *The Road to Hell* (1943)

ELLIS DAVIDSON, HILDA R. *Gods and Myths of Northern Europe* (1964)

— *Scandinavian Mythology* (1969)

— 'The Germanic World' ch.5 or pp.115-141 in *Divination and Oracles* ed. Michael Loewe & Carmen Blacker (1981)

EVANS-PRITCHARD, E. E. *Theories of Primitive Religion* (Oxford, 1965)

FINEGAN, JACK *Handbook of Biblical Chronology* (Princeton, 1964)

FITCH, ERIC *In Search of Herne the Hunter* (Chieveley, 1994)

— 'Ancient Taplow' *At the Edge* 1 (1996) pp.32–35

FONTENROSE, JOSEPH *Python: A study of Delphic myth and its origins* (1959, 1980)

FOOTE, P. G. & R. QUIRK (ed./trans.) *The Saga of Gunnlaug* (1957)

FOOTE, P. G. & D. M. WILSON *The Viking Achievement* (1970)

FÖRSTER, M. (ed.) 'Die Kleinliteratur des Aberglaubens in Altenglischen' *Archiv für das Studium neueren Sprachen* 110 (1903) pp.346-58

— 'Vier neue Donnerbücher' *Archiv* 120 (1908) pp.45-52

— 'Neue Bauernpraktiken' *Archiv* 120 (1908) pp.296-301

— 'Ein neues Traumbuch' *Archiv* 120 (1908) pp.302-305

— 'Windbücher' *Archiv* 128 (1912) pp.55-64

— 'Sonnenscheinbücher' *Archiv* 128 (1912) pp.64-71

— 'Wochenstags-Geburtspronosen' *Archiv* 128 (1912) pp.296-308

— 'Das lateinisch-altenglische Pseudo-Danielsche Traumbuch in Tiberius A III' *Archiv* 125 (1910) pp.39-70

— 'Das zweite altenglische Traumbuch' *Archiv* 134 (1916) pp.264-93

— 'Die altenglische Traumlunare' *Anglia* 60 (1925-6) pp.58-93

FOWLER, ROGER (ed.) *Wulfstan's Canons of Edgar* (Early English Text Society, ordinary series, vol.266, 1972)

FOX, D. & H. PÁLSSON (trans.) *Grettir's Saga* (Toronto, 1974)

FRANTZEN, ALLEN J. *The Literature of Penance in Anglo-Saxon England* (New Brunswick, N.J., 1983)

FRAZER, SIR JAMES *The Golden Bough* (abridged edn, 1922, repr. Ware, 1993)

FRIAR, BRUCE WOODWARD *Libri Annales Pontificum Maximorum: The origins of the annalistic tradition* (Papers & Monographs of the American Academy in Rome, vol.27, 1979)

GARMONSWAY, G. N. (ed.) *Ælfric's Colloquy* (London, 1939) [Latin and Old English texts]

GERVASE OF TILBURY *Le Livre des Merveils* trans. A. Duchsene (Paris, 1992)

GLOSECKI, STEPHEN O. *Shamanism and Old English Poetry* (New York, 1989)

GONZER, PAUL (ed.) *Das anglosächsische Prosa-Leben des hl. Guthlac* (Anglistische Forschungen vol.27, Heidelberg, 1909) [Old English text of Life of St Guthlac]

GRATTAN, J. H. G. & C. SINGER *A-S Magic and Medicine Illustrated specially from the semi-pagan text 'Lacnunga'* (Oxford, 1952)

GREINBERGER, THEODOR 'Das ags. Runengedicht' *Anglia* 45 (1921) pp.201–20

GRIFFITHS, BILL *Anglo-Saxon Times: A study of the early calendar* (1989)

— (ed./trans.) *'The Battle of Maldon': Text and Translation* (Pinner, 1991, 1996)

— (ed.) *Alfred's Metres of Boethius* (Pinner, 1991, 1994)

— *Meet the Dragon: An introduction to Beowulf's adversary* (Seaham, 1995, repr. Wymeswold, 1996)

GRIMM, JACOB *Teutonic Mythology* [originally published 1835 as *Deutsche Mythologie* 2 vols.]; trans. from the 4th edn. by J. S. Stallybrass in 4 vols., vol.1, 1900, vol.2, 1883, vol.3, 1883, vol.4 1888, repr. 1966 [pagination continuous]

GRINSELL, L. V. *The Ancient Burial Mounds of England* (2nd edn., 1953)

GRÖN, FREDRIK 'Earliest Medical Conditions in Norway and Iceland' pp.143-153 (vol.1) in *Science Medicine and History: Essays in honour of Charles Singer* ed. E. A. Underwood (2 vols., Oxford, 1953)

GUMMERE, F. B. *Germanic Origins* (NY, 1892)

J. C. H. 'On the Names of the Days of the Week' pp.1-73 in *The Philological Museum* vol.1 (Cambridge 1832)

HACIKYAN, A. 'The Runes of Old English Poetry' *Revue de l'Université d'Ottawa* 43 (1973) pp.53–76

HALSALL, MAUREEN (ed.) *The Old English Rune Poem: A critical edition* (Toronto, 1981)

HATT, JEAN-JACQUES *The Ancient Civilization of Celts and Gallo-Romans* (1970)

HEMPL, G. 'Hickes's Additions to the Runic Poem' *Modern Philology* 1 (1903–4) pp.135-141

HENDERSON, WILLIAM *Notes on the Folklore of the Northern Counties* (1866)

HENEL, H. (ed.) 'Altenglischer Mönchsaberglaube' *Englische Studien* 69 (1934-5) pp.329-349 [Esp. texts relating to 'good' and 'bad' days]

— *Aelfric's De Temporibus Anni* (Early English Text Society, ordinary series 213, 1942)

HERBERT, KATHLEEN *Looking for the Lost Gods of England* (Pinner, 1994)

HICKES, GEORGE *Linguarum Veterum Septentrionalium Thesaurus Grammatico-Criticus et Archaeologicus* (Oxford, 1705)

HIGHAM, N. J. *An English Empire: Bede and the Early Anglo-Saxon kings* (Manchester, 1995)

HILLS, CATHERINE 'Anglo-Saxon cremation cemeteries, with particular reference to Spong Hill, Norfolk' pp.197-207 in *Anglo-Saxon Cemeteries 1979* ed. P. Rahtz, 1980.

— *Blood of the British* (1986).

HODGES, RICHARD *The Anglo-Saxon Achievement: Archaeology and the beginnings of English society* (1989)

HOFFMAN-KRAYER, E. & HANS BÄCHTOLD-STÄUBLI *Handwörterbuch des deutschen Aberglaubens* vol.6, Berlin & Leipzig, 1934-5 [includes article on *Notfeuer*]

HORNE, DOM ETHELBERT 'Cowrie shells in Anglo-Saxon graves' *Antiquaries Journal* 13 (1933) p.167

HOWE, NICHOLAS *The Old English Catalogue Poems* (*Anglistica* vol.23, Copenhagen, 1985)

— *Migration and Mythmaking in Anglo-Saxon England* (New Haven, 1989)

ISIDORE OF SEVILLE ed. J Oroz Reta et al. *Etymologias* (2 vols., Madrid, 1982)

JACKSON, K. H. (ed./trans.) *A Celtic Miscellany* (Harmondsworth, 1951, rev.1971)

JAMES, EDWARD 'Merovingian cemetery studies and some implications for Anglo-Saxon England' pp.35-55 in *Anglo-Saxon Cemeteries 1979* ed. Rahtz, 1980

JENKINS, CLAUDE 'Saint Augustine and Magic' pp.131-140 (vol.1) in *Science Medicine and History: Essays in honour of Charles Singer* ed. E. A. Underwood (2 vols., Oxford, 1953)

JENTE, RICHARD *Die mythologischen Ausdrücke im altenglischen Wortschatz* (Anglistische Forschungen vol.56, Heidelberg,1921)

JOHNSTON, GEORGE (trans.) *The Saga of Gisli* (London, 1963)

JONES, C. W. *Bedae Pseudographa: Scientific writings falsely attributed to Bede* (Ithaca, N.Y., 1939)

— (ed.) *Bedae Opera de Temporibus* (Cambridge, Mass., 1943)

JONES, GWYN (trans.) *Eirik the Red & other Icelandic sagas.* (1961)

JORDAN, LOUIS 'Demonic Elements in Anglo-Saxon Iconography' pp.283-317 in *Sources of Anglo-Saxon Culture* ed. Paul E. Szarmach (Kalamazoo, Mich., 1983)

JORDANS, WILLIAM *Der germanische Volksglaube von den Toten und Dämonen im Berg* (Bonn, 1933)

DE JUBAINVILLE, HENRI D'ARBOIS 'Des Victimes Immolées per les Constructeurs pour assurer la Solidité des édifices' *Revue Celtique* 26 (1905) p.289

KEEFER, SARAH L. 'A Monastic Echo in an Old English Charm' *Leeds Studies in English* n.s. 21 (1990) pp.71–80 [re charm For Delayed Birth]

KEMBLE, J. 'On Anglo-Saxon Runes' *Archaeologia* 28 (1840) pp.327-372; repr. 1991 ed. Bill Griffiths.

KENDALL, C. B. & P. S. WELLS (eds.) *Voyage to the Other World: The legacy of Sutton Hoo* (Minneapolis, 1992)

KIRBY, D. P. *The Earliest English Kings* (1991)

KIRK, ROBERT *The Secret Common-Wealth* ed. Stewart Sanderson (Cambridge, 1976)

KITSON, PETER 'From Eastern Learning to Western Folklore: the transmission of some medico-magical ideas' pp.57–71 in *Superstition and Popular Medicine in ASE* ed. D. Scragg (Manchester, 1989)

KLEIN, ERNEST *A Comprehensive Etymological Dictionary of the English Language* (Amsterdam, 1971)

LANG, J. T. 'Viking Age Sculpture' in *A Century of Anglo-Saxon Sculpture* (Newcastle upon Tyne, 1977)

LINAHAN, LIZ *Pit Ghosts, Padfeet and Poltergeists* (Barnsley, 1994) [legends from South Yorkshire]

LING, TREVOR *A History of Religion East and West* (1968)

LUCK, GEORG *Arcana Mundi: Magic and the occult in the Greek and Roman worlds* (1987)

MCINTOSH, CHRISTOPHER *The Astrologers and their Creed: An historical outline* (1969)

MAGNUSSON, MAGNUS & HERMANN PÁLSSON (trans.) *Njal's Saga* (Harmondsworth, 1960)

— & — (trans.) *The Vinland Sagas: The Norse Discovery of America* (Harmondsworth, 1965)

MAGOUN, F. P. 'Old English Charm A 13L *Butan heardan beaman*' *Modern Language Notes* 58 (1943) pp.33-4 [re Land Ceremonies Charm]

MAUSS, MARCEL *A General Theory of Magic* (1972)

MEANEY, A. L. *A Gazetteer of Early Anglo-Saxon Burials* (London, 1964)

— *Anglo-Saxon Amulets and Curing Stones* (British Archaeological Reports, British Series no.96, 1981)

— 'Variant Versions of Old English Medical Remedies and the Compilation of Bald's *Leechbook*' *Anglo-Saxon England* 13 (1984) pp.235–68

— 'Women, Witchcraft and Magic in Anglo-Saxon England' pp.9-40 in *Superstitions and Popular Medicine in Anglo-Saxon England* ed. D. G. Scragg, (Manchester, 1989)

MEANS, LAUREL (ed.) *Medieval Lunar Astrology: A collection of representative Middle English texts* (Lewiston, NY, 1993)

MERCER, SAMUEL A. B. *Earliest Intellectual Man's Idea of the Cosmos* (1957)

MERONEY, HOWARD 'The Nine Herbs' *Modern Language Notes* 59 (1944) pp.157-160

— 'Irish in the Old English Charms' *Speculum* 20 (1945) pp.172–182

MERRIFIELD, RALPH *The Archaeology of Ritual and Magic* (London, 1987)

MICHELS, A.G. *The Calendar of the Roman Republic* (Princeton, 1967)

MOLTKE, ERIC *Runes and their Origin* (Copenhagen, 1985)

MOMMSEN, T. (ed.) *Jordanis De Origine Actibusque Getarum* (Monumenta Germaniae Historica, auctorum antiqq., vol.5, pp.53-138, Berlin, 1882)

MORRIS, R. L. *Runic & Mediterranan Epigraphy* (Odense, 1988)

MORRIS, WILLIAM & EIRÍKR MAGNÚSSON (trans.) 'The Story of the Ynglings' pp.11-73 in vol.1 of *The Stories of the Kings of Norway called The Round World (Heimskringla), by Snorri Sturluson* (1893)

MORRISON, J. S. *The Classical World* = ch.4 (pp.87-114) in *Divination and Oracles* ed. Michael Loewe & Carmen Blacker (1981)

MYRES, J. N. L. *Anglo-Saxon Pottery & the Settlement of England* (Oxford, 1969)

— *A Corpus of Anglo-Saxon Pottery of the Pagan Period* (2 vols., Cambridge, 1977)

NICHOLAS, DAVID *The Evolution of the Medieval World* (1992)

NORTH, J. D. *Stars, Minds and fate: Essays in Ancient and medieval cosmology* (1989)

OGILVY, J. D. A. *Books Known to the English 597-1066* (Cambridge, Mass., 1967)

OSBORN, MARIJANE 'Old English Ing and his Wain' *Neuphilologische Mitteilungen* 81 (1980) pp.388–89

— **& LONGLAND, STELLA** 'A Celtic Intruder in the Old English Rune Poem' *ibid.* pp.385-7

OWEN, GALE R. *Rites and Religions of the Anglo-Saxons* (Newton Abbot, 1981)

PADER, ELLEN-JANE 'Material symbolism and social relations in mortuary studies' pp.143-169 in *Anglo-Saxon Cemeteries 1979* ed. P. Rahtz, 1980.

PAGE, R. I. *An Introduction to English Runes* (1973)

PÁLSSON, H. & P. EDWARDS (trans.) *Eyrbyggia Saga* (Edinburgh, 1973)

PARKER, S. J. 'Skulls, Symbols and Surgery: A review of the evidence for trepanation in Anglo-Saxon England and a considerations of the motives behind the practice' pp.73-84 in *Superstitions and Popular Medicine in Anglo-Saxon England* ed. D. G. Scragg, (Manchester, 1989)

PERTZ, G. H. (ed.) *Leges* vol.1 (Monumenta Germaniae Historicae, Hannover, 1835) [contains: Karloman's Capitulare of 742 AD (pp.16-17) and the Capitulare Paderbrunnense (Capitula quae de partibus Saxonie constituta sunt) of 785 AD (pp.48-50)]

PFEIFFER, JOHN *The Cell* (1969)

PHILIP, ALEXANDER *The Calendar: Its history, structure and improvement* (Cambridge, 1921)

PHYTHIAN-ADAMS, CHARLES *Local History and Folklore: A new framework* (1975)

PITTIONI, R. & E. PREUSCHEN 'Untersuchungen im Bergbaugebiet Kelchalm bei Kitzbühe' (*Archaeologica Austriaca* 15, Vienna, 1954)

PLUMMER, C. (ed.) *Venerabilis Bedae Historiam Ecclesiasticam Gentis Anglorum, etc.* (Oxford, 1896)

POLLINGTON, STEPHEN *Rudiments of Runelore* (Hockwold-cum-Wilton, 1995)

POLOMÉ, E. 'The Names of the Runes', pp.421-438 in *Old English Runes and their Continental Background* ed. Alfred Bammesberger (Anglistische Forschungen no.217, Heidelberg, 1991)

PUTNAM, GLENYS 'Spong Hill cremations' pp.217-219 in *Anglo-Saxon Cemeteries 1979* ed. P. Rahtz, 1980.

RAHTZ, PHILIP, T. DICKINSON & L. WATTS (eds.) *Anglo-Saxon Cemeteries 1979* (British Archaeological Reports, British series, vol.82 (1980)

REGINALD OF DURHAM *Libellus de Admirandis Beati Cuthberti Virtutibus* (Surtees Society, 1835)

RITCHIE, ANNA *The Picts* (Edinburgh, 1989

ROBBINS, CHRISTOPHER *Thorsons Introductory Guide to Herbalism* (1993)

ROBERTSON, A. J. (ed.) *Anglo-Saxon Charters* (Cambridge, 1939)

SAGGS, H. W. F. *The Encounter with the Divine in Mesopotamia and Israel* (1978)

SAUPE, ALBIN *Der Indiculus Superstitionum et Paganiarum* (Leipzig, 1891)

SAWYER, P. H. *Anglo-Saxon Charters* (London, 1966)

SAXO: *Saxo Grammaticus: Danorum Regum...Historia Books X-XVI* ed./trans. Eric Christiansen (3 vols., British Archaeological Reports, International Series 118(i), Oxford, 1981)

— *Saxonis Gesta Danorum* ed. J. Olrik & H. Raeder (2 vols., Copenhagen, 1931) [Complete Latin text]

— *The History of the Danes, Books 1-9* ed. H. R. Ellis Davidson, trans. Peter Fisher (2 vols., Cambridge, 1979-80) [vol.1 trans., vol.2 notes]

SCHNEIDER, KARL *Die Germanischen Runennamen* (Meisenheim am Glan, 1956)

SEARLE, WILLIAM G. *Onomasticon Anglo-Saxonicum* (Cambridge, 1897)

SHARPE, ERIC J. 'The Old English Runic Paternoster' pp.41–60 in *Symbols of Power* ed. H. R. Ellis Davidson (Cambridge, 1977)

SHIPPEY, T. A. *Poems of Wisdom and Learning in Old English* (Cambridge, 1976)

SIEVERS, E. 'Bedeutung der Buchstaben' *Zeitschrift für deutsches Alterthum u. deutsche Literatur* 18 (1875) p.297

— 'Bedeutung der Buchstaben' *ZfdA* 21 (1877) pp.189-90

SISAM, K. *Studies in the History of Old English Literature* (Oxford, 1953)

SKEAT, W. W. [note on *-ing*] *Notes & Queries* 6th series, vol.10 (1884) p.110

— 'The Anglo-Saxon names of the months' *Notes & Queries* 7th series, vol.7 (1889) p.301

SKEMP, A. R. 'The Old English Charms' *Modern Language Review* 6 (1911) pp.289-301

SMITHERS, G. V. *The Making of Beowulf* (Durham, 1961)

SPARKS, H. F. D. (trans.) *The Apochryphal Old Testament* (Oxford, 1984)

SPEAKE, GEORGE *A Saxon Bed Burial on Swallowcliffe Down* (1989)

SPIESBERGER, K. *Runenmagie* (Berlin, 1955)

STANLEY, E. G. 'Old English poetic diction and the interpretation of *The Wanderer, The Seafarer,* and *The Penitent's Prayer*' *Anglia* 73 (1955-6) pp.413-466

— *The Search for Anglo-Saxon Paganism* (Cambridge, 1975) [based on his articles in *Notes & Queries* 1964-5]

STANLEY, E. G. *In the Foreground: 'Beowulf'* (Cambridge, 1994)

STENTON, F. M. *Anglo-Saxon England* (2nd edn., 1947)

STEVENS, WESLEY M. *Bede's Scientific Achievement* (Jarrow Lecture, 1985)

— 'Sidereal time in Anglo-Saxon England' ch.8 in *Voyage to the Other World: The legacy of Sutton Hoo* ed. C. B. Kendall & P. S. Wells (Minneapolis, 1992)

STONE, ALBY *Wyrd: Fate and destiny in North European paganism* (Newark, 1989, 1991)

— 'The second Merseburg Charm' *Talking Stick* no.11 (1993)

— 'Archaeologists, ideology and paganism at Sutton Hoo' *Talking Stick* no.14 (1994)

— 'Seiðr' *Talking Stick* no.16 (1994)

— 'A Pagan Gothic Revival' *At the Edge* 2 (1996) pp.8–12

STORMS, G. *Anglo-Saxon Magic* (The Hague, 1948)

SWANTON, MICHAEL (ed./trans.) *Beowulf* (Manchester, 1978)

TACITUS: *Dialogues, Agricola and Germania* trans. W Hamilton Fyfe (Oxford, 1908)

TAYLOR, C. & R. MUIR *Visions of the Past* (1982)

TAYLOR, PAUL B. & W. H. AUDEN (trans.) *The Elder Edda: A selection* (1973)

TENGVIK, GÖSTA *Old English Bynames* (Uppsala, 1938)

TESTER, S. J. *A History of Western Astrology* (Woodbridge, 1987)

THORPE, B. (ed.) 'Liber Poenitentialis Theodori Archiepiscopi Cantuariensis Ecclesiae' pp.277–342 in *Ancient Laws & Institutes of England* (1840)

— (ed.) 'Confessionale Ecgberti' pp.343–389, *ibid.*

— (ed.) *The Sermones Catholici or Homilies of Ælfric* (2 vols, 1844, 1846)

THUN, NILS 'The Malignant Elves: Notes on Anglo-Saxon magic and Germanic myth' *Studia Neophilologica* 41 (1969) pp.378-96

TIERNEY, PATRICK *The Highest Altar: The story of human sacrifice* (1989)

TIMMER, B. J. 'Wyrd in Anglo-Saxon Prose and Poetry' *Neophilologus* 26 (1940–41) pp.24–33, pp.213–228.

TURNER, VICTOR W. 'An anthropological approach to the Icelandic saga' pp.349-374 in *The Translation of Culture* ed. T. O. Beidelman (1971)

TURVILLE-PETRE, E. O. G. *Myth and Religion of the North: The religion of ancient Scandinavia* (1964)

VAN DE NOORT, ROBERT 'The context of Early Medieval barrows in western Europe' *Antiquity* 67 (1993) pp.66-73

VERCOUTTER, J. 'Mathematics and Astronomy [of Egypt]' pp.17-44 in *Ancient and Medieval Science: From prehistory to AD 1450* ed. René Taton (1963)

VICKREY, JOHN F. 'The Narrative Structure of Hengest's Revenge in *Beowulf* *Anglo-Saxon England* 6 (1977) pp.91-103

VIERCK, HAYO 'The cremation in the ship at Sutton Hoo: a postscript' pp.343-355 in *Anglo-Saxon Cemeteries 1979* ed. P. Rahtz, 1980.

VIGFUSSON, G. & F. YORK POWELL (eds./trans.) *Corpus Poeticum Boreale* (2 vols., Oxford, 1883) [includes essay 'Beliefs and worship of the Old Northmen' at 1, pp.401–431]

DE VRIEND, H. J. *The Old English Herbarium and Medicina de Quadrupedis* (Early English Text Society ordinary series, 286, 1984)

WACHER, JOHN *The Roman Empire* (1987)

WACHSLER, ARTHUR A. 'Grettir's fight with a bear: Another neglected analogue of *Beowulf* in the Grettis Saga Asmundarsonar' *English Studies* 66 (1985) pp.381-390

WARD, F. A. B. *Time measurement, Pt 1 Historical review* (3rd edn., HMSO, 1947)

WARNER, RUBY D-N (ed.) *Early English Homilies from the 12th Century MS. Vesp. D.xiv.* (Early English Text Society ordinary series, 152, 1917)

WEBB, J. F. (trans.) *Lives of the Saints* (Harmondsworth, 1965) [Voyage of St Brendan, Bede's prose life of Cuthbert, Eddius Stephanus' Life of Wilfrid]

WESTON, JESSIE L. *The Quest of the Holy Grail* (1913, repr. 1964)

WHITE, LYNN, JR *Medieval Technology and Social Change* (Oxford, 1962)

WHITELOCK, DOROTHY *The Beginnings of English Society* (Harmondsworth, 1952)

WILKINS, ROBERT *The Fireside Book of Deadly Diseases* (1994)

WILKINSON, L. P. *The Roman Experience* (1975)

WILSON, DAVID *Anglo-Saxon Paganism* (1992)

WOOLF, H. B. *The Old Germanic Principles of Name-Giving* (Baltimore, 1939)

ZIPES, JACK *The Brothers Grimm: From enchanted forests to the modern world* (New York, 1988)

[ZUPITZA, J.] .'Kreuzandacht' *Archiv für das Studium neueren Sprachen* 88 (1892) pp.361–365

Part Two

TEXTS

Charms

Where better to start than with four short charms in early German that illustrate many of the tendencies of style (repetition and rhyme as well as alliteration, invocations of powerful aid from any source, the demonstration of knowledge and power in the speaker)? This shared style is more significant than pure date, and does indicate a common background of charm as technological tool, packed with sonic expertise.

1. The Tegernsee Charm

(9th century MS., Münich Clm. 18524, 2)

cf. charm no.13, below, against a wen.

> *Gang uz, Nesso, mit niun nessinchilinon,*
> *uz fonna marge in deo adra, vonna den adrun in daz fleisk,*
> *fonna demu fleiske in daz fel, fonna demo velle in diz tulli.*
> *Ter pater noster.*

> Crawl out, worm, with the nine wormlets,
> out from the marrow into the veins, from the veins into the flesh,
> from the flesh into the skin, from the skin onto this arrow.
> Then you recite The Lord's Prayer three times.

2. The First Merseburg Charm

(10th century MS., Merseburg)

Probably a loosening charm, cf. Bede *Ecclesiastical History*, Bk.4 ch.20; cf. also Bee-Charm no.14, and the '*Wið Færstice*' charm no.10: Grimm, 1900, I p.401 considers the *idisi* to be connected with Valkyries, as also Turville-Petre, 1964, p.221.

> *Eiris sazun idisi, sazun hera duoder;*
> *suma hapt heptidun, suma heri lezidun,*
> *suma clubodun umbi cuoniouuidi.*
> *insprinc haptbandun, inuar uigandun.*

> Once the Idisi ('ladies') alighted here, settled themselves here (and) there;
> some (of them) fettered the prisoners, some hindered the war-group,
> some laid hold of the bonds.
> Make loose the fetters, drive off the enemy!

3. The Second Merseburg Charm

An anecdote charm, cf. Woden and serpent episode in 9 Herbs Charm, no.6, below

> *Phol ende uuodan   uuorun zi holza.*
> *du uuart demo balderes uolon   sin uuoz birenkit.*
> *thu biguol en sinthgunt,   sunna era suister,*
> *thu biguol en friia,   uolla era suister,*
> *thu biguol en uuodan,   so he uuola conda:*
> *sose benrenki,   sose bluotrenki,   sose lidirenki:*
> *ben zi bena,   bluot si bluoda,*
> *lid zi geliden,   sose gelimida sin!*

Phol[1] and Woden travelled to the forest.
Then was for Baldur's foal its foot wrenched.
Then encharmed it Sindgund (and) Sunna her sister,
then encharmed it Frija (and) Volla her sister,
then encharmed it Woden, as he the best could:
As the bone-wrench, so for the blood-wrench, (and) so the limb-wrench
bone to bone, blood to blood,
limb to limb, so be glued.[2]

4. The Lorsch Charm

(9th century MS. from Lorsch, now in the Vatican)
cf. Old English Bee Charm, no.14, below

> *Kirst, imbi ist hucze!*
> *nu fluic du, uihu minaz, hera,   fridu frono*
> *in godes munt   heim zi comonne gisunt.*
> *sizi, sizi, bina: inbot dir sancte maria.*
> *hurolob ni habe du: zi holce ni fluc du.*
> *noh du mir nindrinnes,   noh du mir nintuuinnest.*
> *sizi uilo stillo,   vuirki godes uuillon.*

---

[1] There are some problems of identity here; Grimm, 1, p.228 fn. suggests *Phol* is another name for Baldur; Stone, 1993, suggests *Phol* is the same as *fol* i.e. the foal of line 2; and a further possibility is that *Baldur*, like the Old English common noun, *bealdor*, could mean simply 'leader'. To make best narrative sense, the foal should belong to a 'stranger', and the various attempts to heal it are crowned with success when Woden's fortuitous additional help arrives.

[2] Stanley (1975, p.84) and Stone (1993) both note a similar Norwegian charm, written down in the 19th century: its text is: Jesus himself rode to the heath, / And as he rode, his horse's bone was broken. / Jesus dismounted and healed that: / Jesus laid marrow to marrow, / Bone to bone, flesh to flesh. / Jesus thereafter laid a leaf / So that these should stay in their place.

Could this be taken to imply that in the Merseburg Charm, it is Woden's horse that is injured, and Woden himself that effects the cure?

Christ, the bees are swarming:
Now fly you, beasts mine, hither again, with holy peace
in God's protection home to come safe.
Settle, settle, bees! (so) bids you Holy Mary.
Permission not have you, to the forest not fly you.
Nor you me should-elude, nor you me should-evade.
Sit very still, fulfil God's will!

5. The Land Ceremonies Charm

(BL Cotton MS. Caligula A.vii – early 11th century)

With this we begin an impressive sequence of Old English charms. The text was written down in the 11th century, perhaps as a sort of compendium of different elements brought together to make one large impressive ritual.

The purpose of such rites was a sort of pre-modern insurance – for what would sheer effort of cultivation avail if mischance of weather or plant disease spoiled the crop? Christianity was aware of such needs just as much as paganism was, and the words and actions are often specifically Christian in this text. The charm reaches a climax with the invocation of the unknown 'Erce' over the body of the plough, which Herbert (1994, p.14) sees as a symbolic rendering fertile of the plough for its forthcoming union with the soil (cf. Magoun, 1943, p.34, who views the salve as "a fertilizing liquid."). However, it is worth noting that the words of the Erce verse have no direct application to a plough as such, and rather could be evidence that pre-existing texts are being adapted here to suit the concerns of developing Anglo-Saxon technology.

Bearing all these problems in mind, I hope, will not detract from your enjoyment of the verse, which is among the most direct and effective of its kind in the literature of magic. (By contrast, the prose instructions seem sometimes to be deliberately complex, as if the effect depends on making the ritual exacting, as befits the dignity of a large estate.)

Her ys seo bot, hu ðu meaht þine æceras betan gif hi nellaþ wel wexan oþþe þær hwilc ungedefe þing on gedon bið on dry oððe on lyblace.

Here is the remedy, how you can improve your fields if they will not produce properly or if any improper influence has been exercised upon them by magic or witchcraft.

Genim þonne on niht, ær hyt dagige, feower tyrf on feower healfa þæs landes, and gemearca hu hy ær stodon. Nim þonne ele and hunig and beorman, and ælces feos meolc þe on þæm lande sy, and ælces treowcynnes dæl þe on þæm lande sy gewexen, butan heardan beaman, and ælcre namcuþre wyrte dæl, butan glappan anon, and do þonne haligwæter ðær on, and drype þonne þriwa on þone staðol þara turfa, and cweþe ðonne ðas word:

Crescite, wexe, et multiplicamini, and gemænigfealda, et replete, and gefylle, terre, þas eorðan. In nomine patris et filii et spiritus sancti sit benedicti.

And Pater noster swa oft swa þæt oðer.

Take by night, before it dawns, four turfs from the four corners of the plot, and make a note of where they belonged. Then take oil and honey and yeast, and milk from each beast that is on the land, and a portion of each type of tree that is growing on the land, apart from the harder woods, and a portion of each nameable plant, excepting buck-bean only, and then apply holy water and let it drip thrice on the underside of the turfs and say then these words:

Crescite, grow, *et multiplicamini,* and multiply, *et replete,* and fill, *terre,* the earth.

And say the Lord's Prayer the same number of times.

And bere siþþan ða turf to circean, and mæssepreost asinge feower mæssan ofer þan turfon, and wende man þæt grene to ðan weofode, and siþþan gebringe man þa turf þær hi ær wæron ær sunnan setlgange. And hæbbe him gæworht of cwicbeame feower Cristes mælo and awrite on ælcon ende: Matheus and Marcus, Lucas and Iohannes. Lege þæt Cristes mæl on þone pyt neoþeweardne, cweðe ðonne:

Crux Matheus, crux Marcus, crux Lucas, crux sanctus Iohannes.

And then carry the turfs to a church and let the mass-priest sing four masses over the turfs, and let the green side be turned to the altar; and then let the turfs be returned to where they originally were before the sun's setting. And let him have made of aspen four tokens of Christ [i.e. crosses] and write on each arm: Matthew and Mark, Luke and John. Lay the token of Christ in the bottom of the hole, then say: Cross of Matthew, cross of Mark, cross of Luke, cross of Saint John.

Nim ðonne þa turf and sete ðærufon on and cweþe ðonne nigon siþon þas word, Crescite, and swa oft Pater noster, and wende þe þonne eastweard, and onlut nigon siðon eadmodlice, and cweð þonne þas word:

Eastweard ic stande, arena ic me bidde,
bidde ic þone mæran domine, bidde ðone miclan drihten,
bidde ic ðone haligan heofonrices weard,
eorðan ic bidde and upheofon
and ða soþan sancta Marian
and heofones meaht and heahreced,
þæt ic mote þis gealdor mid gife drihtnes
toðum ontynan, þurh trumne geþanc
aweccan þas wæstmas, us to woruldnytte

gefyll[an][1] *þas foldan,   mid fæste geleafan*
wlitigan þas wancgturf,   swa se witega cwæð
þæt se hæfde are on eorþrice,   se þe ælmyssan
dælde domlice   drihtnes þances.

Then take the turfs and lay (them) on top and then say nine times these words: *Crescite*, and the same number of times the Lord's Prayer, and then turn yourself to the east and bow humbly nine times and then say these words:

Eastwards I face, for favours I ask,
I ask the glorious Lord, I ask the great God,
I ask the Holy Guardian of Heaven,
I ask the earth and heaven above
and the just, holy Mary
and heaven's might and the high-hall,
that I might be able this charm, by God's grace,
with my teeth intone, [and] with fixed purpose
make these crops start growing, [and] for our benefit,
fill the earth, [and] with firm faith
beautify the surface, for the prophet said[2]
that he should have recompense on earth who alms
distributed justly, according to the Lord's will.

Wende þe þonne III sunganges, astrece þonne on andlang and arim þær letanias and cweð þonne: Sanctus, sanctus, sanctus oþ ende. Sing þonne Benedicite aþenedon earmon and Magnificat and Pater noster III, and bebeod hit Criste and sancta Marian and þære halgan rode to lofe and to weorþinga and to are þam þe þæt land age and eallon þam þe him underðeodde synt.

Then turn yourself round three times clockwise, then lie at full length and recite the Litany and then say the Sanctus through to its end. Then chant the Benedicite with your arms outstretched and the Magnificat and the Lord's Prayer three times, and commend it [the land] to Christ and holy Mary and to the praise of the holy rood and to the honour and benefit of him that owns the land and to all them that are subject to him.

Ðonne þæt eall sie gedon, þonne nime man uncuþ sæd æt ælmesmannum and selle him twa swylc, swylce man æt him nime, and gegaderie ealle his sulhgeteogo togædere; borige þonne on þam beame stor and finol and gehalgode sapan and gehalgod sealt.

---

[1] MS. *gefylle*

[2] Perhaps in reference to *Matthew* 6:4, or *Luke* 6:38.

When all that is done, take some unidentified seed from a charity-seeker and give him twice [the value of] whatever is taken from him, and then gather all the ploughing gear together; then insert in the wood frankincense and fennel and hallowed paste and hallowed salt.

Nim þonne þæt sæd, sete on þæs sules bodig, cweð þonne:

> *Erce, Erce, Erce,   eorþan modor,*
> *geunne þe se alwalda,   ece drihten,*
> *æcera wexendra   and wriðendra,*
> *eacniendra   and elniendra,*
> *sceafta he[hra],   scir[ra]*[1] *wæstma,*
> *and þære bradan   berewæstma,*
> *and þære hwitan   hwætewæstma,*
> *and ealra   eorþan wæstma.*
> *Geunne him   ece drihten*
> *and his halige,   þe on [h]eofonum synt,*
> *þæt hys yrþ si gefriþod   wið ealra feonda gehwæne,*
> *and heo si geborgen   wið ealra bealwa gehwylc,*
> *þara lyblaca   geond land sawen.*
> *Nu ic bidde ðone waldend,   se ðe ðas woruld gesceop,*
> *þæt ne sy nan to þæs cwidol wif   ne to þæs cræftig man*
> *þæt awendan ne mæge   word*[2] *þus gecwedene.*

Then take the seed, put it in the body of the plough, then say:

> Erce, Erce, Erce,[3] Mother of Earth,
> may the Almighty, the eternal Lord, grant you
> fields growing and thriving,
> increasing and strengthening,
> tall stems (and) fine crops,
> both the broad barley
> and the fair wheat,
> and of all the crops of the earth.
> May the eternal God grant,
> and his saints, that are in heaven,
> that his crops be protected against all and any enemies,

---

[1] MS. *hen se scire*

[2] In the MS, *woruld* is altered to produce 'word'.

[3] *Erce* is problematical. "Attempts have been made to interpret Erce as the name of a forgotten earth goddess, but the word may be no more than a cry of invocation." (Ellis Davidson 1964, p.114.) It is not an obvious Old English word or name, though the name *Ertae* is claimed as an interpretation of the difficult right-hand end panel of the Franks Casket; and similar words are found in formulas supposed to derive from Irish (Meroney, 1945); but its impact may indeed derive from its unusualness as much as its meaning.

and be guarded against all ills of any kind,
against the sorcery spread throughout the land.
Now I pray the Creator who made this world
that there should be no woman so word-skilled, no man so cunning
as to be able to change the words thus spoken.

Þonne man þa sulh forð drife and þa forman furh onsceote, cweð þonne:

> *Hal wes þu, folde,   fira modor!*
> *Beo þu growende   on godes fæþme,*
> *fodre gefylled   firum to nytte.*

When you drive the plough forth and cut the first furrow, say:

> Greetings to you, earth, mother of men!
> May you be full of growth in God's protecting arms,
> filled with food for the benefit of mankind.

Nim þonne ælces cynnes melo and abacæ man innewerd[r]e[1] handa bradnæ hlaf and gecned hine mid meolce and mid haligwætere and lecge under þa forman furh. Cweþe þonne:

> *Ful æcer fodres   fira cinne,*
> *beorhtblowende,   þu gebletsod weorþ*
> *þæs haligan noman   þe ðas heofon gesceop*
> *and ðas eorþan   þe we on lifiaþ;*
> *se god, se þas grundas geworhte,   geunne us growende gife,*
> *þæt us corna gehwylc   cume to nytte.*

Cweð þonne III Crescite in nomine patris, sit benedicti. Amen and Pater noster þriwa.

Then take meal of each type and bake a loaf as broad as the palm of the hand, and kneed it with milk and holy water and lay it in the first furrow. Then say:

> Field full of food for mankind,
> brightly seeding, you shall be blessed
> in the holy name [of him] that created this heaven
> and this earth that we live on;
> may the god who made these grounds grant us the gift of growth
> so that for us each grain (of seed) shall come to fulfilment.

Say then thrice: Grow in the name of the Father, be blessed. Amen and the Lord's Prayer thrice.

---

[1] MS. *-dne*

6. The Nine Herbs Charm

(BL MS. Harley 585 – ca.1000 AD)

This long verse charm is one of the most enigmatic of Old English texts. It is ostensibly for an actual wound (see prose conclusion), but claims to tackle up to nine different poisons or infections – hence the nine base ingredients, presumably. Many sense-emendations are necessary: perhaps because the text has been poorly transmitted and contains a good few errors; but there is also some problem with the order of sections and what, cinematographically, would be called 'continuity' – which could also point to a text made of diverse material i.e. a composite origin. The intended unity is emphasised by the recapitulatory list of ingredients in the closing prose; yet it is hard to reconcile these with the earlier herb stanzas; and neither list is easily compatible with the emphasis on the number 'nine' in the incantatory section that forms the central climax of the work (Meroney, 1944, feels that 'apple' should be excluded from a count of 'herbs'). In Swedish tradition, nine types of wood were sometimes used to kindle special fire (Grimm, 1883, 2, 607): could the present charm be a construct, almost a fantasia, around the figure 9?

In view of these problems, I have retained the MS use of a cross to mark sections, and the sparse use of capitals, in case these provide the reader with a better idea of sectional structure than my own punctuation/division can. I have moved to the fore one line: occurring originally where I have dots in the text, this seems to me a title that has later been wrongly incorporated in the text (cf. Meroney, 1944, p.160).

ðas VIIII ongan   wið nygon attrum.[1]

these nine [stand] in opposition against 9 poisons.

Gemyne ðu, mucgwyrt,   hwæt þu ameldodest,
hwæt þu renadest   æt regenmelde.
Una þu hattest,   yldost wyrta.
Ðu miht wið III   and wið XXX,
þu miht wiþ attre   and wið onflyge,[2]
þu miht wiþ þa[m] laþan   ðe geond lond færð.

---

[1] This line moved from below
[2] A Glosecki, 1989, p.121, suggests *onflyge* may be an actual flying dart or arrow.

Recall, mugwort,[1] what you declared,
what you established, at the Great Council.[2]
'Unique'[3] you are called, most senior of herbs.
You prevail against 3 and against 30[4]
you prevail against poison and against infection,
you prevail against the harmful one[5] that throughout the land travels.

Ond þu, wegbrade, wyrta modor,
eastan op[e]n[o],[6] innan mihtigu;
ofer ðy cræte curran, ofer ðy cwene reodan,
ofer ðy bryde bryodedon, ofer þy fearras fnærdon.
Eallum þu þon wiðstode and wiðstunedest;
swa ðu wiðstonde attre and onflyge
and þæm laðan þe geond lond fereð.

And you, waybroad/plantain, mother of herbs,
open by the east, inwardly powerful,
over you wagons rolled, over you women rode,
over you brides made cry, over you bulls snorted.
All you then withstood and confronted,
so may you withstand poison and infection
and the harmful one that throughout the land travels.

stune hætte þeos wyrt: heo on stane geweox;
stond heo wið attre, stunað heo wærce.
stiðe heo hatte, wiðstunað heo attre,
wreceð heo wraðan, weorpeð ut attor.

---

[1] Of mugwort we are later told:
    For womens matters it is excellent.
    And he that shall this herbe about him beare,
    Is freed from hurt or daunger any way,
    No poisned Toade nor Serpent shall him feare
    No wearinesse his limmes shall ought assay..."
                R. Chester 'A Dialogue' line 197ff re Mugwort.

[2] Braekman, 1980, relates this to one of the Lord's last pronunciations before the Ascension (Mark 16:18), as a "'Great Proclamation'... of the virtues of herbs by Our Lord." (p.463)

[3] Re *Una*: Braekman, 1980, p.464, links this to a Latin charm in a 15th century MS involving the herb '*pervinca*' (periwinkle). Should *Una* begin a new herb entry?

[4] Multiples of three are common in 'Solomon & Saturn 2' – here reinforcing power of nine?

[5] 'harmful one' is identified by Bonser (1963, p.71) as an epidemic, perhaps the yellow plague, personified in Welsh sources as "a most strange creature from the sea marsh... his hair, his teeth, and his eyes being as gold."

[6] MS. *opone*

'Stune' (lamb's cress) is called this herb: it on stone grows;
it resists poison, combats pain.
'Resolute' it is called, it assails poison,
it drives away the evil one(s), casts out poison.

+ *þis is seo wyrt   seo wiþ wyrm gefeaht;*
þeos mæg wið attre,   heo mæg wið onflyge,
heo mæg wið ða[m] laþan   ðe geond lond fereþ.
fleoh þu nu, attorlaðe,   seo læsse ða maran,
seo mare þa læssan,   oððæt him beigra bot sy.

This is the herb that against the serpent fought;
this avails against poison, it avails against infection,
it avails against the harmful one that travels round the land.
Now put to flight, Attorlothe,[1] as lesser the greater,
as greater the lesser, until there be a cure for him of both.

Gemyne þu, mægðe,   hwæt þu ameldodest,
hwæt ðu geændadest   æt alorforda:
þæt næfre for gefloge   feorh ne gesealde
syþðan him mon mægðan   to mete gegyrede.

Recall, Mayweed/Chamomile, what you declared,
what you made certain at Alderford:
that never for infection anyone should yield their life
once Mayweed had been prepared for them to eat.

Þis is seo wyrt   ðe wergulu hatte;
ðas onsænde seolh   ofer sæs hrygc
ondan attres   oþres to bote.

This is the herb that is called '*wergulu*';[2]
this the seal sent over the sea's horizon,
to the harm of the other poison, a remedy.
..............[3]

---

[1] De Vriend, 1984, herb no.45, glosses *Attorlaþe* as Cockspur Grass; Dobbie 1942
p.cxxxiii as Betony; in literal Old English it is 'poison-loather'.

[2] *Wergulu* can only be identified by reference to the closing prose list; as nettle, perhaps?

[3] From here I have moved a line to the opening, which seems to me title material. Some
would feel that not only this line but the following section on Woden are out of place, and
should come after the last herbs (chervil and fennel) are named. However, the section with
Woden serves to illustrate the potency of apple, so can form part of the main listing.

+ *wyrm com snican,   toslat he nan,*[1]
ða genam woden   VIIII wuldortanas,
sloh ða þa næddran   þæt heo on VIIII tofleah.
Þær geændade   æppel and attor
þæt heo næfre ne wolde   on hus bugan.

A serpent came crawling (but) it destroyed no one
when Woden took nine twigs of glory,
(and) then struck the adder so that it flew into nine (pieces).
There achieved apple and poison
that it never would re-enter the house.

+ *fille and finule,   felamihtigu twa:*
þa wyrte gesceop   witig drihten,
halig on heofonum,   þa he hongode;
sette and sænde   on VII worulde
earmum and eadigum   eallum to bote.
stond heo wið wærce,   stunað heo wið attre,
seo mæg wið III   and wið XXX,
wið [feondes][2] *hond   and wið freab[r]egde,*[3]
wið malscrunge · minra[4] *wihta.*

Chervil and Fennel, very powerful pair:
those herbs the wise Lord created,
holy in the heavens, when he was hanging;[5]
He confirmed and sent (them) into the seven worlds
for rich and poor, for all a remedy.
It resists pain, it contends against poison,
it avails against three and against thirty,
against the fiend's/enemy's hand and against mighty trickery,
against enchantment by evil beings.

---

[1] Dobbie emends *nan* to *man*, which is more purposeful.

[2] MS. *wið þæs hond; feondes* restores alliteration.

[3] MS. *wið frea begde; færbregde* 'sudden trickery' restores sense, but the element *frea-* might be capable of retention.

[4] Dobbie changes to *manra*, from adj. *man*, 'evil'; Bosworth & Toller, Supplement, give *min* = evil.

[5] In a Christian context 'hanging in heaven' would refer to the crucifixion; but (remembering that Woden was mentioned a few lines previously) there is also a parallel, perhaps a better one, with Odin, as his crucifixion was associated with learning.

+ *nu magon þas VIIII wyrta   wið nygon wuldorgeflogenum,*
wið VIIII attrum   and wið nygon onflygnum:
wið ðy readan attre,   wið ð[y]¹ runlan attre,
wið ðy hwitan attre,   wið ðy wedenan² attre,
wið ðy geolwan attre,   wið ðy grenan attre,
wið ðy wonnan attre,   wið ðy wedenan attre,
wið ðy brunan attre,   wið ðy basewan attre;
wið wyrmgeblæd,   wið wætergeblæd,
wið þorngeblæd,   wið þys[tel]geblæd,³
wið ysgeblæd,   wið attorgeblæd,
gif ænig attor cume   eastan fleogan
oððe ænig norðan cume⁴
oððe ænig westan   ofer werðeode.

Now these nine herbs avail against nine super-spirits[5]
against nine poisons and against nine infections:
against the red poison, against the ?foul poison,
against the white poison, against the blue poison,
against the yellow poison, against the green poison,
against the dark poison, against the blue poison,
against the brown poison, against the scarlet poison;
against the snake-radiance,[6] against water-radiance,
against thorn-radiance, against thistle-radiance,
against ice-radiance, against poison-radiance,
whether any poison come airborn from the east
or any from the north come
or any from the west upon mankind.

---

[1] MS. ða

[2] Grattan & Singer 1952 change first ex. of *wedenan* to *hæwenan* 'purple' to avoid
repetition.

[3] MS. *þys geblæd*

[4] Grattan & Singer 1952 expand this line with *genægan cume* = come approaching; but it
may form one heavy line with the preceding.

[5] Clark Hall's dictionary suggests 'one who has fled from glory' i.e. demon.

[6] *Blæd* should not imply 'blister' (*blædre*) but have the meaning of a blast of air. Thus in
Ælfric's 'Life of Cuthbert' it is used of (seals') breath and (fire's) blast, in the latter
case paralleling *ða ættrigan flan deoflicere costnunge* (the poisonous arrows of devilish
temptation).

+ *crist stod ofer a[dl]e*[1]   *ængan cundes.*
Ic ana wat   ea rinnende
7 [þær] þa nygon   nædran behealdað.
motan ealle weoda nu   wyrt[r]um[2] *aspringan,*
sæs toslupan,   eal sealt wæter,
ðonne ic þis attor   of ðe geblawe.

Christ stood over disease of any kind.
I alone know of a running stream
and there the nine adders keep guard.
May all plants now dwindle to their roots,
seas [and] all salt water disperse
when I blow this poison from you.

mugcwyrt, wegbrade þe eastan open sy, lombescyrse, attorlaðan, mageðan,
netelan, wudusuræppel, fille and finul, ealde sapan: gewyrc ða wyrta to
duste, mængc wiþ þa sapan and wiþ þæs æpples gor. Wyrc slypan of wætere
and of axsan; genim finol, wyl on þære slyppan and beþe mid
[æg]gemo[n]gc,[3] *þonne he þa sealfe on d[o],*[4] *ge ær ge æfter. sing þæt*
galdor on ælcre þara wyrta, III ær he hy wyrce and on þone æppel ealswa;
ond singe þon men in þone muð and in þa earan buta and on ða wunde þæt
ilce gealdor, ær he þa sealfe on d[o].[5]

Mugwort, plantain that is open at the east, lamb's cress, ?betony, mayweed
(chamomile), nettle, crab-apple, chervil and fennel, old salve: pound the
herbs to a powder, mix with the salve and with the apple's juice. Make a
paste of water and ashes; take the fennel, boil in the paste and anoint (him)
with (this?) egg-mixture, when putting the (herb) ointment on, either before or
after. Sing the charm over each of the herbs, thrice before processing them,
and on the apple likewise; and sing the same charm into the man's mouth and
into both ears and over the wound, before putting the ointment on.

---

[1] MS. *alde*

[2] MS. *wyrtum*; *wyrtrum* 'roots' seems to give better sense than *wyrtum* 'plants'; *aspringan*
can mean either to 'spring up' or 'to dwindle' – confusingly!

[3] MS. *aagemogc*

[4] MS. *de*

[5] MS. *de*

7. Wið Cyrnel (against a Lump)
(BL MS Harley 585 – ca. 1000 AD)

This is virtually a counting charm, a formula for diminution.

> *Wið cyrnel:*
>> *Neogone wæran Noðþæs sweoster;*
>> *þa wurdon þa nygone to VIII*
>> *7 þa VIII to VII,*
>> *7 þa VII to VI,*
>> *7 þa VI to V,*
>> *7 þa V to IIII.*
>> *7 þa IIII to III,*
>> *7 þa III to II,*
>> *7 þa II to I,*
>> *7 þa I to nanum.*

> *Þis þe lib be cyrneles 7 be scrofelles 7 weorme[s] 7 æghwylces yfeles. Sing bendicite nygon siþum.*

For Lumps:
> Nine were Noth's[1] sisters
> Then changed the 9 into 8
> and the 8 into 7
> and the 7 into 6
> and the 6 into 5
> and the 5 into 4
> and the 4 into 3
> and the 3 into 2
> and the 2 into 1
> and the 1 into none.

[Let] this [be] your remedy for a lump and for scrofula and for worms and for every kind of harm. Sing the Benedicite nine times.

---

[1] *Noð* is recorded as a personal name (meaning 'boldness, daring') in Searle 1897 p.359 (and cf. *Nottes*, genitive, *ibid.* p.xxii), but has, as far as I can discover, no supernatural connotations. Some lost story in which an (evil?) family is reduced might be posited, to parallel the decrease in lumps. Grattan & Singer (1952, p.184) suggest *noð* as deriving from Latin *nodus*, 'ganglion'.

8. A List of Herbs

(BL MS Harley 585 – ca. 1000 AD)

This is a list or recipe rather than a specific charm; but it is a tour de force that may not simply be poetic: the alliteration and rhyme surely implies something special about the order or the unity or the process. If no more than a fancy way of remembering a large number of ingredients, is that not a sort of practical magic? It soon develops into a complex ritual, whose Latin and beyond-Latin content is typical of a series of short prose charms. Indeed, we may note, with Grattan & Singer, that "The juxtaposition of (a) the gibberish chant, (b) the use of spittle, (c) the blowing on the wound, and (d) the Christian chant of the priest, is impressive as a summary of Anglo-Saxon magic." (1952, p.124, note 8)

To haligre sealfe:

Sceal betonican   7 benedicte
7 hindhæleðe, hænep
7 hindebrer, isenhearde,
salfige   7 safine,
bisceopwyrt   7 boðen,
finul   7 fifleafe,
healswyrt   7 hune,
mucgwyrt, medewyrt   7 mergelle,
agrimoni[a]¹   7 æðelferðingwyrt,
rædic 7 ribbe   7 seo reade gearuwe,
dile, oportanie,   draganse,
cassuc 7 cawlic,   cyleðenie 7 wyirrind
[wudu-]weax, wudurofe   7 wrættes cið
saturege   7 sigelhweorfa,
brunewyrt 7 rude   7 berbene,
streawberian wise   7 blæces snegles dust,
ealhtre, fanan,   merce, pollegian,
attorlaðe,   haran spicel,
wudufille,   wermod,
eoforþrote,   æncglisc cost,
hæwene hnydele   [hofe, cymen]²
vi[n]ca pervi[n]ca,   feferfuge
7 lilige, levastica,   ale[h]sandrie,³
petresilige,   grundeswylige.

Þysra feo[we]r wyrta man sceal mæst don to 7 eallra oðra ælcre efenfela.

---

¹ MS. *agrimonis*
² Follows *feferfuge* in MS.
³ MS. *ale'n'sandrie*

For a holy salve:

Must (be used) betony and bennet,
and hindheal (and) hemp
and raspberry, ironhard,
sage and savine,
bishopwort and rosemary,
fennel and fiveleaf (cinquefoil),
halswort (throatwort) and horehound,
mugwort, meadowsweet and maregall,
agrimony and aethelfarthingwort,
radish and ribwort and the red yarrow,
dill, abrotanon and dragonwort,
hassuck and cawlic, celandine and wir-rind,
wood-waxen,[1] woodruff and wræt-sprout
saturea and solsequia,
brownwort and rue and vervain,
strawberry-stalk and dark snail's dust,
lupin, flag, marche, pennyroyal,
cockspur grass, viper's bugloss,
wood chervil, wormwood,
boarthroat and English costmary,
purple deadnettle, hove, cumin,
perwinkle and feverfew,
lily, lovage, alexanders,
parsley, groundsel.

Of these last four plants, one should put in most, and an equal amount of all the others.

7 ðus man sceal ða buteran gewrycean to ðære haligan sealfe: æt anes heowe[s] cy, þæt heo sy eall reod oððe hwit 7 unmæle, mon ða buteran aðwere, 7 gif ðu næbbe buteran genoge, awæsc swiðe clæne [7] mængc oðre wið. 7 ða wyrta ealle gescearfa swiðe smale tosomne, 7 wæter gehalga fonthalgunge, 7 do ceac innan in ða buteran. Genim þonne ænne sticcan 7 gewyrc hine feðorbyrste; writ onforan ðas halgan naman: Matheus, Marcus, Lucas, Iohannes. Styre þonne mid ðy sticcan ða buteran, eal þæt fæt. Ðu sing ofer ðas sealmas, Beati immaculati, ælcne ðriowa ofer, 7 Gloria in excelsis Deo, 7 Credo in Deum Patrem, 7 letanias arime ofer, þær is[2] ðara haligra naman 7 Deus meus et pater, et In principio, 7 þæt wyrmgealdor.

---

[1] Wax would be an anomaly in such a list; Clark Hall gives *wuduweax* as 'genista tinctoria'.
[2] MS. his

And thus one must make the butter for the holy salve: of a one-coloured cow, that is all red or white, without marking, churn the butter; and if you have not enough butter, wash some other butter very clean and mix with it. And shred all the plants up very small, together, and put a bowl-full into the butter. Then take a stick and fashion it with four prongs; write upon (them) these holy names: Matthew, Mark, Luke, John. Then stir the butter with the stick (and mix) all the vessel. You should sing over (it) these psalms, Psalm 119, each (?verse) thrice, and the Gloria and the Credo, and recite litanies over (it), that is the names of the saints and 'Deus meus et pater' and 'In principio' [sections of the Mass], and the worm charm.

7 þis gealdor singe ofer:

Acre arcre arnem nona ærnem beoðor ærnem nidren arcun cunað ele harassan fidine.

Sing ðis nygon siðan 7 do ðin spatl on 7 blaw on 7 lege ða wyrta be ðæm ceace 7 gehalg[ie][1] *hy syððan mæssepreost.*

And sing this charm upon (it):

"_____?"[2]

Sing this nine times and add your spittle to (it?) and blow on (the remaining herbs?) and place the plants by the bowl and let a priest hallow them.

Singe ðas oration[e]s ofer:

Domine sancte, pater omnipotens, eterne deus, per inpositionem manum mearum refugiat inimicus diabolus a capillis, a capite, ab oculis, a naribus, a labi[i]s, a linguis, a sublinguis, a collo, a pectore, a pedibus, a calcaneis, ab uniuersis con[p]aginibus membrorum eis, ut non habeat potestatem diabolus, nec loquendi nec tacendi, nec dormiendi nec resurgendi, nec in die nec in nocte, nec in somno nec in gressu, nec in uisu nec in risu, nec in tangendo nec in legendo. Sed in nomine domini Iesu Christi, qui nos suo sancto sanguine redemit, qui cum patre uiuit et regnat deus in secula seculorum. Amen.

Sing these prayers over (?them):

Holy Lord, Almighty Father, Eternal God, by the laying on of my hands let the hostile devil flee from the hair, from the head, from the eyes, from the nostrils, from the lips, from the tongue, from below the tongue, from the neck, from the chest, from the feet, from the heels, from all the joints of his limbs, so that the devil should have no power, neither over his speaking nor his silence, neither his sleeping nor his rising, neither by day or by night, neither in sleep nor in motion, neither over seeing nor smiling, neither over

---

[1] MS. *gehalga*

[2] Unfortunately gibberish, as otherwise it might throw light on 'Erce' in the Land Ceremonies Charm; but no translation is possible, though a few words might be Gaelic.

touching nor reading. But (be safe) in the name of the Lord Jesus Christ, who redeemed us with his holy blood, (and) who lives and reigns with God the Father for ever and ever. Amen.)[1]

9. Wið Dweorh (Against a Dwarf or a Fever)

(BL MS.Harley 585 – ca. 1000 AD)

This again is an intriguing combination of overt Christian material, and potentially pagan or at least popular material. The verse, indeed, has a surreal effect, though this may result simply from the probable corruption of the opening line, psychoneurotic emendations thereof, and the basic uncertainty who is being addressed – the patient or the cause of the disease. There are interesting discussions of this charm in Cameron (pp.151–3) and Meaney (1981, pp.15–17).

> *Wið dweorh man sceal niman VII lytle oflætan, swylce man mid ofrað, and writtan þas naman on ælcre oflætan: Maximianus, Malchus, Iohannes, Martimianus, Dionisius, Constantinus, Serafion. Þænne eft þæt galdor, þæt her æfter cweð, man sceal singan, ærest on þæt wynstre eare, þænne on þæt swiðre eare, þænne [b]ufan[2] þæs mannes moldan. And ga þænne an mædenman to and ho hit on his sweoran, and do man swa þry dagas; him bið sona sel.*

Against a dwarf one must take seven small holy wafers, such as one makes holy communion with, and write these names on each wafer: Maximian, Malchus, John, Martimian, Dionysius, Constantine, Serafion.[3] Then again the charm, which hereafter is quoted, one must sing, first in the left ear, then in the right ear, then upon the top of the man's head. And then go to a maiden and (let her) hang it around his neck, and do so for three days; it will speedily be better for the patient.

> *Her com in gangan, in spiden wiht,[4]*
> *hæfde him his haman on handa, cwæð þæt þu his hæncgest wære,*
> *leg[d]e þe his teage an sweoran. Ongunnan him of þæm lande liþan;*
> *sona swa hy of þæm lande coman, þa ongunnan him ða liþu colian.*

---

[1] Other Latin prayers follow, which may or may not be associated with this action.

[2] MS. *hufan*

[3] The names are those of the 'seven sleepers'. Storms speculates that they could be invoked to produce calm sleep and that thus the charm is for a fever. (1948, p.168).

[4] The first line of the chant is probably beyond recovery. *spiden* is often altered to 'spider', after Cockayne's suggestion, but the allusion to riding makes no obvious sense then; *inwriþen*, a swathed creature – Grattan's emendation – leads only to worse nightmares. I conjecture that *spiden* may go back to *swiðe* (strong, powerful), since minuscule 'þ' and 'w' are very alike. *Wiht*, corresponding to Icelandic *vættr*, may denote a supernatural being in its own right.

Þa com in gangan   deores[1] sweostar;
þa geændade heo   and aðas swor
ðæt næfre þis ðæm adlegan   derian ne moste,
ne þæm þe þis galdor   begytan mihte,
oððe þe þis galdor   ongalan cuþe.
Amen. Fiað.

Here came entering in a ?powerful being
he had for him his coat at hand, said that you were his steed,[2]
laid his reins on your neck. They began to move out of the area;
as soon as they got out of the area, then his limbs began to cool.
Then came entering in the beast's sister;
then she settled it and swore oaths
that never this would harm the sick person,
nor (harm) anyone for whom this charm could be obtained,
or who knew how to intone this charm.
Amen. Fiat. (So be it.)

10. Wið Færstice (for a Sudden Stitch)

(BL MS. Harley 585 – ca. 1000 AD)

Here some sort of sudden or stabbing pain is to be tackled, and it is assumed this is caused by an invisible spear or arrow sent by some evil agency (portrayed rather like the valkyries, though a number of possible agencies are covered). A magic knife (of dwarfish make?) is used to locate and remove the shot which is sent back to its source, or banished to a mountain, or transferred to running water. Difficulties of interpretation apart, the imagery and diction are very striking.

> *Wið færstice: feferfuige and seo reade netele, ðe þurh ærn inwyxð, and*
> *wegbrade; wyll in buteran.*

For a sudden pain, (take) feverfew and the red nettle that grows between buildings, and plantain; boil in butter. [And recite:]

> *Hlude wæran hy, la, hlude,   ða hy ofer þone hlæw ridan;*
> *wæran anmode,   ða hy ofer land ridan.*
> *Scyld ðu ðe nu, þu ðysne nið   genesan mote.*
> *Ut, lytel spere,   gif her inne sie!*
> *Stod under linde,   under leohtum scylde,*

---

[1] *Deores* (the animal's) is often emended to *dweores* (the dwarf's) – which prejudges the purpose of the text, and asserts that *dweorh* of the title means dwarf not fever. In that case, this is the defeated dwarf's sister petitioning for a settlement.

[2] This powerful being seems to be able to control the cause of illness, whatever shape that properly possesses. He then redefines (or identifies and claims control of) the cause in horse-shape, and so is able to ride it away – bringing relief for the patient.

þær ða mihtigan wif   hyra mægen beræddon
and hy gyllende   garas sændan;
ic him oðerne   eft wille sændan,
fleogende flane   forane togeanes.
Ut, lytel spere,   gif hit her inne sy!

Loud were they, lo, loud, when they rode over the burial mound;
they were fierce, when they rode over the land.
Shield yourself now (so that) you this evil attack might survive.
Out, little spear, if here (any) be within!
(I) stood beneath a linden(-shield), under a light shield,
where the mighty women ?revealed their power,
and they, yelling, sent forth spears;
I to them another one back will send,
a flying arrow straight towards [them].
Out, little spear, if it be here within!

Sæt smið,   sloh seax lytel,
[...] iserna,.   wund[rum] swiðe.
Ut, lytel spere,   gif her inne sy!
Syx smiðas sætan,   wælspera worhtan.
Ut, spere,   næs in, spere!

The smith sat, hammered out a little knife,
(an article of) iron, very wondrously.
Out, little spear, if (any) here be within!
Six smiths sat, made killing-spears.
Out, little spear, not in, spear!

Gif her inne sy   ise[r]nes dæl,
hægtessan geweorc,   hit sceal gemyltan.
Gif ðu wære on fell scoten   oððe wære on flæsc scoten
   oððe wære on blod scoten
oððe wære on lið scoten,   næfre ne sy ðin lif atæsed;
gif hit wære esa gescot   oððe hit wære ylfa gescot
oððe hit wære hægtessan gescot,   nu ic wille ðin helpan.
Þis ðe to bote esa gescotes,   ðis ðe to bote ylfa gescotes,
ðis ðe to bote hægtessan gescotes;   ic ðin wille helpan.
Fle[oh]¹ þær on fyrgenh[ea]fde!²
Hal westu,   helpe ðin drihten!

---

¹ MS. *fled*
² MS. *-hæfde*

If there be here within a portion of iron,
the work of hags, it shall melt away.
If you were in the skin shot or were in the flesh shot
                                   or were in the blood shot
or were in a limb shot, never be your life jeopardised;
whether it was Æsir's shot or it was elves' shot
or it was hags' shot, now I shall help you.
(Let) this (be) a remedy for you for Æsir's shot, this a remedy to you for
                                   elves' shot,
this a remedy to you for hags' shot; I shall help you.
Flee there to the mountain-head!
May you be healthy, may God assist you!

Nim þonne þæt seax, ado on wætan.

Then take that knife, put [it] in liquid.[1]

11. For Delayed Birth

(BL MS. Harley 585 – ca. 1000 AD)

This is apparently a series of different precautions for a range of natal problems, not just one item as suggested by our title and the formula it derives from in the Old English. First there is a general charm for the problems of a safe delivery; then what sounds like a ritual for conception; then a precautionary act for early pregnancy; followed by a ritual to avoid any repetition of a miscarriage; and lastly what could be a plea for proper lactation. The appropriate actions vary widely, from a graveside chant in the opening paragraph to a Christian 'confession' in the third, suggesting we have a group of charms from different origins.

*Se wifman, se hire cild afedan ne mæg, gange to gewitenes mannes
birgenne and stæppe þonne þriwa ofer þa byrgenne and cweþe þonne þriwa
þas word:*

þis me to bote   þære laþan lætbyrde,
þis me to bote   þære swæran swærbyrde,[2]
þis me to bote   þære laðan lambyrde.

The woman who cannot manage to have children, should go to a departed (i.e. dead) man's grave and then step over the grave three times and then say these words thrice:

(Let) this (be) my remedy for the horrible delayed birth,
(Let) this (be) my remedy for the grievous difficult birth,
(Let) this (be) my remedy for the horrible lame (i.e. deformed) birth.

---

[1] Skemp, 1911, p.291, suggests this 'liquid' is the salve mentioned at the very opening of
  the charm, rather than 'water'.
[2] MS. *swærtbyrde*

And þonne þæt wif seo mid bearne and heo to hyre hlaforde on reste ga,
þonne cweþe heo:

> *Up ic gonge,   ofer þe stæppe,*
> *mid cwican cilde,   nalæs mid cwellendum,*
> *mid fulborenum,   nalæs mid fægan.*

And when that woman is with child and she goes to bed with her husband,
let her say:

> Up I go, over you I step,
> With a living child, not a dying (one),
> with a properly-born (child), not a doomed (one).)

And þonne seo modor gefele þæt þæt bearn si cwic, ga þonne to cyrican,
and þonne heo toforan þan weofode cume, cweþe þonne:

> *Criste, ic sæde,   þis gecyþed!*

And when the mother can feel that the baby is alive, she should go to
church, and when she comes before the altar, say:

> Christ, I said, (let) this (be) fulfilled![1]

Se wifmon, se hyre bearn afedan ne mæge, genime heo sylf hyre agenes
cildes gebyrgenne dæl, wry æfter þonne on blace wulle and bebicge to
cepemannum and cweþe þonne:

> *Ic hit bebicge,   ge hit bebicgan,*
> *þas sweartan wulle   and þysse sorge corn.*

The woman who cannot produce her children alive, should herself take a
portion of her own child's grave, wrap (it) then in black (or uncoloured?)
wool and sell (it) to traders and then say:

> I sell it (to you), may you sell it in,
> this dark wool and this sample of sorrow.

Se [wif]man, se [n]e[2] mæge bearn afedan, nime þonne anes bleos cu meoluc
on hyre handæ and gesupe þonne mid hyre muþe and gange þonne to
yrnendum wætere and spiwe þær in þa meolc and hlade þonne mid þære
ylcan hand þæs wæteres muð fulne and forswelge. Cweþe þonne þas word:

> *Gehwer ferde ic me þone mæran   magaþihtan,*
> *mid þysse mæran   meteþihtan;*
> *þonne ic me wille habban   and ham gan.*

---

[1] Keefer, 1990, relates this to the Magnificat, and Elisabeth's declaration in Luke 1:41.
[2] MS. *þe*

*þonne heo to þan broce ga, þonne ne beseo heo, no ne eft þonne heo þanan
ga; and þonne ga heo in oþer hus oþer heo ut ofeode and þær gebyrge metes.*

The woman who cannot rear her children easily should take the milk of a
cow of one colour in her (cupped) hand and then sip (it) with her mouth and
then do running water and spit out the milk into it and then with the same
hand scoop up a mouthful of the water and swallow (it). Then let her say
these words:

> Everywhere I carried with me the wonderful ?stomach-strength,
> along with this wonderful ?nourished-strength;
> then I wish to have (success) for myself and return home (with it).

When she goes to the brook, she should not look round, nor when she
leaves; and then she should go into some other house than the one she came
from and there take some food.

12. For the Water-Elf Disease

(BL Royal MS. 12 D.xvii – mid 10th century)

Cameron 1993 suggests (p.154) for chickenpox or measles. The 'wounds'
mentioned are real blemishes, in this case, rather than symbolic wounds through
which disease enters.

*Gif mon biþ on wæterælfadle, þonne beoþ him þa handnæglas wonne and
þa eagan tearige and wile locian niþer. Do him þis to læcedome:
eoforþrote, cassuc, fone nioþoweard, eowberge, elehtre, eolone,
merscmealwan crop, fenminte, dile, lilie, attorlaþe, polleie, marubie, docce,
ellen, felterre, wermod, streawbergean leaf, consolde. Ofgeot mid ealaþ, do
hæligwæter to, sing þis gealdor ofer þriwa:*

If someone is suffering from water-elf-disease then the nails of his hands are
discoloured and the eyes watery and he prefers to look down (i.e. avoid
light). Prepare this for his medicine: carline thistle,[1] cassock, the tuber of
iris, yew-berry, lupin, elecampane, the heads of marshmallow, water-mint,[2]
dill, lily, attorlothe, pennyroyal, horehound, dock, elder, centaury,
wormwood, strawberry leaves, comfrey. Steep in ale, add holy water (and)
sing this charm over [it] thrice:

*Ic b[e]nne³ awrat   betest beadowræda,
swa benne ne burnon,   ne burston,
ne fundian,   ne feologan,   ne hoppettan,
ne wund waxsian,*

---

[1] Cameron, 1993, p.154 as Boarthroat.
[2] Cameron as fen-mint.
[3] MS. *binne*

ne dolh diopian;
ac him self healde   halewæge,
ne ace þe þon ma,   þe eorþan on eare ace.
Sing þis manegum siþum:

Eorþe þe onbere eallum hire mihtum and mægenum.

Þas galdor mon mæg singan on wunde.

> I inside have inscribed the best of war-bandages,
> so wounds shall not burn nor burst,
> nor spread nor ?multiply, nor ?throb,
> nor wound grow,
> nor injury deepen,
> but to him I myself proffer a cup of healing;
> let it not pain you any the more than earth hurts earth.[1]

(Then) sing this many times: "Let earth reduce you with all her might and power." These charms one can sing over the wound.

13. Against a Wen

(BL Royal MS. 4 A.xiv – 12th century)

A wen is a tumour or goitre, not necessarily dangerous, but disfiguring and unpleasant, especially if a large growth; here it is subjected to a course of insult and imaginative ill-treatment that would make quite a startling performance if the action were also mimed.

Wenne, wenne,   wenchichenne,
her ne scealt þu timbrien,   ne nenne tun habben,
ac þu scealt norþ eonene   to þan nihgan berhge,
þer þu hauest, ermi[n]g,   enne broþer.
He þe sceal legge   leaf et heafde.
Under fot uolmes,   under ueþer earnes,
under earnes clea,   a þu geweornie.
Clinge þu   alswa col on heorþe,
scring þu   alswa scerne awage,
and weorne   alswa weter on anbre.
Swa litel þu gewurþe   alswa linsetcorn,
and miccli lesse   alswa anes handwurmes hupeban,
and alswa litel þu gewurþe   þet þu nawiht gewurþe.

> Wen! wen! ugly little wen!
> Here you shall not build, nor no home set up,
> but you must go north from here to the nearby hill,

---

[1] Old English *ear* can mean 'ear' (of head, of wheat), or (as in *Rune Poem*) the ground itself.

where you have, you unhappy thing, a brother.
He shall place a leaf on your head.
Under the foot of the ?wolf,[1] under the wing of the eagle,
under the claw of the eagle, continually you will be worn away.
May you be consumed like burning coal in the hearth,
may you shrink away like dung
and evaporate like water in a crock.
You will become as tiny as a linseed,
and much smaller than a ?cricket's hip-bone,
and thus you shall be so small that you change into nothing.

14. For a Swarm of Bees

(MS CCCC 41 – mid 11th century, with charm in margin)

Annually, bees emigrate from their hive to seek out a new home. The bee-keeper is keen at this time to relocate the bees on his own land for future use.

> *Wið ymbe: nim eorþan, oferweorp mid þinre swiþran handa under þinum*
> *swiþran fet and cwet:*

> *Fo ic under fot,   funde ic hit.*
> *Hwæt, eorðe mæg   wið ealra wihta gehwilce*
> *and wið andan   and wið æminde*
> *and wið þa micelan   mannes tungan.*

Against bees (swarming): take earth, throw (it) with your right hand under your right foot, and say:

> I catch (it) under my foot, I have reclaimed it.
> Lo, earth prevails over all creatures,
> and over malice and over jealousy
> and over the tongue [i.e. spell] of the powerful person.

> *And wiðon forweorp ofer greot, þonne hi swirman, and cweð:*

> *Sitte ge, sigewif,   sigað to eorþan!*
> *Næfre ge wilde   to wuda fleogan.*
> *Beo ge swa gemindige   mines godes,*
> *swa bið manna gehwilc   metes and eþeles.*

And from above cast the soil over (the bees) when they swarm, and say:

> Settle ye, war-women, sink to the ground!
> Never should you, wild, to the wood fly.
> Be ye as respectful of my welfare
> as is every man of food and shelter.

---

[1] Reading *wolues* for MS. ?*folmes* 'of the hand'.

15. For Loss of Cattle

(BL MS. Harley 585 – ca.1000 AD)

Cattle could easily stray; it was also very likely that cattle raiders would be responsible for animals going amiss. This was a major concern of the period – see the Lawcode 5 Athelstan, where ch.2 includes new practical provisions for following the tracks of lost cattle. In this charm the dilemma of not knowing where the cattle have got to is tackled: the fame of Bethlehem is cited as an aid to revelation, and the recovery of the Cross by St Helena (see the Old English poem *Elene*), after the Jews had hidden it in the ground, is cited as a powerful example of how information must come to light.

> *þonne þe mon ærest secge þæt þin ceap sy losod, þonne cweð þu ærest, ær þu elles hwæt cwepe:*
>
>> *Bæðleem hatte seo buruh   þe Crist on acænned wæs,*
>> *seo is gemærsod   geond ealne middangeard;*
>> *swa þyos dæd for monnum   mære gewurþe*
>> *þurh þa haligan Cristes rode! Amen.*

When some first informs you that your cattle are missing, then you must say first, before you say anything else:

> Bethlehem is called the town in which Christ was born;
> it is famed throughout all the world.
> So may this deed among men famous (i.e. widely known, or clear) become, with the help of Christ's holy cross! Amen.

Gebide þe þonne þriwa east and cweþ þonne þriwa: Crux Christi ab oriente reducað.

Gebide þe þonne þriwa west and cweð þonne þriwa: Crux Christi ab occidente reducat.

Gebide þe þonne þriwa suð and cweþ þriwa: Crux Christi ab austro reducat.

Gebide þonne þriwa norð and cweð þriwa: Crux Christi ab aquilone reducað, crux Christi abscondita est et inuenta est. Iudeas Crist ahengon, dydon dæda þa wyrrestan, hælon þæt hy forhelan ne mihtan. Swa þeos dæd nænige þinga ferholen ne wurþe, þurh þa haligan Cristes rode. Amen.

Address yourself then thrice to the east and say then thrice: 'The cross of Christ brings back (what is lost) from the east.

Address yourself then thrice to the west and say then thrice: 'The cross of Christ brings back (what is lost) from the west.

Address yourself then thrice to the south and say thrice: 'The cross of Christ brings back (what is lost) from the south.'

Address then thrice the north and say thrice: 'The cross of Christ brings back (what is lost) from the east; the cross of Christ was hidden and found again. The Jews crucified Christ, committed the worst of deeds, concealed that which they could not hide. So let this deed in no way be hidden, with the help of Christ's holy cross. Amen.

16. For Theft of Cattle

(MS.CCCC 41 – mid 11th century – with charm in margin)

This piece is something like an advertisement. The opening invokes confidence, followed by warnings (designed to reach the ear of anyone involved?).

> *Ne forstolen ne forholen nanuht, þæs ðe ic age,*
> *þe ma ðe mihte Herod urne drihten.*
> *Ic geþohte sancte Eadelenan and ic geþohte Crist on rode ahangen:*
> *swa ic þence þis feoh to findanne,   næs to oðfeorrganne,*
> *and to witanne,   næs to oðwyrceanne,*
> *and to lufianne,   næs to oðlædanne.*

Let nothing (be) stolen or lost of that I own,
any the more than Herod could (harm) our Lord.
I invoked St E—[1] and I invoked Christ hanged on the cross;
so I determine on finding these cattle, not to let them be taken away,
and to keep them, not to let them be harmed,
and to cherish them, not to have them snatched away.

> *Garmund,   godes ðegen,*
> *find þæt feoh   and fere þæt feoh*
> *and hafa þæt feoh   and heald þæt feoh*
> *and fere ham   þæt feoh.*
> *Þæt he næfre næbbe landes,   þæt he hit oðlæde,*
> *ne foldan,   þæt hit oðferie,*
> *ne husa,   þæt he hit oðhealde.[2]*
> *Gif hyt hwa gedo,   ne gedige hit him næfre!*
> *Binnan þrym nihtum   cunne ic his mihta,*
> *his mægen and his mihta   and his mundcræftas.*
> *Eall he weornige,   swa sy[re][3] wudu weornie;*
> *swa breðel [s]eo[4]   swa þystel,*
> *se ðe ðis feoh   oðfergean þence*
> *oððe ðis orf   oðehtian ðence.   Amen.*

---

[1] *Eadelena* perhaps for *eadig(u) Helena*, 'blessed Helen', mother of Constantine and finder of the Cross.

[2] MS. *he hit oðhit healde*

[3] MS. *syer*

[4] MS. *þeo*

Garmund,[1] servant of God,
find the cattle and move the cattle
and take possessession of the cattle and guard the cattle
and bring the cattle home!
See that he never have any land, he that took them away,
nor fields, him that snatched them,
nor house, him that withheld them.
And if he do have any, never let it work out for him!
Within three days I will know of his powers,
his strength and his powers and his protections.
He shall wear them all out like dust-dry wood crumbles;
Let him be as limp as a thistle,
he that hopes to get away with this cattle
or hopes to ?drive away this livestock!

17. For Loss of Cattle

(Textus Roffensis p.50 – 12th century – with BL Cotton MS. Tib.A.iii and transcript in BL Cotton MS.Julius C.2 f.97b; via Cockayne vol.3, 286–9)

This charm has points in common with the preceding, especially the invocation of the Cross. A variant is printed by Storms, 1948, no.12, from CCCC 41. Our text then changes into what I take to be a rough verse, which is a sort of formula for defending an inheritance against any counter-claim. This might be taken as a separate item (as by Skemp, 1911. pp.298–9) except that it fits in here as an assertion of ownership in general, relevant to the just return of lost or stolen items.

Gyf feoh sy underfangen: gif hit hors sy sing on his feteran oþþe on his bridele; gif hit sy oðer feoh, sing on þæt fotspor 7 ontend þreo candela 7 dryp on þæt [h]ofræc þæt wex þriwa. Ne mæg hit þe nan mann forhelan. Gif hi[t] sy innorf, sing þonne on feower healfe þæs huses 7 æne onmiddan 'Crux Christi reducat. Crux Christi per furtum periit inuenta est. Abraham tibi semitas uias montes concludat, Iob et flumina, [ad] iudici[um] ligatum perducat.'

If livestock be stolen: if it is a horse sing (the following) on his fetters or his bridle; if it is some other animal, sing upon the footprints and kindle three candles and drip the wax thrice on the hoofprint. (Then) no man will be able to conceal (the truth) from you. If it is (a matter of) household animals, then sing on the four sides of the house and once in the centre: 'Let the Cross of Christ bring it back. The Cross of Christ (which) was lost by theft was found again. Let Abraham close to you paths, roads, hills and rivers. Let Job bring ? him bound to judgement.'

---

[1] Garmund perhaps St Germanus, bishop of Auxerre, who visited Britain in the mid 5th century to combat heresy; but Garmund is recorded as an Old English proper name in its own right, and a *Garmundi via* ('street of Garmund') is noted near Durham – see Searle, 1897, p.254.

Iudeas Crist ahengon þæt heom com to wite swa strangum;
gedydon him dæda þa wirrestan hy þæt drofe onguldon,
hælan hit heom to hearme micclum forþam [þe] hi hit forhelan ne mihtan.

The Jews hanged Christ: that resulted for them in a such severe punishment.
They did to him the worst of deeds: they paid for it grievously.
They concealed it [the Cross?] to their great harm, for they could not hide it.

Hit becwæð 7 becwæl
se ðe hit ahte mid fullan folcrihte
swa swa hit his yldran mid feo 7 mid feore
rihte begeatan 7 lætan 7 læfdan
ðam to gewealde ðe hy wel uðan
7 swa ic hit hæbbe swa hit se sealde ðe to syllanne ahte
unbryde 7 unforboden
7 ic agnian wille to agenre ahte
ðæt ðæt ic hæbbe 7 næfre ðæt [m]yntan
ne plot ne ploh
ne turf ne toft
ne furh ne fotmæl
ne land ne læse
ne fersc ne mersc
ne ruh ne rum,
wudes ne feldes
sandes ne strandes
wealtes ne wæteres
butan ðæt læste ða hwile ðe ic libbe.

He bequeathed it and died,
he that owned it with full common right
as his forebears with money and life
justly obtained it, and transferred it, and handed it down
into the possession of him to whom they properly granted it
and so I have it as he gave it who had it to give
honest and lawful,
and I wish to own as my own property
that which I have and never to yield it,
neither plot nor ploughland,
neither turf nor toft
neither furrow nor foot's space
neither land nor meadow
neither fresh nor marsh
neither rough nor clear,
of woodland or field
of sand or strand

of forest or water,
provided that it last me as long as I live.

Forðam [ðe] [n]is se man on life ðe afre gehyrde
ðæt man cwidde oððon crafode
hine on hundrede   oððon ahwar on gemote
on ceapstowe   oþþe on cyricware
ða hwile he lifde.   Unsac he wæs on life
beo on legere swa swa he mote.   Do swa ic lære:
beo ðu be ðinum   7 læt me be minum;
ne gyrne ic ðines
ne læðes ne landes
ne sace ne socne;
ne ðu mines ne ðærft   ne mynte ic ðe nan þing.

For there is no one alive that ever heard
that anyone sued or summoned him
in the hundred court or in any public court,
in the market or before the congregation,
as long as he lived. Alive, he was free of accusation:
now in the grave let him be as he must be. Do as I teach:
you be (concerned) with yours, and leave me with mine;
I do not yearn for yours,
neither lathe nor land,
neither criminal jurisdiction nor civil,
nor should you take action against mine, nor do I yield you anything.

18. A Journey Charm
(MS. CCCC 41 – mid 11ᵗʰ century)

This charm is notable for employing much of the diction of 'classical' Old English verse (though with *weorc* used in the southern sense of 'effort' rather than the poetic/Anglian one of 'pain'); it also evidences the pious content so much admired in elegiac, allegorical verse. Here too the journey is more than a literally physical experience: it can stand for the adventure of learning, or the journey through life to heaven.

> *Ic me on þisse gyrde beluce   and on godes helde bebeode*
> *wið þane sara s[t]ice,   wið þane sara slege,*
> *wið þane grymma gryre,*
> *wið ðane micela egsa   þe bið eghwam lað,*
> *and wið eal þæt lað   þe in to land fare.*

I entrust myself to this staff,[1] and commend (myself/it?) to God's
                                            guardianship
(for protection) against the pricking of afflictions, against the blow of afflictions,
against the awful horror,
against the great terror that is hateful to each person,
and against all that evil that invades the land.

> *Sygegealdor ic begale,   sigegyrd ic me wege,*
> *wordsige and worcsige.   Se me dege;*
> *ne me mer[e] ne gemyrre,   ne me maga ne geswence,*
> *ne me næfre minum feore   forht ne gewurþe,*
> *ac gehæle me ælmihtig[2] [and] sunu   and frofre gast,*
> *ealles wuldres   wyr[ð]ig[3] dryhten,*
> *swa swa ic gehyrde   heofna scyppende.*

A charm of victory I intone, a rod of victory I carry with me,
(to be) powerful of speech, powerful of deed. Let it be serviceable to me,
that no ?nightmare confuse me, nor my stomach vex me,
nor may it ever happen that I (should be) in fear of my life,
but let the Almighty and the Son and the Comforting Spirit save me,
(for he is) the Lord worthy of all glory,
just as I have been obedient to the Creator of the Heavens.

---

[1] Storms (1948, p.217) trans. "I draw a protecting circle around myself with this rod…"
[2] MS. *ælmihtigi*
[3] MS. *wyrdig*

Abrame and Isace
and swilce men,   Moyses and Iacob,
and Dauit and Iosep
and Evan and Annan   and Elizabet,
Saharie and ec Marie,   modur Cristes,
and eac þæ gebroþru,   Petrus and Paulus,
and eac þusend   þi[n]ra engla
clipige ic me to are   wið eallum feondum.
Hi me ferion and friþion   and mine fore nerion,
eal me gehealdon,   me¹ gewealdon,
worces stirende.   Si me wuldres hyht,
hand ofer heafod   haligra [h]rof,
sigerofra sceote,   soðfæstra engla.

Abraham and Isaac
and similar figures, Moses and Jacob,
and David and Joseph
and Eve and Anna and Elizabeth,
Sarah and also Mary, the Mother of Christ,
and also the 'brothers', Peter and Paul,
and also a thousand of your angels
I call upon as a help for me against all enemies.
Let them lead me and protect me and preserve my travel,
in every thing directing and guiding me,
steering (me in my) work. Let there be for me the hope of salvation,
a hand [i.e. symbol of protection] over my head, a roof of saints,
a ?canopy of heroes, of righteous angels.

Biddu ealle   bliðu mode
þæt me beo hand   ofer heafod
Matheus helm,   Marcus byrne,
leoht, lifes rof,   Lucos min swurd,
scearp and scirecg,   scyld Iohannes,
wuldre gewlitegod   w[i]ga[r]² Serafhin.

I beseech them all with grateful heart
that there be a protection over my head,
Matthew my helmet, Mark my coat of mail,
renowned, famous of life, Luke my sword,
sharp and bright-edged, John my shield,
(and) a wondrously adorned spear the Seraphim.

---

¹ MS. *men*
² MS. *wega*

Forð ic gefare: frind ic gemete,
eall engla blæd,   eadiges lare.
Bidde ic nu sigere[s] god   godes miltse,
siðfæt godne,   smylte and lihte
wind[as on] werepum.   Windas gefran,
circinde wæter   simbli gehale[d]e[1]
wið eallum feondum.   Freond ic gemete wið,
þæt ic on þ[æ]s ælmih[t]gian frið[2]   *wunian mote,*
belocun wið þa[m] laþan,   se me lyfes eht,
on engla blæd[3]   *gestaþelod,*
and inna halre hand   h[e]ofna rices[4]
þa hwile þe ic on þis life   wunian mote.
Amen.

I go forth: let me encounter friends,
all the encouragement of the angels, the exhortation of the blessed.
Now I beg the God of Victory for good favour,
a safe journey, gentle and easy
winds on the coasts. Winds I have heard of,
(and) rolling water[5] (that) continually protected (people)
from all foes. May I meet with friends
so that I may remain within the Almighty's safekeeping,
secure from the evil one who seeks my life,
(rather) confirmed in the spirit of the angels,
and within the holy guardianship of the heavenly kingdom
so long as I shall remain in the life.
Amen.

19. A Prose Charm Against Conspiracy

(MS CCCC 391 – 11th-12th century)

The prose charms in Anglo-Saxon MSS are generally less attractive in that they tend to be short formulas in Latin, sometimes obscurely mixed with misunderstood Greek or Irish or Hebrew. (Curiously, Irish words could be absorbed via Norse intermediation – see Grön, 1953, p.146.) The texts of many of them can be viewed in Grattan & Singer, 1952. Many of the verse charms above have prose elements, but here is an example of a purely prose charm, via Zupitza 1892 pp.364–5.

---

[1] MS. *gehaleþe*
[2] MS. *þis ælmihgian on his frið*
[3] MS. *bla blæd*
[4] MS. *hofna rices blæd*, '?power of the kingdom of (glorious) dwellings'.
[5] *Exodus* 14:21 specifies wind as the agent that parts the waters of the Red Sea.

Gyf ðe ðynce þæt ðine fynd þwyrlice ymbe þe ðrydian, ðonne gang þu on gelimplicere stowe 7 þe ða halgan rode to gescyldnesse geciig, 7 asete þe aðenedum earmum 7 cwæð þus ærest: Ave alma crux que mundi pretium portasti, que vexilla regis eterni ferebas; in te enim Christus triumphavit: in te et ego miser peccator, famulus tuus, nomine --- ; sancta crux, omnes in nos insurgentes vincamus per... Sing ðonne þas salmas oð ende: Domine deus meus in te speravi; Usque quo domine; Exaudi, domine; III Kyrrieleison. Pater noster.

If it seems to you that your enemies are considering unpleasant measures towards you, then go to a suitable place and invoke the Holy Cross as your protection, and compose yourself with outstretched arms and first say this: Hail sustaining Cross that carried the ransom of the world, and that bears the banners of the eternal king; as through thee Christ was triumphant, and through you may I also, wretched sinner, your servant, by name ---; O Holy Cross, let us overcome those rushing against us... Then sing these psalms through to the end: Domine deus meus [Ps.7], Usque quo domine [Ps.12]; Exaudi domine [Ps.16]; thrice the Kyrie. And the Lord's Prayer.

20. Charm for a Horse

(BL Royal MS.12 D.xvii – mid 10th century)

It was not only human welfare that was the concern of Anglo-Saxon medicine, animals like horses, oxen and cows were of considerable worth and can feature in healing charms. This example, though of uncertain application, is interesting as linking elves with disease, and for this reason was edited and discussed by Thun, 1969, p.385.

Gif hors ofscoten sie, nim þonne þæt seax þe þæt hæfte sie fealo hryþeres horn 7 sien iii ærene næglas on. Writ þonne þam horse on þam heafde foran Cristes mæl, þæt hit blede; writ þonne on þam hricge Cristes mæl 7 oṅ leoþa gehwilcum þe þu ætfeolan mæge. Nim þonne þæt winestre eare, þurhsting swigende; þis þu scealt don: genim ane girde, sleah on þæt bæc, þonne biþ þæt horse hal. 7 awrit on þæs seaxes horne þas word: Benedicite omnia opera domini dominorum. Sy þæt ylfa þe him sie, þis him mæg to bote.

If a horse be shot with illness, take a knife whose hilt is of yellow horn of the ox, and let there be three iron nails in it. Then inscribe on the front of the head of the horse the sign of Christ [i.e. the Cross], so that it bleeds; then inscribe the sign of Christ on the spine and on such limbs as you can get to. Then take the left ear, and pierce it, keeping silence. This (also) you shall do: take a wand, hit (the horse) on the back, and it shall be well again. And (make sure you) write on the horn (handle) of the knife these words: Blessed be all the works of the Lord of Lords. If it is a question of elves in this case, this may well help.

Augury

21. The Old English Rune Poem (see page 147 for Hickes' runes)

(Surviving only in printed form in G.Hickes (1705) p.135; with rune-signs and names filled in from another source (discussed in Hempl 1903–4).)

The sort of runes and rune-names exhibited in this poem make it probable we are looking at an Anglian (or Anglian-aware) poem. e.g. *eh* for horse; the possible affinities of *tir* to Old Norse *Tyr* (Tiw), and *yr* to the nominative form of the Old Norse word for bow make a post-Viking date worth considering; its occasional riddle-like tone is similar to the indirect allusion (kenning) in Scandinavian verse. As Page (1973, p.34) notes: "Far from letting runes fall into desuetude, the church in north England seems to have preserved them and extended their use."

Its role as a poem, I suggest, is decorative and mnemonic, rather than obviously divinatory, but the uncertainty of some of the actual rune-names encourages further debate and research.

Following each entry, the form and meaning of the rune-name in the later Icelandic and Norwegian Runic Poems are given.

F (feoh) byþ frofur   fira gehwylcum.
Sceal ðeah manna gehwylc   miclun hyt dælan
gif he wile for Drihtne   domes hleotan.

Wealth is an advantage to all men.
Must though each man freely share it
if he wishes before God credit to win.)

[Ice/Norw. Fé 'wealth']

U (ur) byþ anmod   and oferhyrned,
felafrecne deor,   feohteþ mid hornum,
mære morstapa –   þæt is modig wuht.

The Aurochs[1] is fierce and immoderately horned,
a very dangerous beast, it fights with its horns,
renowned moor-walker – it is a brave creature.

[Ice. Úr 'rain', Norw. Úr 'iron slag']

---

[1] The aurochs (Latin, *urus*) is seemingly not the European bison or wisent, but *bos primigenius*, a large bull with spreading horns. It was probably extinct in Britain before the Roman invasion, but may have been reintroduced by Germanic settlers. See discussion in G. Kenneth Whitehead's *The Ancient White Cattle of Britain and their Descendants* (London, 1953) ch.2; for refs. on aurochs horns in literature see Saxo, 1980, 2, p.145 note 159.

Ð *(ðorn) byþ ðearle scearp;   ðegna gehwylcum*
anfeng ys yfyl,   ungemetun reþe
manna gehwylcun   ðe him mid resteð.

Thorn is terribly sharp; for each person
contact with it is bad, (but it is) excessively unkind
to anyone who on it sits.

[Ice./Norw. Thurs 'giant']

O *(os) byþ ordfruma   ælcre spræce,*
wisdomes wraþu   and witena frofur,
and eorla gehwam   eadnys and tohiht.

Mouth[1] is the source of all speech,
wisdom's support and a pleasure to the learned,
and for all people a help and a hope.

[Ice. Óss 'Odin', Norws. Óss 'rivermouth']

R *(rad) byþ on recyde   rinca gehwylcum*
sefte, and swiþhwæt   ðam ðe sitteþ
onufan meare mægenheardum   ofer milpaþas.

Travel[2] is, in the hall, for each person,
sweet, yet severe for him that sits
upon a sturdy mare over miles-long pathways.

[Ice./Norw. Reith 'riding']

C *(cen) byþ cwicera gehwam   cuþ on fyre,*
blac and beorhtlic,   byrneþ oftust
ðær hi æþelingas   inne restaþ.

Torch[3] is for all living beings evident by its light,
shining and bright it burns typically
where noblemen repose themselves indoors.

[Ice./Norw. Kaun 'ulcer']

---

[1] *os* has no meaning in Old English, except as an element in personal names e.g. *Oswald*. In the context here, the Latin *os* meaning 'mouth' seems to give the best sense.

[2] Kemble (as explained in Bosworth & Toller) assumes a meaning for *rad* of equipment (a Norse derivation?) permitting a pun: the furniture of a house, the trappings of a horse. But perhaps 'riding' or 'travel' is simpler, the contrast being between recollection and action. Or is the concept involved that of 'bouncing'?

[3] A pine torch is implied; the resin in pine-wood gives long burning and bright light, though inclined to splutter and spark. The rune for 'c' (treated as 'ch' here) stood for 'k' in Scandinavian speech, hence the variation of rune-names.

G (gyfu) gumena byþ   gleng and herenys,
wraþu and wyrþscype,   and wræcna gehwam
ar and ætwist   ðe byþ oþra leas.

Generosity is in all men a fine trait and a cause for praise,
a source of support and honour, and for all outcasts
benefit and sustenance – for them that would be otherwise without.

W (wen)ne bruceþ   ðe can weana lyt,
sares and sorge,   and him sylfa hæfþ
blæd and blysse   and eac byrga geniht.

Joy he may claim that knows few cares
or suffering or sorrow, and for himself has
plenty and bliss and also town [i.e. civilised] comfort(s).

H (hægl) byþ hwitust corna;   hwyrft hit of heofones lyfte,
wealcaþ hit windes scura;   weorþeþ hit to wætere syððan.

Hail is the whitest of grains, it spins down from heaven's air,
the wind's blasts whirl it; it returns to water thereafter.

[Ice./Norw. Hagall 'hail']

N (nyd) byþ nearu on breostan;   weorþeþ hi[t] ðeah oft niþa bearnum
to helpe and to hæle gehwæþre,   gif hi his hlystaþ æror.

Neediness[1] presses on the heart; yet it often becomes, for the sons of men,
an aid and a source of improvement to each, if they heed it early enough.

[Ice. Nauth, Norw. Naiuthr, 'neediness']

I (is) byþ oferceald,   ungemetum slidor;
glisnaþ glæshluttur,   gimmum gelicust,
flor forste geworu[h]t,[2]   fæger ansyne.

Ice is very cold, inordinately slippery;
it glitters clear as glass, most like to jewels,
a floor (or flat surface) made out of frost, pretty of aspect.

[Ice. Íss, Norw. Ís, 'ice']

---

[1] The word implies both lack and a context of coercion.
[2] Hickes: *ge worulit*

G (ger) byþ gumena hiht,   ðon god læteþ,
halig heofones cyning,   hrusan syllan
beorhte bleda   beornum and ðearfum.

A good year (or harvest) is the hope of men, when God allows
– holy King of Heaven – the earth to produce
bright crops for (prosperous) people and the needy.

[Ice./Norw. Ár (for 'A') 'fruitful year']

EO (eoh) byþ utan   unsmeþe treow,
heard, hrusan fæst,   hyrde fyres,
wyrtrumun underwreþyd,   wyn[]¹ on eþle

Yew is on the exterior an unsmooth tree,
tough, firm in the ground, a keeper of fire,[2]
with roots undertwined, a joy (to have) on the estate.

P (?peorð) byþ symble   plega and hlehter
wlancum [ond wisum]   ðar wigan sittaþ
on beorsele   bliþe ætsomne.

—[3] is always a source of entertainment and laughter
for the proud and the wise where war-men sit
in the beer-hall, blithely companionable.

EO (eolhx⁴)sec[g] [e]ard⁵ hæfþ   oftust on fenne;
wexeð on wature,   wundaþ grimme,
blode breneð   beorna gehwylcne
ðe him ænigne   onfeng gedeð.

Bullrush has its base oftenest in fenny land;
it grows in water, (and) wounds severely,
burns with blood anyone
who achieves a grip on it.

---

[1] Hickes: *wynan on*

[2] Yew is a good fire wood.

[3] No satisfactory meaning for *peorth*, the assumed rune-name (cf. *cweorð* for 'cw'), has been proposed. (The poet may not have felt obliged to stick to a formal rune-name in any case.) A musical instrument? A board game (Ice. *peth* 'a chess-pawn')? A dice-cup? (see Bauschatz, 1982, p.70)? For a sample of possible solutions, some a little disconcerting, see Arntz 1944, esp. pp.208-9; and Polomé 1991.

[4] The 'eo' rune is usually named *eolh* ('elk'); here a compound *eolhxsecg* ('elk-sedge') is preferred for the sake of making a plausible verse; the word is also recorded as a gloss for *papyrus*.

[5] Hickes: *seccard*

S (segel¹) semannum   symble biþ on hihte,
ðonn hi hine feriaþ   ofer fisces beþ,
oþ hi brimhengest   bringeþ to lande.

Sail for seamen is always dependable
when they bear it over the fish's bath [i.e. sea]
till the ocean-steed [i.e. ship] brings them to land.
[Ice./Norw. Sól 'sun']

T (Tir) biþ tacna sum,   healdeð trywa wel
wiþ æþelingas;   a biþ on færylde
ofer nihta genipu,   næfre swiceþ.

Mars² is one of (a group of) signs, it keeps trust properly
with people; it is always in motion
above the night's shades, never fails/deceives.
[Ice./Norw. Týr, 'Tiw']

B (beorc) byþ bleda leas,   bereþ efne swa ðeah
tanas butan tudder;   biþ on telgum wlitig,
[h]eah³ on helme   hrysted fægere
geloden leafum   lyfte getenge.

Birch is bereft of seed, (but) even so bears
off-shoots without (specific) fruiting; it is showy in its branches,
high in its crown it is adorned fairly,
laden with leaves close to heaven.
[Ice./Norw. Bjarkan 'birch-tree']

E (eh) byþ for eorlum   æþelinga wyn,
hors hofum wlanc,   ðær him hæleþe ymb,
welege on wicgum,   wrixlaþ spræce;
and biþ unstyllum   æfre frofur.

A steed is, in public, fine men's display,
a horse noble with its hoofs, where men around it,
wealthy on their mounts, exchange speech;
and for the restless, (a horse) is always a comfort.

---

¹ The expected rune-name for 's' is *sigel* ('sun'). But as Kemble noted, the verse here
  seems more suited to *segel* ('sail').
² Old English *tir* ('glory') has little relevance here; the connection seems rather to be
  through the Norse form *Týr* for *Tiw*, equated with the planet Mars.
³ Hickes: *þeah*

M (man) byþ on myrgþe   his magan leof;
sceal þeah anra gehwylc   o[ð]rum¹ swican;
for ðam dryhten wyle   dome sine
þæt earme flæsc   eorþan betæcan.

The human, being merry, is much to his friends;
but each, just the same, betrays the other;
for which reason God chooses, by His decree,
the miserable flesh to commit to the earth.

[Ice./Norw. Mathr 'man']

L (lagu) byþ leodum   langsum geþuht
gif hi sculun neþun   on nacan tealtum,
and hi sæ yþa   swyþe bregaþ,
and se brimhengest   bridles ne gym[eð].

The sea by (lands)men is deemed everlasting
if they have to venture onto a tilting boat,
and the sea's waves greatly scare them,
and the ocean-steed [i.e. ship] won't heed its bridle!

[Ice. Lögr, Norw. L@gr – 'water']

NG (Ing) wæs ærest   mid Eastdenum
gesewen secgun;   oþ he siððan e[f]t²
ofer wæg gewat,   wæn æfter ran;
ðus Heardingas   ðone hæle nemdun.

Ing³ was originally among the East Danes
seen by men; later back again
over the waves he travelled, his chariot along sped;
thus the Heardings named the hero.

OE (eþel) byþ oferleof   æghwylcum men,
gif he mot ðær rihtes   and gerysena on
brucan on b[ol]de,⁴   bleadum oftast.

Family property is beloved of everyone,
if he can there (his) due right and privileges
enjoy in the hall, especially with prosperity.

---

¹ Hickes: *odrum*

² Hickes: *est*, possibly for 'east'

³ Osborn 1980 suggests *Ing* is the constellation of Boötes; since it rises in east, sets in the west; and the 60 horsemen could be the 60 days of its visibility as a constellation.

⁴ Hickes: *blode*

D (dæg) byþ Drihtnes sond,   deore mannum,
mære Metodes leoht,   myrgþ and tohiht
eadgum and earmum,   eallum brice.

Day is God's sending, dear to men,
magnificent light of the Creator, joy and encouragement
to rich and poor, a pleasure to all.

A (ac) byþ on eorþan   elda bearnum
flæsces fodor,   fereþ gelome
ofer ganotes bæþ;   garsecg fandaþ
hwæþer ac hæbbe   æþele treowe.

Oak is, upon earth, for the sons of men,
flesh's food [as mast for pigs?], (and) carries (men) often [as boat]
over the gannet's bath [i.e. the sea]; the ocean tests
whether oak holds proper reliability.

Æ (æsc) biþ oferheah,   eldum dyre,
stiþ on staþule,   stede rihte hylt,
ðeah him feohtan on   firas monige.

Ash is very tall, valued by men,
firm on its base it maintains its station [when made into a shield?]
though many men attack it.

Y (yr) byþ æþelinga   and eorla gehwæs
wyn and wyrþmynd;   byþ on wicge fæger,
fæstlic on færelde,   fyrdgea[t]ewa[1] sum.

A bow[2] is for nobles and for every man
a joy and an honour; it is fine (to the view) on horseback,
firm in its place, an item of battle equipment.

[Ice./Norw. Ýr 'yew']

IO (iar/io[r]) byþ eafixa [sum],   and ðeah a bruceþ
fodres on faldan;   hafaþ fægerne eard,
wætre beworpen,   ðær he wynnum leofaþ.

?Beaver[1] is one of the river-fish, and yet always partakes
of its food on land; it has a fair home,
lapped round with water, where it lives with pleasure.

---

[1] Hickes: *fyrd geacewa*

[2] *Yr* as 'bow' depends on an Old Norse form; the word occurs once in Old English in the
phrase *æxe yre*, used of the reverse of a Viking axe-head [*Chronicle C*, 1011].

EA (ear) byþ egle eorla gehwylcun
ðonn fæstlice flæsc onginneþ,
hraw colian, hrusan ceosan
blac to gebeddan; bleda gedreosaþ,
wynna gewitaþ, wera geswicaþ.

Ground[2] is horrid to all men
when certainly the flesh begins
– a corpse – to cool, to choose the earth
– pale – as its bedfellow; riches fail,
joyous memories depart, friendships cease to matter…

22. The Icelandic Runic Poem

(Copenhagen MS. AM,687 of 15th century; the text used here is based on Dickins'
edition of 1915, pp. 28–33.)

Dickins (p.7) considers this could have been written as late as the fifteenth century.
This seems a late estimate: the poem makes use of traditional diction and alliteration.
It lacks the moral dimension of the Anglo-Saxon poem, and occasional resemblances
between the two poems may be coincidental, a matter of shared poetic formulae,
though *óss* as 'god' is an unexpected case (Dickens p.141). Following each stanza,
the MS places a Latin equivalent of the head-word, and a compatible Icelandic term
from a range of synonyms for the concept 'ruler'.

F

Fé er frænda róg
   ok flæðar viti
   ok grafseiðs gata

aurum   *fylkir*

Wealth is friends' falling-out, and sea's fire, and grave-marvel's [i.e.
dragon's] road.

---

[1] The solution for this rune name was suggested by Osborn & Longland, 1980, after a
 Celtic source. "The beaver was designated a fish by the early Church (hence edible
 during Lent), apparently because of its scaly tail." p.386

[2] *Ear* is a rare word in Old English but is attested with the meaning 'soil' as well as the
 obvious 'ear', and a poetic meaning 'ocean'. Though Hickes notes at least three further
 runes (*cweorth, stan,* and *gar*) capable of being set to verse, we can be fairly certain that
 the finality of this verse on 'ea' was the intended end of the Old English poem, if only
 because the unusual meaning of *ear* was chosen above others more appropriate to the
 visual character of the rune (as ear of corn, or trident of Poseidon as *garsecg*).

U

Úr er skýja grátr
> of kára þverrir
> ok hirðis hatr.

[i]mb[er]   *vísi*

Shower is clouds' greeting, and harvest's ruin, and shepherd's horror.

TH

Þurs er kvenna kvöl
> ok kletta búi
> ok varðrúnar verr.

Saturnus   *þengill*

Giant is women's downfall, and cliff-dweller, and Varðrun's[1] husband.

O

Óss er aldingautr
> ok ásgarðs jǫfurr,
> ok valhallar vísi.

Jupiter   *oddviti*

God is the ancient Gautr [i.e. Odin], and Asgard's prince, and Valhalla's lord.

R

Reið er sitjandi sæla
> ok snúðig ferð
> ok jórs erfiði.

iter   *ræsir*

Riding is horseman's joy, and speedy journey, and steed's labour.

K

Kaun er barna böl
> ok bardag[a för]
> ok holdfúa hús

flagella   *konungr*

Ulcer is bairns' grief, and painful place, and decay's dwelling.)

---

[1] *Varðrún* is a giantess of legend.

H

Hagall er kaldakorn
        ok krapadrífa
        ok snáka sótt

grando   *hildingr*

Hail is cold grain, and sleet-shower, and snakes' sickness [i.e. winter]

N

Nauð er þýjar þrá
        ok þungr kostr
        ok vássamlig verk.

opera   *niflungr*

Constraint is slave-girl's woe, and oppressive conditions, and wearisome work.

I

Íss er árbörkr
        ok unnar þak
        ok feigra manna fár.

glacies   *jöfurr*

Ice is river-bark [i.e.coating], and waves' roof, and doomed men's peril.

A

Ár er gumna góði
        ok gott sumar
        ok algróinn akr

annus   *allvaldr*

A fine harvest/season/year is men's benefit, and a good summer, and well-grown fields.

S

Sól er skýja skjöldr
        ok skínandi röðull
        ok hverfandi hvél[1]

rota   *siklingr*

Sun is clouds' shield, and shining ray, and circling wheel.

---

[1] Variant text has *ísa aldrtregi* (ice's destroyer) for third line.

T

Týr er einhendr áss
>> ok ulfs leifar
>> ok hofa hilmir

Mars   *tiggi*

Tyr [Tiw] is the one-handed god,[1] and wolf's remnants, and temples' prince.

B

Bjarkan er laufgat lim
>> ok lítit tré
>> ok ungsamligr viðr

abies   *buðlungr*

Birch is a leafy twig, and little tree, and young and fresh shrub.

M

Maðr er manns gaman
>> ok moldar auki
>> ok skipa skreytir

homo   *mildingr*

Man is man's delight, and earth's outgrowth, and ships' adorner.

L

Lögr er vellanda vatn[2]
>> ok víðr ketill
>> ok glömmungr grund

lacus   *lofðungr.*

Water is surging stream, and broad geysir, and fishes' base.

Y

Ýr er bendr bogi
>> ok brotgjarnt járn
>> ok fífu fárbauti[3]

arcus   *ynglingr.*

Yr is bent bow, and (also means) brittle iron, and arrow's giant.[4]

---

[1] One-handed, etc., as the wolf Fenris had bitten off Tiw's hand, put in his mouth as a pledge.

[2] Variant text has *vim(u)r* (flood-tide) for *vatn*.

[3] A variant text has *fenju fleygir* ('arrow's speeder') for the third line.

[4] Two meanings of *yr* are developed here; one, 'bow', the other, 'iron'. *Fárbauti* is the name of a specific giant, Loki's father.

23. The Norwegian Runic Poem

(Survives only in 17th Century transcript; the text used here is based on Dickins' edition of 1915, pp. 24–7.)

The composition of this work is placed by Dickins (p.7) in late 13th century; Vigfusson & Powell (2, p.369) say "not older than twelfth century." But these estimates are based on metrical features. The couplets are linked by alliteration and rhyme, but the second line has little subject relevance to the head-word in most cases. This may derive from a gnomic tradition of constructing poems from varied proverbial material; but this in turn might have a competitive, oral basis – one poet proposing a first line, a second having to match it, at least metrically, from the same pool of commonplaces. The Y-stanza has a possible comparison to the Old English equivalent; but the resemblances throughout to the Icelandic poem are more noticeable and significant.

F

Fé vældr frænda róge:
føðesk ulfr í skóge.

Wealth causes friends' discord: lives the wolf in the forest.

U

Úr er af illus jarne:
opt løypr ræinn á hjarne.

Dross comes from bad iron: often leaps the reindeer over the icy snow.

TH

Þurs vældr kvinna kvillu:
kátr værðr fár af illu.

Giant causes women's anguish: merry are few from ill-luck.

O

Óss er flæstra færða
før: en skalpr er sværða.

Estuary is most journies' route: but scabbard is (the travel-goal) of swords.

R

Ræið kveða rossom væsta:
Reginn sló sværðet bæzta.

Riding they say is horses' worst (task): Reginn[1] forged of swords the finest.

K

Kaun er barna bǫlvan:
bǫl gǫrver nán fǫlvan.

Ulcer is bairns' affliction: death makes a corpse pale.

H

Hagall er kaldastr korna:
Kristr skóp hæimenn forna.

Hail is the coldest of grains: Christ created the world of old.

N

Nauðr gerer næppa koste:
nǫktan kælr í froste.

Neediness makes for scant choice: a naked man gets chilly in the frost.

I

Ís kǫllum brú bræiða:
blindan þar at læiða.

Ice we call the bridge (that is) broad: a blind man must be led.

A

Ár er gumna góðe:
get ek at ǫrr var Fróðe.

A good season is men's benefit: say I that generous was Frothi.[2]

S

Sól er landa ljóme:
lúti ek helgum dóme.

Sun is the lands' light: bow I to the divine decree.

---

[1] Reginn was Fafnir's brother, and unfortunate foster-father to Sigurd.
[2] Frothi, the Danish king contemporary with Christ's life, was famed for his wealth; his story is told in Saxo Bk.5.

T

Týr er æinendr ása:
opt værðr smiðr blása.

Tyr (Tiw) is the one-handed god: often must a smith blow.

B

Bjarkan er laufgrønstr líma:
Loki bar flærða tíma.

Birch is the greenest-leaved of any bush: Loki bore deceit's long (consequences).[1]

M

Maðr er moldar auki:
mikil er græip á hauki.

Man is the ground's outgrowth: great is the claw of the hawk.

L

Lǫgr er, fællr ór fjalle
foss: en gull ero nosser.

Water is – that falls from the fells – a foss (i.e. waterfall): but golden are ornaments.

Y

Ýr er vetrgrønstr viða:
vænt er, er brennr, at sviða.

Yew is the greenest of trees in winter: it is liable, as it burns, to crackle.

---

[1] Dickins, 1915, p.27, translates the second half, 'Loki was fortunate in his deceit'. In either case the reference would be to his role in Baldur's death.

24. Alphabet Divination

(BL Cotton Tiberius D.27, f.55b–56b)

This text was printed by Sievers 1877 as 'Bedeutung der Buchstaben'. The letters explained are those of the Latin, not the Old English alphabet, suggesting the text was being used in conjunction with random opening of a Bible or Psalter.

A. *He gangeð 7 biþ his siðfæt gesund.*

He (should) proceed and his journey will be safe/successful.

B. *God þu fintst, gyf ðu hit onginst 7 þe bið wel.*

You will come upon good things if you undertake it (i.e. this project), and (all) will be well for you.

C. *Bliðnysse getacnaþ, nis hit on þissum leohte.*

It signifies joy, but it is not of this world/realm.

D. *Ne gewealdest þu þæs ðu wilt ne þu hit æfre fintst.*

You will never possess/control that you wish to, nor will you ever find it.

E. *Becume blisse ðe 7 þu bist symble gesund.*

Joy will come to you and you will be always healthy/successful.

F. *Tacnað deaþ fram deaþe; on þyssum geare bide god godes.*

It signifies the extinction of death; in this year expect the grace of God.

G. *Þu scealt geðeon be þisse geþohtunge.*

You shall prosper by this idea/advice.

H. *Ð(æt) ðe ne biþ geseald; þenc þu on oðer.*

That will not be granted you; think of something else.

I. *Ongin þ(æt) þu wille, þ(æt) þe bið geendod.*

Undertake what you please, it will be (successfully) concluded.

K. *Beorh þe þ(æt) þu ne gange on frecnysse.*

Guard yourself against getting into danger.

L. *Hera ðu god on ealle tid þines lifes.*

Obey God at every moment of your life.

M. *God þe gemiclað þ(æt) ðe forþ gespewð þ(æt) þu don wilt.*

God will empower you so that what you wish to do will succeed.

N. *Hylt þu þæt to donne; ne bið seald þinum dædum.*

Do not proceed with it; (success) will not be accorded to your actions.

O. *Ealle friðsumaþ god on eallum his mihtum.*

God will reconcile everyone with all His powers.

P. *Gyf þu riht nimst, nelt þu wifes wesan.*

If you choose the right (course), you will not partake of that fate.

Q. *Forþam micel god is 7 nergendlic swyðe 7 þu fintst blisse.*

Because God is great and very merciful and you will find peace.

R. *Forlæt alda syn.*

Give up former sins – or: abandon men's wickedness

S. *Þu bist hal gyf þu to gode gehwyrfst, se sit hal 7 mihtig.*

You will be safe if you turn to God, who is ever dependable and mighty.

T. *Ny fyrhteð þa þe on synnum lyfiað 7 yfel þencað.*

Do not fear those that live in sin and admire evil.

U. *Blis seo ðe biþ geseald*
   7 weg on geweald.

This joy (i.e.wish) will be granted you, and a route to success.

X. *Blise 7 weg 7 ece lif.*

Joy and advancement and eternal life (i.e. salvation)

Y *Bycna[ð] sibbe 7 gesynta.*

Signifies concord and health/prosperity.

Z. *Wuldor sy ðe 7 wurðmynt,   wereda drihten,*
   fæder on foldan,   fægere gemæne
   mid sylfan sunu   7 soðum gaste;
                        amen.

   Glory be to you and honour, Lord of Hosts,
      Father on Earth, happily united
      with Your own Son and the True Spirit;

Sievers (1875) printed two further alphabets from continental MSS., one in Latin, one in German. These are later works with no obvious connection to the Old English text given above, but do give instructions on how such an interpretative alphabet could be used:

> *Si quis aliquid sompnauerit, querat librum quemcunque uoluerit, et dicat 'in nomine patris et filii et spiritus sancti, amen,' et per primam literam quam scriptam inueniet in prima pagina quando liber aperitur significationem sompni inueniet.*

> If someone dreams something, let him seek out a book – whichever he pleases – and say 'in the name of the Father and the Son and the Holy Ghost, amen,' and according to the first letter that he finds written on the first page (he lights on) when he opens the book, he will discover the meaning of the dream.

In the similar German instructions, the psalm 'Miserere mei deus' is to be sung before invoking the Trinity, and the book to be consulted must be a Psalter.

25. De Somniorum Eventu

(Bodleian MS. Junius 23 f.150b–152b, and sim. in BL Cotton Tiberius A.ii.f.36a-37b, via Cockayne vol.3 pp.168–177; I also use his translation.)

This extensive text covers pretty well everything an Anglo-Saxon might be expected to encounter in the dream-world. For reasons of space, I have extracted as a sample the entries relating to animals. Occasionally these are given a cultural bias (as the eagle as an imperial symbol); many of the implications are of a literal kind, but not all are obviously so.

> *Gyf mon meteð þæt he gefeo earn on his heafod ufan gesettan, þæt tacnað micel weorðmynd.*

> If a man dreams that he sees an eagle settle on his head, that betokeneth much honour.

> *Gif him þince þæt he feala earna ætsomne geseo, þæt bið yfel nið 7 manna sætunga 7 særa.*

> If it seems to him he sees many eagles at once, that shall be harm and assaults and plots of men.

> *Gyf him þince þæt he geseo beon hunig beran, þæt byð þæt he on eadegum hadum feoh gestreonað.*

> If it seems to (him) that (he) sees bees carrying honey, it shall prove to be the earning of money from wealthy persons.

> *Gyf hine beon stingen, þæt byð þæt his mod byð swiðe onstired fram ælþeodegum mannum.*

> If bees sting him, that signifies that his mind shall be much disturbed by foreigners.

Gyf him þince þæt he geseo beon in to his huse fleogan, þæt byð þes huses awestnes.

If he fancy he sees bees fly into his house, that shall be the destruction of the house.

Gyf him þince þæt he geseo fela fugla ætsamne, þæt byð æfest 7 gecid.

If he fancy that he sees many fowls together, that shall be jealousy and chiding.

Gyf he fuglas geseog betwenan heom winnan, þæt byð þæt rice hadas winnað heom betweonan.

If he seeth fowls fight one another, that shall be that powerful persons are in contest.

Gyf his nædre ehte, beorge him wyð ifle wifmen.

If a snake pursue him, let him be on his guard against evil women.

Þonne him þynce þæt his earn ehte, þæt bið dead.

When it seems an eagle pursues him, that is death.

......

Gif him þince þæt he dracan geseo, god þæt biþ.

If he fancies that he sees a dragon, that is good.

......

Gif him þince þæt he huntige, beorge him georne wið his fynd.

If he fancies he is a hunting, let him be well on his guard against his enemies.

Gif him þince þæt he hundas geseo 7 hi hine gretan, beorge him eac wið his fynd.

If he thinks he sees hounds, and they bay him, let him be on his guard against his enemies.

Gif him þince þæt he geseo hundas yrnan, þæt byþ micel good toweard.

If he thinks he sees hounds run, that stands for much coming good.

Þonne him þince þæt he fiscas geseo, þæt byð regn.

When he thinks that he sees fishes, that signifies rain.

......

Gif mon mete þæt he hwit hors hæbbe, oððe on ride, þæt byð weorðmind.

If he dreams that he has or rides upon a white horse, that portends honour.

Gif him þince þæt he on blacum horse ride, þæt byð his modes angnes.
If he thinks he is riding on a black horse, that is anxiety of mind.

Gif him þince þæt he on readum horse ride, þæt byð his goda wanigend.
If he fancies he is riding on a bay horse, that is decay of fortune.

Gyf him þince þæt he on fealawan horse ride, þæt byð god – oððe grægan, þæt byð god swefn.
If he fancies he is riding on a dun or grey horse, that is a good dream.

......

Gif him þince þæt he næddran geseo, þæt bið yfeles wifes niþ.
If he fancies he sees an adder, that means a wicked woman's spite.

......

Gif him þince þæt he hæbbe hwit sceap, þæt tacnað god.
If he dreams he has a white sheep, that portends good.

Gif him þince þæt he hæbbe ferr hryðer, ne byð þæt naþor ne god ne yfel.
If he fancies he has a bull, that is neither good nor harm.

......

Gif man mæte þæt he feola swyna ætsamne geseo, þonne mæg he wenan broces.
If a man dreams that he sees many swine together, then he may look out for trouble.

Gif him þince þæt he feala henna geseo oððe hæbbe, þæt bið god.
If he fancies he sees or possesses many hens, that is good.

Gyf man mæte þæt he henne æegeru hæbbe oððe þicge, ne deah hym þæt.
If a man dreams that he has or eats hens' eggs, that avails nought.

Gyf mon mete þæt he gæt geseo, þonne mæg he wenan þæs laðwendan feondes him on neawyste.
If a man dreams he sees a goat, then he may reckon on the near neighbourhood of the evil being, the fiend.

Gyf mon mæte þæt he feola stodhorsa habbe oððe geseo, awestnesse his goda ðæt tacnað.
If a man dreams he has many stud horses, or sees such, that betokens devastation of his goods.

Gyf man mete þæt he fela gosa hæbbe, god þæt byð.

If a man dreams that he has many geese, that is good.

Gif him þince that he sceap pullige, ne bið þæt god.

If one dreams he is pulling [i.e. plucking] sheep, that is not good.

26. The Import of Dreams by State of the Moon

(Bodleian Hatton 115 f.148a – late 11th century – via Foerster 1935–6 pp.90–92.)

In this text, the efficacy of a dream is assessed in relation to the phase of the moon, the full moon having least impact.

Ðære ærestan nyhte, þonne niwe mone byð ecymen, þæt mon þonne in sweofne gesihþ þæt cymeð to gefean.

On the first night, when the new moon is come, whatever one sees in a dream will turn out well.

Þære æfteran niht 7 þore ðriddan nyht, ne byoð þæt naðer ne god ne yfel.

On the second and the third night, it will (mean) neither good nor evil.

Ðære feorðan nyht 7 þeora fiftan wene heo godre gefremednesse.

On the fourth and fifth nights, she (the moon) presages a good outcome.

Þære syxtan niht, þæt þu gesyx[t], swa hyt byoð, 7 þeo wyð eorfoþu geoscilt.

On the sixth night, whatever you see will come about, and you will be shielded from any bad consequence.

Þere seofoðan nyht, þæt þu gesixt, swa hyt byð, 7 æfter mycelre tyde agæð.

On the seventh night, what you see will come about, and after a long time will occur.

Þære viii niht 7 þere nigoþan, raþe þu gesihst swefn, þæt bið a[d]le[1] oðþe trega.

On the eighth night and the ninth, as soon as you see the dream, it will (mean) illness or misfortune.

[there is no entry for tenth or eleventh night]

Þeore xii niht 7 þeore xiii niht, ine þrim dagum þu gesihst þin swefn.

On the twelfth and thirteenth night, within three days you will see your dream (come about).

Þeore xiiii nihti ne hafað þat nane gefremednesse.

---

[1] MS. *able*

On the fourteenth night, it has no effect.

Þeore xv niht hit hafað litle gefremædnesse.
On the fifteenth night it has little effect.

Þeore xvi niht æfter mycelre tide agæð þin sweofn.
On the sixteen night, after a long time your dream will come about.

Ðere xvii niht 7 xviii 7 nigontene in iii 7 c-um daga bið go[d][1] *swefn.*
On the seventeenth, eighteenth and nineteenth, within 103 days' time the dream will make good.

Ðonne se mona bið xx niht 7 i 7 xx niht, þæt bið scir oððe ceap in þem swefne toweard.
When the moon is twenty or twenty-one nights (old), what (you see) in the dream will affect your position or possessions.

Þonne heo byð ii 7 xx niht eald, þæt þu gesihst, hit lengeð to gode gefean.
When she (the moon) is twenty-two nights old, what you see will result in great joy.

Þonne heo bið iii 7 xx nihta eald, þæt bið cid 7 geflit.
When she (the moon) is twenty-three nights old, it will (mean) strife and contention.

Ðonne heo bið iiii 7 xx nihta eald, 7 v 7 xx, 7 vi 7 xx nihta eald, þæt bið weorðlic ege[s]: on nigon dagum oððe on x þin swefn agæð.
When she (the moon) is twenty-four nights old, and twenty-five and twenty-six nights old, what (you dream) is worthy of serious alarm: within nine or ten days your dream will come about.

Þonne heo bi[ð] vii 7 xx, 7 viii 7 xx nihta eald, ealne gefean þæt bicneð.
When she (the moon) is twenty-seven and twenty-eight nights old, it signifies complete happiness.

Þonne heo bið ix 7 xx 7 fulle xxx nihta eald, þæt bið æfre buton fræcnesse.
When she (the moon) is twenty-nine and the complete thirty nights old, it (the dream) is always without harm.

---

[1] MS. *goð*

27. Import of Dreams by Content

(BL Cotton MS. Tib.A.iii – 11th century – edited by Förster in Archiv *120, pp.302–5)*

This limited text is probably Latin-based (since the significances form a group of 'f' and 'g' words in Latin, appropriate to a translation of a section of a larger text), and shows some variety of approach, from the directly significant dream like no.13, to the obliquely meaningful like no.12, and the directly contradictory interpretation, as in nos.8 or 21. Reality is slightly challenged in no.10.

1. *Gif him mæte þæt his onsyne fæger si, god þæt bið 7 him bið wurðmynt toweard; 7 gif him þince unfæger, yfel þæt bið.*

   If he has a dream that his face is fair, that is good and there will honour coming to him; and if that his face is unfair, that will be evil.

2. *Gif him mæte þæt he se mid æniges cynnes irene slægen, ymbhydu þæt beoð 7 sorge þæt tacnað.*

   If he has a dream that he be struck with any thing iron, that is (a sign of) anxiety and it signifies sorrow.

3. *Gif him mæte þæt he sweord wege, orsorhnesse yfela þæt bioþ.*

   If he has a dream that he carries a sword, that is (a sign of) freedom from evil cares.

4. *Gif him þince þæt he gimmas sceawige, þæt bioð mænigfeald 7 uncuðlic þing.*

   If it seems to him that he looks upon jewels, that is (a sign of) a complex and mysterious business.

5. *Gif man mæte þæt he micel rice hæbbe, þæt bið wurðmynt.*

   If someone dreams that he has great power, that is (a sign) of honour to come.

6. *Gif man mæte þæt he on wyllan þwea,*[1] *þæt byð gestreon.*

   If someone dreams that he washes in a spring, that is (a sign of) wealth coming.

7. *Gif man mæte þæt he fela hunda ætsomne geseo, þonne scilde he hine wið his fynd ful georne.*

   If someone dreams that he sees many dogs together, then he should be on guard against his enemies very keenly.

---

[1] MS. *þwean*

8. *Gif man mæte þæt he deadne mann cysse, langsam lif 7 gesæliglic him biþ towerd.*

   If someone dreams that he kisses a dead person, a long and happy life is coming to him.

9. *Gif man mæte þæt he penegas oððe mancas finde, þæt tacnað æfæste/æfst*

   If someone dreams that finds pennies or half-crowns, that signifies enmity.

10. *Gif man mæte þæt he finde 7 ne grete/oðrine, þæt tacnað bliðes mannes onsion; gif he nimþ, ne deah him þæt.*

    If someone dreams that he finds (money) and does not touch it, that signifies the countenance of a happy person; but if he picks it up, it will not benefit him.

11. *Gif him þince þæt his earn swyþe eahte, þæt byþ mycel gefea.*

    If it seems to him that an eagle pursues him assiduously, that is (a sign of) great joy to come.

12. *Gif he geseo twegen monan þæt byþ micel gefea.*

    If he sees two moons, that is (a sign of) great joy to come.

13. *Gif he geseo þæt man operne man slea, beorge him wiþ broc.*

    If he sees someone strike down another person, let him guard himself against harm.

14. *Gif him mæte þæt he geseo hwitne ocsan oððe onufan sitte, þæt bið wurðmynt.*

    If he has a dream that he sees or sits upon a white ox, that is (a sign of) honour coming.

15. *Gif him þince blæc oððe red, yfel þæt byþ 7 broc.*

    If (the ox) seems to him black or red, that will (signify) evil and misfortune.

16. *Gif man mæte þæt he geseo hwitne oxan 7 miclene, þæt bið gefea.*

    If someone dreams that he sees a large white ox, that is (a sign of) joy.

17. *Gif he hornlease oxan geseo, þonne ofercymð he his find.*

    If he sees a hornless ox, then he will overcome his foes.

18. *Gif him mæte þæt his earmes beon fægere gegerede, þæt bið freondscype.*

    If he has a dream that his arms are beautifully clothes, that is (a sign of) friendship.

19. *Gif man mæte þæt he micles þinges geweald age, þæt bið þæt he him his fynd to gewealde getihð.*

If someone dreams that he has responsibility in some great enterprise, that means that he will bring his enemies under control.

20. *Gif him þince þæt he yrne swyþe, þonne byð him broc towerd.*

If it seems to him that runs hard, then there will be misfortune coming to him.

21. *Gif him þince þæt he micel god hæbbe, þæt bið his goda wanung.*

If it seems to him that he has a lot of possessions, that is (a sign of) a decrease in his possessions.

22. *Gif man mæte þæt he stele, þæt þe wurð underne 7 cuð, þæt he ær ana witan sceolde.*

If someone dreams that he ?rushes forward, then something will become revealed and widely known that he alone previously kept knowledge of.

23. *Gif him mæte þæt him si his swura gebunden, beorge him þonne georne wið ealle frecne þing.*

If he has a dream that his neck is tied, let him guard himself keenly against all dangerous things.

24. *Gif man mæte þæt he of heahre dune fealle, god þæt bið þearfan, 7 þam weligan yfel.*

If someone dreams that he falls from a high cliff, that is a good sign for a poor man but a bad one for a rich person.

25. *Gif man mæte þæt he si upahafen, god þæt tacnað.*

If someone dreams that he is raised aloft, that signifies good to come.

28. Import of New Year's Day

(BL Cotton MS. Vesp.D.xiv f.75b; via Warner 1917 p.66)

This is representative of a large class of prognostications, in which the combination of (human-devised) calendar elements are imbued with supernatural significance.

Đonne forme gearesdæig byð Sunendæig, hit byð god winter, 7 windig læncte[n]tid, dryge sumer, god hærfest, 7 scep tyððrigeð, 7 hit byð grið 7 wæstme manigfeald.

When the first day of the New Year is a Sunday, it will be a clement winter, and a windy spring, a dry summer, a good harvest, and it will favour sheep, and there will be peace and a good return on crops.

Ðonne hit byð Monendæig, hit byð scurfah winter, 7 god læncten, 7 windig sumer, 7 storemig 7 geswyncfull hærfest.

When it falls on a Monday, it will be a rainy winter and a fine spring and a windy summer and a stormy and arduous harvest.

Þonne hit byð Tywesdæig, hit byð wæt winter, 7 windig læinten, 7 wæt sumer, 7 wifmæn swelteð 7 scipes forfareð 7 cynges sweltað.

When it falls on a Tuesday, it will be a wet winter and a windy spring and a wet summer and women will miscarry and ships perish and kings die.

Þonne hit byð Wodnesdæig, hit byð heard winter, 7 yfel læinten, god sumer 7 geswyncfull hærfest, 7 hunig byð gæsne.

When it falls on a Wednesday, it will be a hard winter and a bad spring, a good summer and an arduous harvest, and honey will be lacking.

Ðonne hit byð Þuresdæg, hit byð god winter, 7 windig læinten, god sumer, 7 god hærfest.

When it falls on a Thursday, it will be a clement winter, and a windy spring, and a good summer, and a good harvest.

Þonne hit byð Fridæg, hit byð hwerefinde winter, 7 god lænten, 7 god sumer, 7 god hærfest.

When it falls on a Friday, it will be a variable winter, and a good spring, and a good summer, and a good harvest.

Ðonne hit byð Sæterdæig, hit byð scurfah winter, 7 windig læinten, 7 ealle wæstmes yfeles gewænde; scep cwelleð 7 ealde mænn.

When it falls on a Saturday, it will be a rainy winter, and a windy spring, and all crops turned bad; sheep will die and so will old people.

29. Weather Signs (Signa Tempestatum vel Serenitatis)

(Bede *De Natura Rerum* c.36 via *Patrologia Latina* vol.90, cols.187–278)

This is an example of 'allowable' prediction, based on the supposed influence of the moon on the sub-lunary sphere or atmosphere as we would call it (cf. Ælfric, below, no.33). It includes the popular 'red sky at night' formula.

Sol in ortu maculosus, vel sub nube latens, pluvium diem praesagit. Si rubeat, sincerum; si palleat, tempestuosum; si concavus videtur, ita ut in medio fulgens radios ad austrum et aquilonem emittat, tempestatem humidam et ventosam; si pallidus in nigras nubes occidat, aquilonem ventum. Coelum si vespere rubet, serenum diem; si mane, tempestuosum significat. Ab aquilone fulgur, et ab euro tonitrus tempestatem, et ab austro flatus aestum portendit. Luna quarta si rubeat quasi aurum, ventos ostendit; si summo in corniculo maculis nigrescit, pluvium mensis exordium; si in medio, plenilunium serenum. Item cum aqua in nocturna navigatione scintillat ad remos, tempestas erit. Et cum delphini undis saepius exsiliunt, quo illi feruntur, inde ventus exsurget, et unde nubes discussae coelum aperiunt.

If the sun is blotched at its rising, or hidden behind a cloud, it presages a rainy day. If it is red, a clear day; if it looks pale, a stormy day; if it looks hollow, such that it sends out from its centre rays to south and north, (it means) wet and windy weather; if pale and hidden in black clouds, a north wind (is coming). If the sky reddens at sunset, (it foretells) a clear day; if in the morning, it means bad weather. Lightning from the north and thunder from the south portend bad weather, wind from the east portends heat. If a quarter-moon is coloured like gold, it portends high winds; if at the tip of a horn it darkens with blotches, (it will be) the commencement of a rainy month; if the marks seem in the centre, a calm month. Also when during a night voyage the sea glitters about the oars, there will be a storm. And when dolphins often leap above the water, by what they say, there will result a wind rising and breaking clouds will open the heavens (in rain).

30. Thunder

(Pseudo-Bede *De Tonitruis Libellus*, printed in *Patrologia Latina* vol.90 cols. 609–614)

This strange, elaborately composed work, is unlikely to be by Bede. Jones (1939 p.45–47) speculates that the Herefrid to whom the work is dedicated could be the late 9th century Bishop of Auxerre; the material could derive from a seventh century Greek text, Lydus' *De Ostentis*. In view of the florid style of the Latin, I substitute a simplified and condensed translation.

1. On the Direction of Thunder:

If thunder arises in the east on the coast, then according to the wise traditions of philosophers, it indicates that during the course of that year there would be a great outpouring of human blood [i.e. a battle].

If the thunder comes from western regions, then… it is said to presage death for the offspring of Adam, and a terrible plague approaching in the course of that year.

If the thunder is in the south, then, as wise and astute philosophers assert… it foretells that the inhabitants of the ocean [i.e. fish] will die off in some great misfortune.

When thunder is heard in the north… it signifies the death of the worst transgressors, that is of pagans and of heretic Christians.

2. Significance by Month

With a translation of the Latin I parallel a translation of an Old English text from Cotton Vesp.D.xiv, f. 103b, via Warner 1917 p.91, for contrast.

Latin: If thunder occurs in January (as the astuteness of Philosophers reports), then in the course of that year many men and beasts, such as cattle and sheep, will die, and also orchards and woods will remain sterile and unproductive.

OE: In the month of January, if it thunders, it presages great winds, and the crops of the earth will turn out well, and there will be a battle (or, war).

Latin: If thunder occurs in the moth of February, then (they say) it will seriously damage the ears of anyone that hears it...

OE: In the month of February, if it thunders, it foretells the death of many people and most of the kingdom.

Latin: Thunder in March...has dangerous connotations, and foretells a great mortality or a day of tremendous judgement [i.e. a communal disaster]

OE: In the month of March, thunder signifies great winds, and crops turning out well, and discord among people.

Latin: April thunder, as they say, signifies approaching danger for crops and fruits, and means it is very dangerous to be sailing on the waves of the ocean.

OE: In April, thunder betokens a happy year, and the death of evil people.

Latin: If in any year the thunder peals out in May, then those who have researched such matters maintain that the coming year will be one of good rainfall and a plenitude of crops and great fertility.

OE: In May, thunder presages a hungry year.

Latin: If thunder occurs in June... it is said to indicate that a great many different shoals of all kinds of fish will come in the ocean waves.

OE: In the month of June, thunder signifies great winds, and madness among wolves and lions.

Latin: Thunder in the month of July... is said to signify the approach of the risk of death in the course of the same year, and also a great unfruitfulness in trees.

OE: In the month of July, thunder signifies crops turning out well, and livestock perishing.

Latin: If thunder peals out in August... it is said to indicate the likelihood of many fish of all kinds dying, and of a plague of snakes.

OE: In the harvest month, thunder signifies a good yield, and people will sicken.

Latin: If thunder arises in September…it is said mystically to indicate a huge crowd of secular people on the move in large groups

OE: In September, thunder means a good harvest, and the killing of powerful (or rich) people.

Latin: October thunder… is asserted to mean very strong gales and mighty winds before the end of the year.

OE: In October thunder foretells a great gale, and crops yet to come, and a lack of fruits from trees.

Latin: Thunder in November… is said to signify approaching sterility and lack of fecundity for all things.

OE: In November thunder bodes a happy year, and crops yet to come.

Latin: By fortunate and careful investigation, noble and learned doctors have discerned in the spiritual mirror of nature, that December thunder predicts nothing harmful or evil for men or animals or crops, but rather indications of prosperity and health.

OE: In December, thunder predicts a good harvest from the soil, and harmony, and peace.

3. Thunder according to the seven days.

Here the text attributed to Bede may be contrasted with an Old English text from Cotton. Tiberius A.ii.f.38a via Cockayne vol.3 p.180, for which I use Cockayne's translation.

Latin: If it thunders on Sunday… this is considered to presage an extensive mortality of monks and nuns.

OE: If the first thunder comes on Sunday, it signifies the death of children of your kin.

Latin: If thunder arises on a Monday…, they say it indicates that a large number of married couples will die, and crops will be damaged if there is an eclipse.

OE: If it thunders on Monday, that presages great bloodshed in some nation.

Latin: If thunder occurs on Tuesday… there is no doubt it signifies a coming magnificent and abundant supply of the fruits of the earth.

OE: If it thunders on Tuesday, that signifies a failing of crops.

Latin: Of thunder on Wednesday... there is no doubt it presages idle and scandalous prostitutes will pass in a throng from the prison of the flesh, or a great shedding of human blood.

OE: If it thunders on Wednesday, that means the death of land-workers and mechanics [*cræftigra*].

Latin: They say... that however many times Jupiter roars out on his own day (Thursday), will be that much multiplied the abundance of the fruits of the earth, and a great and rich multitude of the inhabitants of the sea [i.e. fish] will fill again and again the streams and rivers.

OE: If it thunders on Thursday, that means the death of womenfolk.

Latin: On Friday... if thunder occurs, it presages the soon-following killing of a king, or a very violent war, or other disaster involving a great number of lives, or a great number of cattle about to die.

OE: If it thunders on Friday, that means the death of sea-creatures.

Latin: On the Sabbath (Saturday)... if thunder arises, then not long after there will come a great plague affecting humans, or a very violent war.

OE: If it thunders on Saturday, that means the death of judges and officials.

31. De Diebus Malis (Concerning Unlucky Days)

(Bodleian MS Harley 3271 ff.90b–91a, mid 11th century, via Henel 1934–5 pp.336-7; sections 3–6 precede 1–3 in MS.)

When you had decided what to do, it was almost as important to do it at the right time. (Read the instructions on the medicine bottle carefully!) To the Romans, the equivalent was a list of days to be avoided, implying an astrological dimension to medical treatment, and a sympathy between the cycles of the body and the planets.

1. *Þa ealdan læcas gesettan on ledenbocum þæt on ælcum monðe beoð æfre twegen dagas þe syndan swyðe derigendlice ænigne drenc on to ðicgenne, oððe blod on to lætenne, forðan þe an tid is on ælcum þæra daga gif man ænige æddran geopenað on þære tide þæt hit bið his lifleast oððe langsum sar. Þæs cunnode sum læce, let his horse blod on þære tide and hit læg sona dead.*

   The ancient doctors laid down the precept in Latin texts that in each month there are always two days which are very perilous to take any (medicinal) draught on, or to let blood on, because there is one hour in each of those days on which if one opens a vein then it means loss of life or permanent injury; one doctor investigated this: he drew blood from his horse at that hour and it fell down dead at once.

2. *Nu synd hit þas dagas, swa swa us seicgaþ bec:*
   se forma dæg on martio, þæt is on hlydan monþe, 7 se feorþa dæg ærþam þe he
   fare aweg;
   on þam oþran monþe, þe we apriles hatat, se tyoþa dæg is dergendlic, 7 se
   endlyfta dæg ær his utgange;
   eft is on þan monþe þe we maios hatet se þridda dæg dergendlic 7 se seoueþa ær
   his ende;

   on iunius se teoþa 7 ær his ende se fifteoþa;
   on iulius se þreotteoða 7 ær his ende se teða;
   on augustus se forma 7 ær his ende se oðer;
   on september se ðridda 7 ær his ende se teoða;
   on october eac se ðridda 7 ær his ende se teoða;
   on november se fifta 7 ær his ende se þridda;
   on december se twelfta 7 ær his ende se seofanteoða;
   on ianuarius se forma 7 ær his ende se seofoða;
   on februarius se feorða 7 ær his ende se ðridda.

Now these are the days, according to what books tell us:

the first day in March, that is on the month (called) Hlyda, and the fourth day before it (the month) passes away; in the second month, which we call April, the tenth day is dangerous and the eleventh day before its (the month's) ending; then in the month we call May is the third day dangerous, and the seventh before its end; in June the tenth, and before its ending the fifteenth; in July the thirteenth, and before its end the tenth; in August the first, and before its end the second; in September the third and before its end the tenth; in October likewise the third and before its end the tenth; in November the fifth, and before its end the third; in December the twelfth, and before its end the seventeenth; in January the first and before its end the seventh; in February the fourth, and before its end the third.

3. *We gesetton on foreweardan on þysre endebyrdnesse þone monaþ martius, þe menn hatat hlyda, forþan he is angin æfter rihtum getele ealles þæs geares, 7 se ælmihtiga god on þam monþe gescop ealle gesceafta.*

We have placed at the head of this list the month March, we people (here) call Hlyda, because it is the beginning in proper reckoning of the whole year and almighty God in that month formed all creation.

4. *Nu æft be þam monan is miclum to warnienne þæt mon on fyuwer [sic] nihtan
   monan oþþe on fif nihta men blod ne læte, swa swa us secgað bec, ærþan þe se
   mona 7 syu sæ beon anræde.*

   Now though concerning the moon, it is much to be guarded against that anyone
   during the (first) four nights of the (new) moon or on the fifth should draw out
   blood, according to what books tell us, before the moon and the sea be in
   agreement.

5. *Eac we gehyrdan seggan sumne wisne man þæt nan man ne lyfode þe him lete
   blod on ealra halgena mæssedæig, oþþe gif he gewundad wære. Nis þis nan
   wigelung, ac wise men hit afundan þuruh þæne halgan wisdom, swa swa him
   gedihte godd.*

   Also we have learned that a certain wise man said that no one would live if his
   blood were let on Allhallows, or if he (then) were wounded. This is no
   witchery, but wise men discovered it through holy wisdom, as God intended
   they should.

6. *Gyt her to eacan is to warnienne þæt man ne þicge goseflæsc on þane
   æftemestan dæi hlydan monþes, ne on þæne æftemestan dæig december
   monþes. Goseflæsc byþ æfre unhalwende þam untruman, swa swa ma oþra
   metta þe we ne magan her secggan.*

   Yet here also it must guarded against that no gooseflesh be eaten on the last
   day of the month of March,[1] nor on the last day on the month of December.
   Gooseflesh is always unwholesome to invalids, as are other foods that we may
   not here list.

---

[1] This taboo may relate to Roman superstition; in England eating goose does not seem to
have been discouraged; it was traditional to Michaelmas.

Science & Knowledge

32. Alfred on the Solar System.

Alfred's 'Metres of Boethius' – translations of the Latin poems in Boethius' 'De Philosophiae Consolatione' – is a brave attempt to render Boethius' complex statements on Graeco-Roman philosophy and science. The following passage from Metre 20 (lines 161-175) is an explanatory extra in the Old English version, tackling the problem of what keeps the earth in its place, with the metaphor of an egg.

> Þu gestaðolest þurh þa strongan meaht,
> weroda wuldorcyning, wundorlice
> eorðan swa fæste þæt hio on ænige
> healfe ne helde, ne mæg hio hider ne þider
> sigan þe swiðor þe hio symle dyde.
> Hwæt, hi þeah eorðlices auht ne halde,
> is þeah efneðe up 7 ofdune
> to feallanne foldan ðisse,
> þæm anlicost þe on æge bið
> gioleca on middan, glideð hwæðre
> æg ymbutan. Swa stent eall weoruld
> stille on tille: streamas ymbutan,
> lagufloda gelac, lyfte 7 tungla,
> 7 sio scire scell scriðeð ymbutan
> dogora gehwilce – dyde lange swa.

You, glorious King of Hosts, marvellously established, through your great power, the earth so firm (in its place) that it never tilts to any side, nor can it this way or that settle any more than it ever did. Look! though nothing material holds it (in place), yet it would be equally easy for this earth to fall up as down, very like the yolk in the middle of an egg, which can move about (within the confines of) the egg. Similarly the world remains still in its station: outside, the play of the waters, the sky and the stars, and the bright shell itself [=the firmament] revolve around it every day – long has it done so!

33. Ælfric's *De Temporibus Anni* (extracts)

(full text in Henel 1942)

This is based on Bede's work, and contains many details about the phases of the moon, and the agreement of moon and tides, which is informative but dull. I have selected only a few brief examples to give an idea of the style and content. The earth (round or flat?[1]) is the centre of the universe and about it all the planets and the sun rotate; outermost is the boundary of the firmament, a permanent shell in which the stars are embedded. The result is a sort of compendium of biblical and Graeco-Roman data.

1.4–1.6

On ðam oðrum dæge gesceop God heofonan, seo þe is gehaten firmamentum; seo is gesewenlic 7 lichamlic ac swa ðeah we ne magon for ðære fyrlenan heahnysse 7 þæra wolcna þicnysse 7 for ure eagena tyddernysse hi næfre geseon. Seo heofen belicð on hire bosme ealne middaneard 7 heo æfre tyrnð onbuton us swyftre ðonne ænig mylenhweowul, eal swa deop under þyssere eorðan swa heo is bufan. Eall heo is sinewealt 7 ansund 7 mid steorrum amett.

On the second day God created the heaven, which is called the firmament; that is visible and corporeal but yet we never manage to see it because of its remote altitude and the thickness of the clouds and because of our eyes' weakness. The heaven encloses in its interior all middle earth and it continually turns about us quicker than any mill-wheel, as deep under this earth as it is above. It is entirely round and whole and studded with stars.

1.18–20

Soðlice seo sunne gæð be Godes dihte betwux heofenan 7 eorðan: on dæg bufan eorðan 7 on niht under ðysse eorðan eal swa feorr adune on nithlicere tide under þære eorðan swa heo on dæg bufon upastihð. Æfre heo bið yrnende ymbe ðas eorðan 7 eal swa leohte scinð under ðære eorðan on nihtlicere tide swa swa heo on dæg deð bufon urum heafdum. On ða healfe ðe heo scinð þær bið dæg, 7 on ða healfe ðe heo ne scinð þær bið niht.

Truly the sun at God's command runs between the heaven and the earth: during the day above the earth and during the night below this earth, as far down in the night-time below the earth as it in day-time rises above. Continually it is circling round the earth and shines just as brightly below the earth at night-time as it does in the day-time above our heads. On that side on which it shines there is day, and on that side on which it does not shine there is night.

---

[1] *Istorius sæde þæt þyses middangeardes lenge wære XII þusend mila 7 bræde six þusend 7 þreo hundred butan litlum ealandum.* (Istorius said that this earth's length was 12,000 miles and its breadth 6,300 excluding little islands.) – BL MS Cotton Julius A.2 f.140b quoted in *Anglia* 11 (1889) p.5.

1.31–33

*Soðlice se mona 7 ealle steorran underfoð leoht of ðære micclan sunnan 7
heora nan næfð nænne leoman buton of ðære sunnan leoman; 7 ðeah ðe seo
sunne under eorðan on nihtlicere tide scine, þeah astihð hire leoht on
sumere sidan þære eorðan þe ða steorran bufon us onliht; 7 ðonne heo
upagæð heo oferswið ealra ðæra steorrena 7 eac þæs monan leoht mid hire
ormætan leohte. Seo sunne getacnað urne hælend Crist, se ðe is
rihtwisnysse sunne swa swa se witega cwæð.*

Truly the moon and all the stars receive their light from the great sun and
none of them has any brightness except from the sun's light; and although
the sun shines under the earth during the night-time, yet its light rises to the
other side of the earth and illuminates the stars above us; and when it rises
itself, it overpowers the light of all the stars and the moon as well with its
tremendous brightness. The sun signifies our saviour Jesus Christ, who is
the 'sun of righteousness' as the prophet says.[1]

1.35–36 & 8.11–8.14

*Se mona ðe weaxð 7 wanað getacnað þas andwerdan gelaðunge ðe we on
sind; seo is weaxende þurh acennedum cildum 7 wanigende þurh
forðfarendum...*

*Nu cweðað sume men þe ðis gescead ne cunnon þæt se mona hine wende be
ðan ðe hit wedrian sceall on ðam monðe, ac hi ne went næfre naðor, ne
weder ne unweder of ðam ðe his gecynde is. Men magon swa ðeah þa ðe
fyrwite beoð cepan be his bleo 7 be ðære sunnan oððe þæs roderes hwilc
weder toweard bið. Hit is gecyndelic þæt ealle eorðlice lichaman beoð
fulran on weaxendum monan þonne on wanigendum; eac ða treowu þe beoð
aheawene on fullum monan beoð heardran wið wyrmætan 7 langfærran
þonne ða þe beoð on niwum monan aheawene.*

The moon that waxes and wanes signifies the present community of which
we are part; it grows by childbirth and contracts by death...

Now some, who do not know this information [about the moon reacting to
the sun], say that the (new) moon changes itself according to whether it will
be stormy in that month. But neither good weather or bad proceeds from the
aspect of the moon. However men who are keen can deduce by its aspect, as
by that of the sun and the sky, what the weather will be. It is inevitable that
all earthly bodies are fuller under the waxing moon than under the waning
one; also, trees that are cut down at the full moon are hardier against worm-
attack and more enduring than those felled at the new moon.

---

[1] Malachi 4:2

34. Adrian and Ritheus (extracts)

(BL Cotton MS. Julius A.II f.137b.)

In this prose tract, unlike Bede, Alfred and Ælfric, there is little concern with plausible explanation: even the argument that the sun must be very big but far away because of its heat felt so markedly and evenly on earth is reduced to a formula to be taken on trust. It is unlikely that any of the esoteric material found here is invention; but it attests to the problem of depending exclusively on a 'superior' past civilisation – there is no longer any scope for critical discrimination.

Saga me, hwær scyne seo sunne on niht?

Ic þe secge, on þrim stowum: ærest on þæs hwales innoðe, þe is cweden Leviathan, and on oðre tid heo scynð on helle; and þa ðridda tid heo scynð on þam ealond þæt is Glið nemned, and þar restað haligra mann[a] saula oð domes dæig.

Q. Tell me, where does the sun shine at night?

A. I say to you, in three places: firstly in the insides of the whale who is called Leviathan; and at another time it shines in hell; and for a third period it shines upon the island that is called Glith and (that is) where the souls of holy men remain till Doomsday.

Saga me, forhwam scyne seo sunne swa reade on ærne morgien?

Ic þe secge, forþam ðe heo kymð up of þære sæ.

Q. Tell me, why does the sun shine so red in the early morning?

A. I say to you, because it comes up out of the sea.

Saga me, forhwam byð seo sunne swa read on æfen?

Ic þe secge, forþan þe heo lokað ufan on helle.

Q. Tell me, why is the sun so red in the evening?

A. I say to you, because it looks down on hell.

Saga me, hu mycel seo sunne sy.

Ic þe secge, heo ys mare þonn eorðe, forþam heo byð on ælcum lande hat.

Q. Tell me, how big the sun is.

A. I say to you, it is greater than the earth, because it is equally hot in each country.

Saga me, hwilc sy seo sunne?

Ic þe secge, Astriges se dry sæde þæt hit wære byrnende stan.

Q. Tell me, what is the sun (made of)?

A. I say to you, Astriges the magician said that it was a burning stone.

35. Solomon & Saturn 2 (extract)

(MSS. CCCC 41 and 422)

The dialogues of Solomon and Saturn, which comprise prose and verse items in Old English, are not included in the average anthology, presumably because most people consider that "as a literary text the dialogue can have no merit."[1] The content is obscure and slightly odd to modern taste, but its arrangement for two speakers (perhaps indicating the manner of performance) is not without dramatic interest: Solomon represents the true biblical tradition of knowledge, Saturn a defective alternative tradition, perhaps supposed to be that of Babylonian/Eastern learning.

The second verse dialogue is printed and translated in Shippey, 1976, pp.86–103. From this poem the two passages below give the impression of very speculative material, but share with Alfred's 'Metres' a concern over the laws and moral dimensions of physics: the way in which the sun shines is the theme of Metre 30; the disparity of fortune and desert is found in Metres 4 and 9, the concept of rewards being unequal in heaven is mooted in Metre 20:229–231; the contest of elements is found at Metre 20:70–72; the competition of all living things in Metres 13 and 27; the theme of fire tending upwards at Metre 20:124–130, 150–158; the combination of fire in other inanimate and animate entities in Metre 20:144–156. This dialogue may not therefore be quite as mystical as it seems, for the themes it presents tackle points of concern to King Alfred and doubtless many other Anglo-Saxons.

1. Saturnus cwæð:

> "Ac forhwon ne mot seo sunne   side gesceafte
> scire geondscinan?   Forhwam besceadeð heo
> muntas and moras   and monige ec
> weste stowa?   Hu geweorðeð ðæt?"

Saturn said: But why cannot the sun shine all at once over (all) the broad creation? Why does it cast shadows on mountains and plains and many other desert places? How does that come about?

Salomon cwæð:

> "Ac forhwam næron eorð[we]lan   ealle [gedæ]led[2]
> leodum gelice?   Sum to lyt hafað,
> godes grædig.   Hine God seteð
> ðurh geearnunga   eadgum to ræste."

---

[1] Shippey, 1976, p.21
[2] MS. *godeled*

Solomon said: Why were not all earth-dwellers accorded the same (wealth) as each other? One may have too little, (being) keen for good. God will place him in repose with the blessed for his merits.

Saturnus cwæð:

> "*Ac forhwan beoð ða gesiðas somod ætgædre,*
> *wop and hleahtor? Full oft hie weorðgeornra*
> *sælða toslitað. Hu gesæleð ðæt?*"

Saturn said: Why are the companions, weeping and laughter, always together? Very often they break up the joy of worthy people. How does that come about?

Salomon cwæð:

> "*Unlæde bið and ormod se ðe a wile*
> *geomrian on gihðe. Se bið Gode fracoðast.*"

Solomon said: Wretched and hopeless is the one who ever prefers to complain in his adversity. Such seems worthless to God.

Saturnus cwæð:

> "*Forhwon ne moton we ðonne ealle mid onmedlan*
> *gegnum gangan in Godes rice?*"

Saturn said: Why may we not all proceed with (equal) glory forward to God's kingdom?

Salomon cwæð:

> "*Ne mæg fyres feng ne forstes cile,*
> *snaw ne sunne somod eardian,*
> *aldor geæfnan, ac hira sceal anra gehwylc*
> *onlutan and onliðigan ðe hafað læsse mægn.*"

Solomon said: The grip of fire and the chill of frost, snow and sun – these cannot abide together or live the same life, but one of them has to bend and yield, that has the lesser strength.

2. [Solomon:]

> *Leoht hafað heow and had haliges gastes,*
> *Cristes gecyndo; hit ðæt gecyðeð full oft.*
> *Gif hit unwitan ænige hwile*
> *healdað butan hæftum, hit ðurh hrof wædeð,*
> *bryceð and bærneð boldgetimbru,*
> *seomað steap and geap, stigeð on lenge,*
> *clymmeð on gecyndo; cunnað hwænne mote*
> *fyr on his frumsceaft on fæder geardas,*

eft to his eðle,   ðanon hit æror cuom.
Hit bið eallenga   eorl[e] to gesihðe,
ðam ðe gedælan can   Dryhtnes ðecelan,
forðon nis nænegu gecynd   cuiclifigende,
ne fugel ne fisc   ne foldan stan,
ne wæteres wylm   ne wudutelga,
ne munt ne mor   ne ðes middangeard,
ðæt he forð ne sie   fyrenes cynnes."

Light has the appearance and form of the Holy Ghost, the (same) nature as Christ; it very often demonstrates that. If unknowing men keep it for any length of time without restraints, it gets away through the roof, it breaks up ad burns the beams of the house, it lingers there, high and wide, then finally ascends, climbs up according to its own nature; being fire, it tests as to when it can (return) to its origin in the courtyards of the Father, (go) back to its home-land, whence it before came. It is entirely visible to the man who knows how to distinguish the torches of the Lord, for there is no living species, neither fowl nor fish nor stone of the earth, neither surge of water nor tree-branch, neither mountain nor moor nor this middle-earth – that is not all at times part of the fiery family.

36. The Signs of the Fifteen Days before Doomsday

(MS. Vesapsian D.xiv, ed. R. D-N Warner, 1917, pp.89–91)

This text is preserved in a book of late Old English homilies, and supplies an apt closing text for my selection. The forthcoming end of the world was a scientific tenet, that is a religious concept accepted as fact – here ornamented by vivid image and moral reflection, tinged perhaps by post-Conquest misanthropy.

On þan formen dæige, se sæ heo onhefð ofer ealle dunen feowertig elnen on hehnysse swa swa weall, 7 swa hit byð fram morgen oð æfen.

On the first day, the sea will raise itself up, forty ells in height above all hills like a rampart, and so it will remain from morning to evening.

On þan oðren dæige, seo sæ besincð inn agean swa deope, þæt uneaðe men gesicð þæt ufemeste, 7 swa hit byð eallne dæig.

On the second day, the sea will sink down as deep again (as it rose), so that it will be difficult for people to see its top, and so it will remain all day.

On þan þridden dæige, heo gecerð to hire rihte gecynde mid eallen hire streamen, þe heo hæfde æt frymðen, þa þa God ærest toscelede wæter fram lande.

On the third day, it (the sea) will return to her proper state with all the watercourses that it had in the beginning when God first divided water from land.

On þan feorðen dæige, ealle sælice deor 7 fissces heo æteowigieð bufe þan yðen 7 bellgigeð swa swa mid mænnisscre reorde, ac þehhweðere ne understant nan mann heora gereord bute God ane; 7 þæt byð to tacnunge þære eorre, þe God cyðð þan synfullen on domes dæige.

On the fourth day, all marine animals and fish will show themselves above the waves and bellow with like a human voice, yet all the same no person will understand their message except God alone; for it will be a symbol of the wrath that God will display towards the sinful on Doomsday.

On þan fiften dæige, ealle wyrte 7 ealle treowwes ageafeð read swat swa blodes dropen. Þæt doð þa wyrtan, for þy þæt þa synfulle mæn heo træden, 7 þa treowwen, for þan þe þa synfulle hæfden freome of heom 7 of heora wæstmen.

On the fifth day, all plants and all trees will give out a red exudation like drops of blood. The plants will do that because sinfull people have been used to trample on them, and the trees because sinful people had benefit of them and their produce.

On þan sixten dæige sculen slean togædere ealle stanes lytle 7 mycele, 7 ælc stan tobrytt on feower hloten, 7 ælc þære hloten fiht wið oðer, oððet heo eall to duste gewurðeð. Þæt heo doð forþan þæt þa arlease mænn of heom worhten steples 7 castles, þæt heo þær mid swæncten geleaffulle mænn 7 Godes þearefen.

On the sixth day all stones small and great will clash together, and each rock will shatter into four lots, and each of those lots will fight with the others, until they are all eroded to dust. They do that because dishonourable men made towers and castles out of them to torment faithful people and God's needy.

On þan seofeðen dæige wurðeð geemnode denen 7 dunen, swa þæt eall eorðe byð smeðe 7 emne. Þæt betacne[ð][1] þæt God ne forsihð þæs þearfendan ansene ne ne wurðeð þæs mihtiges mannes modignysse, ac besicð to ælces mannes gewyrhten.

On the seventh day will be levelled the valleys and the hills, so that all the earth will be smooth and even. That signifies that God will not despise the poor man's appearance nor respect the powerful man's pride, but will pay attention to each man's merits.

---

[1] MS. *betacned*

On þan ehteðen dæige gewurðð swylc eorðstyrung, þæt eall middeneard beofeð fram eastdæle to westdæle, for þan þe he abær þær mannen unrihtwisnysse.

On the eighth day there will happen something like an earthquake, so that all the world will shake from its east end to its west end, because it had to endure men's injustice.

On þan nigeðen dæige tofealleð castles 7 steples 7 hus 7 circen 7 ealle getimbrunge lytle 7 mycele, for þan þe þa synfulle hæfden þæron heora wununge.

On the ninth day will collapse castles and towers and houses and churches and all buildings little and great, because sinful people had their dwellings therein.

On þan tenðen dæige, heo gegaderigeð ealle deaddre manna lymen, swa þæt gyf an mann wære dead on middewearden, 7 his an hand oððe fot wære on eastdæle 7 his oðer lym on westdæle, þehhweðere heo cumeð togædere ælc to his lichame, 7 ælc lichame arist oð his byrigeles brerd.

On the tenth day all the limbs of dead people will reassemble themselves, so that if a person lay dead in a middle region and one hand or one foot were in some eastern region and his others limbs in some western region, yet they would come together again to make a body and each body shall rise as far as the grave's top margin.

On þan ændeleften dæge eorneð wilddeor beo tunen 7 felden 7 manna wunungen swa swa heo beon wittlease.

On the eleventh day wild animals will stampede through towns and fields and people's homes as if they were driven mad.

On þan twelften dæige eorneð mænn geon[d] eall middeneard byfigende 7 drædende Cristes tocyme to demene cwican 7 deaden, swa þæt se were ne gret his wif, ne þæt wif hire were, þeh heo heom gemeten, ac byð swa swa wittlease 7 unspecende. Ne heo ne eteð ne heo ne drincað.

On the twelfth day, people will rush about all the world, trembling and dreading Christ's coming to judge the quick and the dead, so that a husband will not greet his wife, nor a wife her husband, even though they met up, but they will be like mindless and speechless. They will not eat and they will not drink.

On þan þreottende dæige fealleð sunne 7 mone, 7 ealle steorren, forþan þe heo geafen leome þan yfelen mannen.

On the thirteenth day will fall the sun and the moon and all the stars, because they gave light to evil people.

On þan feowertenðen dæige, ealle libbende mænn gewurðeð deade, swa þæt heora nan ne byð gebyrod, ac fyr cumð 7 forbærnð þa eorðe, forþan þe heo fostrede þa synfulle 7 þa arlease.

On the fourteenth day all living people will die so that none of them will receive burial, but fire will come and consume the earth because it fed the sinfull and dishonourable.

On þan fiftenðe dæige cumð flod 7 geswyleð þa æsscen, 7 besæncð ealle þa unclænnyssen into þære eorðe deopnysse, swa þæt on middanearde ne belæfð naht unclænes gesene.

On the fifteenth day will come a flood and swill away the ashes, and wash all the uncleanness down into the earth's depths, so that there will be nothing dirty left visible on the earth.

Some of our other titles

The English Warrior from earliest times to 1066
Stephen Pollington

This is not intended to be a bald listing of the battles and campaigns from the Anglo-Saxon Chronicle and other sources, but rather it is an attempt to get below the surface of Anglo-Saxon warriorhood and to investigate the rites, social attitudes, mentality and mythology of the warfare of those times.

> "An under-the-skin study of the role, rights, duties, psyche and rituals of the Anglo-Saxon warrior. The author combines original translations from Norse and Old English primary sources with archaeological and linguistic evidence for an in-depth look at the warrior, his weapons, tactics and logistics.
>
> A very refreshing, innovative and well-written piece of scholarship that illuminates a neglected period of English history"

Time Team Booklists - Channel 4 Television

Revised Edition

An already highly acclaimed book has been made even better by the inclusion of additional information and illustrations.

£16.95   ISBN 1–898281–42–4   245 x 170mm   over 50 illustrations   304 pages hardback

The Mead Hall The feasting tradition in Anglo-Saxon England
Stephen Pollington

This new study takes a broad look at the subject of halls and feasting in Anglo-Saxon England. The idea of the communal meal was very important among nobles and yeomen, warriors, farmers churchmen and laity. One of the aims of the book is to show that there was not just one 'feast' but two main types: the informal social occasion *gebeorscipe* and the formal, ritual gathering *symbel*.

Using the evidence of Old English texts - mainly the epic *Beowulf* and the *Anglo-Saxon Chronicles*, Stephen Pollington shows that the idea of feasting remained central to early English social traditions long after the physical reality had declined in importance.

The words of the poets and saga-writers are supported by a wealth of archaeological data dealing with halls, settlement layouts and magnificent feasting gear found in many early Anglo-Saxon graves.

Three appendices cover:

- Hall-themes in Old English verse;
- Old English and translated texts;
- The structure and origins of the warband.

£14.95 ISBN 1-898281-30-0   9 ¾ x 6 ¾ inches   248 x 170mm   288 pages   hardback

First Steps in Old English

An easy to follow language course for the beginner

Stephen Pollington

A complete, well presented and easy to use Old English language course that contains all the exercises and texts needed to learn Old English. This course has been designed to be of help to a wide range of students, from those who are teaching themselves at home, to undergraduates who are learning Old English as part of their English degree course. The author is aware that some individuals have difficulty with grammar. To help overcome this and other difficulties, he has adopted a step-by-step approach that enables students of differing abilities to advance at their own pace. The course includes practice and translation exercises.

There is a glossary of the words used in the course, and 16 Old English texts, including the Battle of Brunanburh and Battle of Maldon.

£16.95   ISBN 1-898281-38-6 10" x 6½" (245 x 170mm)   256 pages

Ærgeweorc   Old English Verse and Prose

read by Stephen Pollington

This audiotape cassette can be used with *First Steps in Old English* or just listened to for the sheer pleasure of hearing Old English spoken well.

Tracks: 1. Deor. 2. Beowulf – The Funeral of Scyld Scefing. 3. Engla Tocyme (The Arrival of the English). 4. Ines Domas. Two Extracts from the Laws of King Ine. 5. Deniga Hergung (The Danes' Harrying) Anglo-Saxon Chronicle Entry AD997. 6. Durham 7. The Ordeal (Be ðon ðe ordales weddigaþ) 8. Wið Dweorh (Against a Dwarf) 9. Wið Wennum (Against Wens) 10. Wið Wæterælfadle (Against Waterelf Sickness) 11. The Nine Herbs Charm 12. Læcedomas (Leechdoms) 13. Beowulf's Greeting 14. The Battle of Brunanburh 15. Blacmon – by Adrian Pilgrim.

£7.50   ISBN 1–898281–20–3   C40 audiotape

Wordcraft: Concise English/Old English Dictionary and Thesaurus

Stephen Pollington

This book provides Old English equivalents to the commoner modern words in both dictionary and thesaurus formats. The Thesaurus presents vocabulary relevant to a wide range of individual topics in alphabetical lists, thus making it easily accessible to those with specific areas of interest. Each thematic listing is encoded for cross-reference from the Dictionary. The two sections will be of invaluable assistance to students of the language, as well as to those with either a general or a specific interest in the Anglo-Saxon period.

£9.95   A5   ISBN 1–898281–02–5 256pp

An Introduction to the Old English Language and its Literature

Stephen Pollington

The purpose of this general introduction to Old English is not to deal with the teaching of Old English but to dispel some misconceptions about the language and to give an outline of its structure and its literature. Some basic knowledge of these is essential to an understanding of the early period of English history and the present form of the language.

£4.95   A5   ISBN 1–898281–06–8   48pp

Anglo-Saxon Runes

John. M. Kemble

Kemble's essay *On Anglo-Saxon Runes* first appeared in the journal *Archaeologia* for 1840; it draws on the work of Wilhelm Grimm, but breaks new ground for Anglo-Saxon studies in his survey of the Ruthwell Cross and the Cynewulf poems. It is an expression both of his own indomitable spirit and of the fascination and mystery of the Runes themselves, making one of the most attractive introductions to the topic. For this edition new notes have been supplied, which include translations of Latin and Old English material quoted in the text, to make this key work in the study of runes more accessible to the general reader.

£4.95   A5   ISBN 0–9516209–1–6   80pp

Looking for the Lost Gods of England

Kathleen Herbert

Kathleen Herbert sifts through the royal genealogies, charms, verse and other sources to find clues to the names and attributes of the Gods and Goddesses of the early English. The earliest account of English heathen practices reveals that they worshipped the Earth Mother and called her Nerthus. The tales, beliefs and traditions of that time are still with us in, for example, Sand able to stir our minds and imaginations.

£4.95   A5   ISBN 1–898281–04–1   64pp

Rudiments of Runelore

Stephen Pollington

This book provides both a comprehensive introduction for those coming to the subject for the first time, and a handy and inexpensive reference work for those with some knowledge of the subject. The *Abecedarium Nordmannicum* and the English, Norwegian and Icelandic rune poems are included in their original and translated form. Also included is work on the three Brandon runic inscriptions and the Norfolk 'Tiw' runes.

£4.95   A5   ISBN 1–898281–16–5   Illustrations   88pp

Rune Cards

Brian Partridge & Tony Linsell

"This boxed set of 30 cards contains some of the most beautiful and descriptive black and white line drawings that I have ever seen on this subject."

Pagan News

30 pen and ink drawings by Brian Partridge

80 page booklet by Tony Linsell gives information about the origin of runes, their meaning, and how to read them.

£9.95   ISBN 1-898281-34-3   30 cards 85mm x 132mm - boxed with booklet

Dark Age Naval Power

A Reassessment of Frankish and Anglo-Saxon Seafaring Activity

John Haywood

In the first edition of this work, published in 1991, John Haywood argued that the capabilities of the pre-Viking Germanic seafarers had been greatly underestimated. Since that time, his reassessment of Frankish and Anglo-Saxon shipbuilding and seafaring has been widely praised and accepted.

In this second edition, some sections of the book have been revised and updated to include information gained from excavations and sea trials with sailing replicas of early ships. The new evidence supports the author's argument that early Germanic shipbuilding and seafaring skills were far more advanced than previously thought. It also supports the view that Viking ships and seaborne activities were not as revolutionary as is commonly believed.

> 'The book remains a historical study of the first order. It is required reading for our seminar on medieval seafaring at Texas A & M University and is essential reading for anyone interested in the subject.'
>
> F. H. Van Doorninck, *The American Neptune*

£16.95 ISBN 1-898281-43-2 approx. 10 x 6½ inches (245 x 170 mm) Hardback 224 pages

English Martial Arts

Terry Brown

Little is known about the very early history of English martial arts but it is likely that methods, techniques and principles were passed on from one generation to the next for centuries. By the sixteenth century English martial artists had their own governing body which controlled its members in much the same way as do modern-day martial arts organisations. It is apparent from contemporary evidence that the Company of Maisters taught and practised a fighting system that ranks as high in terms of effectiveness and pedigree as any in the world.

In the first part of the book the author investigates the weapons, history and development of the English fighting system and looks at some of the attitudes, beliefs and social pressures that helped mould it.

Part two deals with English fighting techniques drawn from books and manuscripts that recorded the system at various stages in its history. In other words, all of the methods and techniques shown in this book are authentic and have not been created by the author. The theories that underlie the system are explained in a chapter on *The Principles of True Fighting*. All of the techniques covered are illustrated with photographs and accompanied by instructions. Techniques included are for bare-fist fighting, broadsword, quarterstaff, bill, sword and buckler, sword and dagger.

Experienced martial artists, irrespective of the style they practice, will recognise that the techniques and methods of this system are based on principles that are as valid as those underlying the system that they practice.

The author, who has been a martial artist for twenty-eight years, has recently re-formed the Company of Maisters of Defence, a medieval English martial arts organization.

£16.95 ISBN 1–898281–29-7 10 x 6½ inches - 245 x 170 mm 220 photographs 240 pages

A Guide to Late Anglo-Saxon England

From Alfred to Eadgar II 871–1074

Donald Henson

This guide has been prepared with the aim of providing the general readers with both an overview of the period and a wealth of background information. Facts and figures are presented in a way that makes this a useful reference handbook.

Contents include: The Origins of England; Physical Geography; Human Geography; English Society; Government and Politics; The Church; Language and Literature; Personal Names; Effects of the Norman Conquest. All of the kings from Alfred to Eadgar II are dealt with separately and there is a chronicle of events for each of their reigns. There are also maps, family trees and extensive appendices.

£9.95 ISBN 1–898281–21–1 9½" x 6¾"/245 x 170mm, 6 maps & 3 family trees 208 pages

The English Elite in 1066 - Gone but not forgotten

Donald Henson

The people listed in this book formed the topmost section of the ruling elite in 1066. It includes all those who held office between the death of Eadward III (January 1066) and the abdication of Eadgar II (December 1066). There are 455 individuals in the main entries and these have been divided according to their office or position.

The following information is listed where available:

What is known of their life;

Their landed wealth;

The early sources in which information about the individual can be found

Modern references that give details about his or her life.

In addition to the biographical details, there is a wealth of background information about English society and government. A series of appendices provide detailed information about particular topics or groups of people.

£16.95 ISBN 1–898281–26–2 250 x 175mm / 10 x 7 inches paperback 272 pages

Tastes of Anglo-Saxon England

Mary Savelli

These easy to follow recipes will enable you to enjoy a mix of ingredients and flavours that were widely known in Anglo-Saxon England but are rarely experienced today. In addition to the 46 recipes, there is background information about households and cooking techniques.

£4.95 ISBN 1-898281-28-9 A5 80 pages

Anglo-Saxon Riddles

Translated by John Porter

Here you will find ingenious characters who speak their names in riddles, and meet a one-eyed garlic seller, a bookworm, an iceberg, an oyster, the sun and moon and a host of others from the everyday life and imagination of the Anglo-Saxons. Their sense of the awesome power of creation goes hand in hand with a frank delight in obscenity, a fascination with disguise and with the mysterious processes by which the natural world is turned to human use. This edition contains **all 95 riddles of the Exeter Book in both Old English and Modern English.**

£4.95   A5   ISBN 1–898281–13–0   144 pages

Tolkien's *Mythology for England*

A Guide to Middle-Earth

Edmund Wainwright

Tolkien set out to create a mythology for England and the English but the popularity of his books and the recent films has spread across the English-speaking world and beyond.

You will find here an outline of Tolkien's life and work. The main part of the book consists of an alphabetical subject entry which will help you gain a greater understanding of Tolkien's Middle-Earth, the creatures that inhabit it, and the languages they spoke. It will also give an insight into a culture and way-of-life that extolled values which are as valid today as they were over 1,000 years ago.

This book focuses on *The Lord of the Rings* and shows how Tolkien's knowledge of Anglo-Saxon and Norse literature and history helped shape its plot and characters.

£9·95   ISBN 1-898281-36-X   approx. 10 x 6½ inches (245 x 170 mm)   Hardback   128 pages

Anglo-Saxon Books

Tel. 0845 430 4200   Fax. 0845 430 4201   email: enq@asbooks.co.uk

Please check availability and prices on our web site at www.asbooks.co.uk

See website for postal address.

Payment may be made by Visa / Mastercard or by a cheque drawn on a UK bank in sterling.

UK deliveries add 10% up to a maximum of £2·50

Europe – including **Republic of Ireland** – add 10% plus £1 – all orders are sent airmail

North America add 10% surface delivery, 30% airmail

Elsewhere add 10% surface delivery, 40% airmail

Overseas surface delivery 6 – 10 weeks; airmail 6 – 14 days

Most titles can be obtained through North American bookstores.

Latest Titles

Anglo-Saxon Attitudes – A short introduction to Anglo-Saxonism
J.A. Hilton

This is not a book about the Anglo-Saxons, but a book about books about Anglo-Saxons. It describes the academic discipline of Anglo-Saxonism; the methods of study used; the underlying assumptions; and the uses to which it has been put.

Methods and motives have changed over time but right from the start there have been constant themes: English patriotism and English freedom.

£6.95   A5   ISBN 1–898281–39-4   Hardback 64pp

The Origins of the Anglo-Saxons
Donald Henson

This book has come about through a growing frustration with scholarly analysis and debate about the beginnings of Anglo-Saxon England. Much of what has been written is excellent, yet unsatisfactory. One reason for this is that scholars often have only a vague acquaintance with fields outside their own specialism. The result is a partial examination of the evidence and an incomplete understanding or explanation of the period.

The growth and increasing dominance of archaeological evidence for the period has been accompanied by an unhealthy enthusiasm for models of social change imported from prehistory. Put simply, many archaeologists have developed a complete unwillingness to consider movements of population as a factor in social, economic or political change. All change becomes a result of indigenous development, and all historically recorded migrations become merely the movement of a few hundred aristocrats or soldiers. The author does not find this credible.

£19.95   A5   ISBN 1–898281–40-2   304pp

A Departed Music – Readings in Old English Poetry
Walter Nash

The *readings* of this book take the form of passages of translation from some Old English poems. The author paraphrases their content and discuses their place and significance in the history of poetic art in Old English society and culture.

The authors knowledge, enthusiasm and love of his subject help make this an excellent introduction to the subject for students and the general reader.

£16.95   A5   ISBN 1–898281–37-8   240pp

English Sea Power 871-1100 AD
John Pullen-Appleby

This work examines the largely untold story of English sea power during the period 871 to 1100. It was an age when English kings deployed warships first against Scandinavian invaders and later in support of Continental allies.

The author has gathered together information about the appearance of warships and how they were financed, crewed, and deployed.

Price £14.95   144 pages   hardcover   ISBN 1-898281-31-9

Organisations

Þa Engliscan Gesiðas

Þa Engliscan Gesiðas (The English Companions) is a historical and cultural society exclusively devoted to Anglo-Saxon history. Its aims are to bridge the gap between scholars and non-experts, and to bring together all those with an interest in the Anglo-Saxon period, its language, culture and traditions, so as to promote a wider interest in, and knowledge of all things Anglo-Saxon. The Fellowship publishes a journal, *Wiðowinde,* which helps members to keep in touch with current thinking on topics from art and archaeology to heathenism and Early English Christianity. The Fellowship enables like-minded people to keep in contact by publicising conferences, courses and meetings which might be of interest to its members.

For further details see www.tha-engliscan-gesithas.org.uk or write to: The Membership Secretary, Þa Engliscan Gesiðas, BM Box 4336, London, WC1N 3XX England.

Regia Anglorum

Regia Anglorum was founded to accurately re-create the life of the British people as it was around the time of the Norman Conquest. Our work has a strong educational slant. We consider authenticity to be of prime importance and prefer, where possible, to work from archaeological materials. Approximately twenty-five per cent of our members, of over 500 people, are archaeologists or historians.

The Society has a large working Living History Exhibit, teaching and exhibiting more than twenty crafts in an authentic environment. We own a forty-foot wooden ship replica of a type that would have been a common sight in Northern European waters around the turn of the first millennium AD. Battle re-enactment is another aspect of our activities, often involving 200 or more warriors.

For further information see www.regia.org or contact: K. J. Siddorn, 9 Durleigh Close, Headley Park, Bristol BS13 7NQ, England, e-mail: kim_siddorn@compuserve.com

The Sutton Hoo Society

Our aims and objectives focus on promoting research and education relating to the Anglo Saxon Royal cemetery at Sutton Hoo, Suffolk in the UK. The Society publishes a newsletter SAXON twice a year, which keeps members up to date with society activities, carries resumes of lectures and visits, and reports progress on research and publication associated with the site. If you would like to join the Society please see website: www.suttonhoo.org

Wuffing Education

Wuffing Education provides those interested in the history, archaeology, literature and culture of the Anglo-Saxons with the chance to meet experts and fellow enthusiasts for a whole day of in-depth seminars and discussions. Day Schools take place at the historic Tranmer House overlooking the burial mounds of Sutton Hoo in Suffolk.

For details of programme of events contact:-
Wuffing Education, 4 Hilly Fields, Woodbridge, Suffolk IP12 4DX
email education@wuffings.co.uk   website www.wuffings.co.uk
Tel. 01394 383908 or 01728 688749

Places to visit

Bede's World at Jarrow

Bede's world tells the remarkable story of the life and times of the Venerable Bede, 673–735 AD. Visitors can explore the origins of early medieval Northumbria and Bede's life and achievements through his own writings and the excavations of the monasteries at Jarrow and other sites.

Location – 10 miles from Newcastle upon Tyne, off the A19 near the southern entrance to the River Tyne tunnel. Bus services 526 & 527

Bede's World, Church Bank, Jarrow, Tyne and Wear, NE32 3DY

Tel. 0191 489 2106; Fax: 0191 428 2361; website: www.bedesworld.co.uk

Sutton Hoo near Woodbridge, Suffolk

Sutton Hoo is a group of low burial mounds overlooking the River Deben in south-east Suffolk. Excavations in 1939 brought to light the richest burial ever discovered in Britain – an Anglo-Saxon ship containing a magnificent treasure which has become one of the principal attractions of the British Museum. The mound from which the treasure was dug is thought to be the grave of Rædwald, an early English king who died in 624/5 AD.

This National Trust site has an excellent visitor centre, which includes a reconstruction of the burial chamber and its grave goods. Some original objects as well as replicas of the treasure are on display.

2 miles east of Woodbridge on B1083   Tel. 01394 389700

West Stow Anglo-Saxon Village

An early Anglo-Saxon Settlement reconstructed on the site where it was excavated consisting of timber and thatch hall, houses and workshop. There is also a museum containing objects found during the excavation of the site. Open all year 10am–4.15pm (except Yuletide). Special provision for school parties. A teachers' resource pack is available. Costumed events are held at weekends, especially Easter Sunday and August Bank Holiday Monday. Craft courses are organised.

For further details see www.stedmunds.co.uk/west_stow.html or contact:

The Visitor Centre, West Stow Country Park, Icklingham Road, West Stow,

Bury St Edmunds, Suffolk IP28 6HG   Tel. 01284 728718